The Archaeology and Ethnography of Central Africa

The Archaeology and Ethnography of Central Africa provides the first detailed description of the prehistory of the Loango coast of West-Central Africa over the course of more than 3,000 years. The archaeological data presented in this volume comes from a pivotal area through which, as linguistic and historical reconstructions have long indicated, Bantu-speaking peoples expanded before reaching eastern and southern Africa. Despite its historical importance, the prehistory of the Atlantic coastal regions of West-Central Africa has until now remained almost unknown. James Denbow offers an imaginative approach to this subject, integrating the scientific side of fieldwork with the interplay of history, ethnography, politics, economics, and personalities. The resulting "anthropology of archaeology" highlights the connections between past and present, change and modernity, in one of the most inaccessible and poorly known regions of West-Central and southern Africa.

James Denbow is Professor of Archaeology at the University of Texas, Austin. In the 1980s, he was Senior Curator and Head of the Archaeology Department at the National Museum of Botswana, where he established and ran the Antiquities Program for the Government of Botswana. Between 1987 and 1993, he worked extensively in what is now the Republic of the Congo in Central Africa. His research has been funded by many agencies, including Fulbright, the National Science Foundation, the National Geographic Society, USAID, and the Swedish International Development ment Authority. He is the author of two books, *Cultures and Customs of Botswana* and *Uncovering Botswana's Past*, and has published more than forty scientific articles in journals, including *Science*, *Current Anthropology*, the *Journal of Archaeological Science*, the *Journal of African History*, *History in Africa*, the *Journal of American Folklore*, the *Journal of African Archaeology*, the *African Archaeological Review*, the *South African Journal of Science*, and the *South African Archaeological Bulletin*. His current research focuses on processes of state formation centered on the prehistoric site of Bosutswe on the eastern fringe of the Kalahari Desert.

The Archaeology and Ethnography of Central Africa

James Denbow
University of Texas at Austin, USA,
and
GAES, University of the Witwatersrand,
South Africa

CAMBRIDGE
UNIVERSITY PRESS

CAMBRIDGE
UNIVERSITY PRESS

32 Avenue of the Americas, New York, NY 10013-2473, USA

Cambridge University Press is part of the University of Cambridge.

It furthers the University's mission by disseminating knowledge in the pursuit of
education, learning, and research at the highest international levels of excellence.

www.cambridge.org
Information on this title: www.cambridge.org/9781107040700

First published 2014

Printed in the United States of America

A catalog record for this publication is available from the British Library.

Library of Congress Cataloging in Publication data
Denbow, James R. (James Raymond), 1946–
The archaeology and ethnography of Central Africa / by James Denbow.
pages   cm
Includes bibliographical references and index.
ISBN 978-1-107-04070-0 (hardback)
1. Africa, Central – Antiquities.   2. Ethnology – Africa, Central.   I. Title.
DT352.3.D46   2013
930.10967–dc23   2013024288

ISBN 978-1-107-04070-0 Hardback

Contents

Figures

Figures

Tables

Acknowledgments

I am indebted to a great many people who have contributed to this research and provided comments to improve its content. Above all I am grateful to Dr. Max Pitcher and Mr. Roger Simpson of Conoco (now ConocoPhillips) for initiating the project and providing the considerable financial and logistical resources needed to carry it out. Mr. Bertrand Poirier, Director of Congolaise de Dévelopment Forestier (CDF) in Pointe Noire, was instrumental in continuing the project with Shell funding. This ensured that the plan to survey and conserve sites in the eucalyptus plantation could be completed. Many of the Congolese participants in the project have been mentioned by name at various points in the book, and I would like to extend again my gratitude to them for their hard work, dedication, and friendship.

The people who have read parts or all of the manuscript and provided their commentary have contributed more than they could know. My wife Jocelyne Denbow, who has lived through most of the adventures described here and many more, helped edit the manuscript with good humor and love. My good friend Morongwa Mosothwane also read through and commented on most of the chapters and helped steer me around some pitfalls. Colin Barrett read the manuscript and tried to teach me the arcane and mysterious differences between hyphens, en-dashes, and em-dashes – a subject of which I had been blissfully unaware my whole life. Other readers included Jan Vansina, K. Kris Hurst, Carla Klehm, Ed Wilmsen, Kate de Luna, and an anonymous reviewer who provided detailed comments for which I am extremely grateful. François Camus, Gilbert Courtois, Terry Robinson, Joseph Kimfoko-Maddungou, and Aimé Manima-Moubouha provided help and friendship in many ways during the years in which we worked in the Congo. My student Ruth Hargus helped with early ceramic analyses. I also benefited from conversations and correspondence over the years with Barnard Clist, whom I visited in Gabon, Pierre de Maret who was kind enough to put me up in Brussels, and Eileen Kose who shared her Namiba findings with me.

For my Botswana research I have benefited from so many people that I cannot possibly mention them all in the context of this book. For the work in the Tsodilo Hills and Matlapaneng of Northwestern Botswana, I continue to remember the late Alex Matseka who worked as my assistant for many years. I also miss the late Alec Campbell who was the driving force in founding the National Museum of Botswana and tirelessly encouraged the archaeological investigation of Tsodilo. Ed Wilmsen and I worked together there at Nqoma and Divuyu, and also at Matlapaneng – he under his National Science Foundation grant and I in my position with the National Museum of Botswana. Over the years, Mike and Kerstin Main, Tom Huffman, and Phenyo Thebe and his family have at various times provided vehicles, a roof over my head, friendship, help with bureaucrats, and a feeling of having a home away from home. Thank you.

1

Behind the Scenes of Research

Introduction

The history of the Loango coast between Gabon and Cabinda in equatorial Africa is blessed with many firsthand accounts spanning the last five centuries; these include observers such as Andrew Battell and Duarte Lopez who lived for long periods in Loango and neighboring regions in the late sixteenth and early seventeenth centuries (Purchas 1617; Lopes, Pigafetta, and Hutchinson 1881). Their accounts come at the beginning of more than four centuries of interaction with the West – interactions that ranged from the depredations of the slave trade to the political disenfranchisement and humiliation of colonial conquest. The cultural lens of each observer colored and prejudiced their accounts, but their observations are particularly important because they were informed by many years of residence in what would become the Republic of Congo. With cautious reading, they contain a wealth of information about the countryside, its peoples, and their cultural beliefs and transformations. Records gleaned from Catholic missionary accounts in the middle of the eighteenth century illuminate the changes that took place between the period of initial contact and the height of the slave trade (Proyart 1814; Nsondé 1995). Later, Richard Dennett (1887, 1898, 1968) and Eduard Pechuël-Loesche (1907) provide additional accounts for the nineteenth century. Dennett, in particular, was a long-term observer and trader who used his local knowledge of the Vili language and customs to provide detailed and sometimes acerbic descriptions of Fioté (Vili) beliefs and customs at the beginning of the colonial era.

But until the archaeological research presented here was carried out, there was little information about the region or its peoples before their first encounters with Europeans. For the earlier periods, indigenous responses to the slave and commodity trade along the coast had to be largely deciphered indirectly from the accounts of outsiders. Some sense of local responses can be gleaned, however, from archaeological readings of the earthenware containers, salt-glazed stoneware, glass rum, wine, and gin bottles, locally made clay tobacco pipes, tombstones, and other artifacts found on the coastal plain (Denbow 1990, 1999). Archaeological evidence can expand, supplement, and in some cases provide a corrective or help nuance the accounts of foreign traders, missionaries, and adventurers. But the archaeological excavations reported here span a much

1

longer period – more than 3,000 years – to expose the deeper roots from which later societies and kingdoms such as Loango grew. These data are presented here in detail for the first time.

In places such as the Congo, where archaeological research is so new that its logistical framework and interpretive understandings are still emerging, fluidity in knowledge forms often produces unexpected twists and turns as multiple and cross-cultural perspectives intertwine over the course of day-to-day interaction between archaeologists and their local counterparts. To enrich what otherwise would be a linear précis of excavations and artifacts, this book attempts to illuminate and personalize the archaeological process by foregrounding in some sections the dialogues, interactions, and experiences of archaeologists, family members, and local Congolese as the project unfolded. By setting the scientific work in its broader context, it is hoped that what will emerge is a more multifaceted understanding of the ways in which people interact with their history and communicate their knowledge and attitudes toward life (Geertz 1973: 89).

The book is divided into two sections: the first four chapters establish the logistical, cultural, and environmental setting in which the research took place; the next three chapters present the detailed results of archaeological excavations at fifteen sites chronicled by forty radiocarbon dates and a new ceramic typology. This work provides a first glimpse into 3,300 years of prehistoric settlement in this hitherto unexplored region of equatorial Africa. Chapter 8 explores the relationship of this work to archaeological and linguistic knowledge across the region from Angola to the northern edge of the Kalahari Desert and the Okavango Delta. The final chapter provides a brief summary of the information presented along with a call for better protection for Africa's rapidly vanishing archaeological heritage.

Arrivals

One perhaps could have no better introduction to the Loango coast than to arrive by sea, following a route used by many earlier generations of slavers, explorers, and adventurers. Richard Burton was one of these. Sailing along a route from Fernando Po that paralleled the Gabon coast southward across the Equator to Pointe Indienne in 1863,[1] he caught his first glimpse of Loango Bay and wrote,

> The country looks high and bold after the desperate flatness of the Bights [of Benin], and we note with pleasure that we have left behind us the "impervious luxuriance of vegetation which crowns the lowlands, covers the sides of the rises, and caps their summits." During the rains after October the grass, now showing yellow stubble upon the ruddy, rusty plain, becomes a cane fence, ten to twelve feet tall; but instead of matted, felted jungle, knitted together by creepers of cable size, we have scattered clumps of dark, lofty, and broad-topped trees. A nearer view shows great cliffs, weather-worked into ravines and basins, ribs and ridges, towers and pinnacles. Above them is a joyful open land ... pitted with the crater-like sinks locally called "holes," so frequent in the Gaboon country. Loango is a "pool harbour" ... a spit of shingle, whose bay, north-east and south-west, forms an inner lagoon, bounded landwards by conspicuous and weather-tarnished red cliffs. This "lingual" rests upon a base of terra firma whose westernmost projection is Indian Point. From the latter runs northwards the "infamous" Indian Bar ... a reef some three miles long, which the waves assault with prodigious fury; a terror to slavers, especially in our autumn, when the squalls and storms begin. The light sandy soil of the mainland rests upon compact clay, and malaria rises only where the little drains, which should feed the lagoon, evaporate in swamps. Here and there are clumps of tall cocoas, a copot, pullom or wild cotton-tree, and a neat village upon prairie land, where stone is as rare as on the Pampas.... Guided by a hut upon the beach

fronting French Factory and under lee of the breakers off Indian Bar, I landed near a tree-motte, in a covelet smoothed by a succession of sandpits. (Burton 1876, vol. 2: 3–5)

My own entry in November 1987, like that of most modern travelers, was less picturesque. An hour's flight from Brazzaville, the capital city, in a threadbare Air Congo jet deposited me on the tarmac fronting a two-story corrugated iron shed on which, in faded red lettering, was inscribed "Agostinho Neto Aérogare, Pointe Noire." The airstrip, though patched and rough, was serviceable, and I noted as we landed that the local women were clearing new manioc gardens right up to the edge of the crumbling tarmac. Having landed in what was then the People's Republic of the Congo, ruled by the oldest Marxist-Leninist government in Africa, I quickly learned what that meant in practical terms: those with money or connections could be whisked quickly through to the "Salon d'Honneur" to await their luggage; others less fortunate were left to haggle with a line of eager customs and immigration agents primed to extract fees for the importation of goods such as my laptop computer. On my first visit I was lucky enough to be among the former group. My trip had been arranged by Conoco Oil Company in Houston, which had asked me to examine an archaeological locality discovered by some of their personnel in an area they were planning to bid on for an oil lease from the Congolese government. One of Conoco's "facilitators" met me at the plane and quickly escorted me through the building and upstairs to await my luggage. There I was pleasantly surprised to find that the entire upper story of the sweltering building was taken up with a dimly lit bar cooled by several slowly turning ceiling fans. Refreshments were being served to those waiting to depart, those thankful for having arrived successfully through the bureaucratic gauntlet below, and those simply in need of a drink and a cigarette.

A few years later I would be shockingly reminded of the manioc gardens on the side of the airstrip when a munitions dump left behind by departing Cuban soldiers exploded in a fearful conflagration. The port at Pointe Noire had long been used by the Cuban army to land munitions and supplies for their efforts in support of the Angolan government's side in the civil war in Cabinda. Over the years they had also established a firing range and a "rest farm" for recuperating soldiers in the countryside outside Pointe Noire (Figure 1.1, top). It was not far from the archaeological site of Mvindou, where I would later excavate. The push toward multiparty democracies that spread across Africa in the 1990s following the unraveling of the Soviet Union precipitated a change in government in the Congo in 1991. As a result, the Cubans were asked to leave. They did so the following year, leaving behind two decades' worth of munitions and missiles stacked like firewood at the far end of the airstrip. When the women arrived at the end of the dry season the following year to burn off their now-withered gardens in preparation for a new season, they did not realize that with the Cuban soldiers gone, no one had kept the munitions dump clear of vegetation. Around two in the afternoon, as their fires reached the end of the airstrip, the munitions ignited. I was sitting at a sidewalk café in Pointe Noire 8 kilometers away when massive explosions began, followed by missiles whistling high into the air. Those of us nursing our after-lunch coffees, mostly expatriates, shot uneasy glances at one another.

"A coup d'état?" one asked.
"The explosions are all coming from the direction of the airport."

Heavy concussions shook the ground around us and shattered the store windows. They continued far into the night, littering the airstrip with shrapnel and disrupting air traffic for days. I later learned that many children, fearing the worst, had fled their homes to seek safety in the surrounding forest. Some did not return to their worried families for days.[2]

That same year the vivid, red oil paintings of Karl Marx, Vladimir Lenin, and Che Guevara that had graced the dusty parade ground in front of the district offices in Madingo-Kayes, a small village 70 kilometers north of Pointe Noire, were removed (Figure 1.1, bottom). The red flag of

Figure 1.1. **(top)** A view of the Cuban "farm" and firing range outside Pointe Noire where soldiers fighting in the civil war in Angola were sent for rest and recovery. Several archaeological sites were found near the buildings and firing range. Scattered signboards in Spanish such as this one contained inspirational quotations, including this one from Che Guevara urging "Nos forjaremos en la acción cotidiana creando un hombre Nuevo con una nueva técnica" or, roughly, "Through our daily actions we will forge ourselves into new men with new skills." The Cubans abandoned the camp when they were asked to leave Angola as part of the general settlement of the Angolan Civil War; **(bottom)** The parade ground in Madingo-Kayes as it appeared in 1988 with large oil paintings of Marx, Lenin, and Guevara flanking the red flag of the People's Republic of the Congo.

the Marxist regime, with its gold star and crossed hammer and hoe flanked by green fronds, was replaced with a new one bearing the pan-African colors of green, gold, and red. It appeared to symbolize new hopes for a fledgling democracy.

Our archaeological team first heard of the change in government while surveying an area 40 kilometers northeast of Pointe Noire where the coastal savanna surrenders to tropical forest on the mist-shrouded flanks of the Mayombe Mountains. There had been a lot of talk about political change, but everything seemed confused and intangible. Then, as we were walking across the savanna looking for artifacts, Romain Mougani, one of the younger Congolese workers who was never without his portable radio with its twisted-piece-of-wire antenna, called out in French, "Hey, everyone, come here and listen."

We gathered around the radio as it was announced that the Congo would no longer be a Marxist republic. A look of utter astonishment spread over the face of Casimir Kissiboula, an older worker in his forties and a staunch Catholic.

"I don't understand. How can they just abandon this philosophy?" he asked. "I have been taught most of my life how important Marxism is and how we must constantly struggle to build a new and better society. And now they just throw it away like that?" he said, snapping his fingers. "Like it was nothing?"

His comments were all the more poignant because he had faced his own personal difficulties because of the practice of his religion, which, while not forbidden, was not looked on with favor by the political elite or "Bouton Rouge" as they were called after the circular red badge they wore in their lapels.

The following year it was my turn to be surprised as I counted the number of small village churches that had sprung up like flowers along the drive from Pointe Noire to Madingo-Kayes. Most were simple clearings in the forest where bamboo crosses were set up facing a few rows of roughly hewn log benches. Woven walls of split bamboo sometimes surrounded the open-air chapels. Although perhaps coincidental, their appearance suggested that new spiritual needs were being addressed – or that older ones, once suppressed, were now finding expression.

Landscapes and Constructed Meanings

A few times during the course of the archaeological reconnaissance, sacred groves and springs were pointed out to me, but most of the time my Congolese crew and I passed by or through them unaware of their existence. During my first visit in 1987, I was taken to one such spring deep in the gallery forest that shaded the bottom of Diosso Gorge. To get to the spring, I had to descend the sheer sand face of the gorge by inserting my feet, one below the other, into small, crumbling toeholds cut into the smooth wall of the cliff. About 10 meters down, the primitive stairway ended in a faint trail that wound for 500 meters through the jungle to a small spring. Little distinguished it from other locations, and I would not have known of its ritual significance had I not been told. A few fragments of broken porcelain and glass and a few scraps of tattered cloth were the only indications that anyone visited this quiet glade. On another occasion, while surveying 40 kilometres northwest of Madingo-Kayes, we came upon a small jungle clearing. Inside, a "bed" of earth had been raised 15 centimeters above ground level and surrounded by a low wall of cut saplings; little else suggested that this space had spiritual meaning. In other spots, tombstones on the deserted savanna marked the locations of now-vanished villages. Depictions of the sun, moon, stars, and other figures molded on them evoked the spiritual meanings with which they once had been imbued, although these were now only dimly understood (Dennett 1968; Denbow 1999).

In the nineteenth and early twentieth centuries, the Loango terrain was replete with such sacred places and meanings. R. E. Dennett, an English trader and resident of Loango for more than two decades, was fortunate enough to be led through the countryside by guides more spiritually informed than mine. They pointed out to him more than 100 sacred groves, trees, and springs that configured a cultural landscape redolent with cosmologic imagery:

> As we passed through the village of Zulu, we cast a last look at the sea and the pretty Bay of Luango, with its lighthouse at Point Indienne. Just beyond the point, on the way to Black Point [present-day Pointe Noire], one can see the wood that contains the sacred grove of Nymina; and nearer to Luango may be noticed the tall mangrove trees that mark the grove sacred to Lungululubu. We next crossed the Xibanda [Tchibanda]³ valley, and came to a place where once a town stood, called Ximpuku. Looking north from this place we noted upon the crest of the opposite hill the grove sacred to Mpuku Nyambi, while to the south, and not far from our standpoint, a minor grove, spoken of as the offspring of Mpuku Nyambi, topped the hill. This grove is called Xilu Xinkukuba, and is near the linguister Juan's town. Then 14 or 15 miles south, behind Black Point, near to the River Ximani and the town of Nvuxi, stands the grove of Xivuma, and as many miles north, at Xissanga upon the sea coast, is situated the grove sacred to the double personages Nxiluka and Xikanga; while far away to the north, on the ruddy cliffs behind Konkwati, 60 miles from here, is the grove called Xinjili. (Dennett 1968: 9)

Today, other objects continue to inscribe cultural meaning onto local places, things, and landscapes. On the crest of the hill that overlooks Loango Bay to the south and the archaeological site of Tchissanga (Dennett's Xissanga) to the north, an oil company had erected a now-rusting iron tower to transmit radio signals from its workers in the field to its headquarters in Pointe Noire. When I passed the tower for the first time, I was surprised to see next to it an unusual "fetish" that consisted of a pole topped by a wooden platform holding a piece of broken mirror and several water-worn, white quartzite cobbles. Affixed to a wooden plaque on the side of the pole was a picture of a Mercedes-Benz, neatly torn from a magazine. Nearby, the whitewashed lid of a paint can dangled from a piece of electrical cable attached with a strip of red cloth to another pole. Two paint-spattered gloves stuck onto a bush at its base completed the contraption (Figure 1.2, top). My first thought was that the fetish had been constructed to protest the seeming omnipotence of multinational corporations and their minions who rarely stopped to visit with local people as they sped through the area in their air-conditioned 4×4s. That thought was quickly replaced by another: perhaps this fetish had been built to harness in some way the power of these foreign companies, turning it to local use. It was not until a year later that I accidentally stumbled on the fetish's origin and purpose.

Our archaeological camp, a rough three-room wooden shed with a wide veranda, had been built for us on the beach below Tchissanga by Conoco in 1988. Fishermen from a village on the heights above beached their dugouts nearby. The fishermen sometimes remained on the ocean for several days at a time, "camping out" in their small canoes and warding off the cold by huddling over wood fires built over a bed of earth in the bottom of their vessels. In the evenings, we would often see their fires reflecting off the low clouds far out to sea. Over the course of our project, I came to know many of them, including one roguish old man named Bernard who was particularly talkative and friendly. The Congolese crew quickly nicknamed him "Dracula" behind his back because of his blackened and broken set of sawlike front teeth.

One afternoon while visiting with Bernard as he hammered yet another tin patch onto the side of his weather-beaten canoe (Figure 1.2, bottom), I brought up the topic of the fetish near the radio tower.

"I wonder who built that?" I asked idly.

"Why, I did," he said with some pride. "The oil company pays me to look after the tower and make sure no one vandalizes it. I can't be there all the time, so I built the fetish to keep vandals away. I haven't had any problems."

Figure 1.2. **(top)** Bernard's fetish on the hilltop overlooking Tchissanga as it appeared in 1987; **(bottom)** Bernard patching his fishing canoe on the beach just north of our archaeological camp, which can be seen in the background.

The same hilltop with the radio tower and Bernard's fetish was also the site of a monument of historical, if not ritual, significance. Brazzaville, in the present Republic of Congo, had been the symbolic capital of Free France between 1940 and 1943. Fears of a German attack had led to the posting of a small garrison of soldiers on the tower hill as lookouts because it had an excellent view over Loango Bay. I never learned who the soldiers were; they were likely local villagers recruited into the French army. In 1943, Central and West Africans made up more than half of the Free French army (Shillington 1995: 362–372). Their stay must have been memorable because after the war they constructed a small cement monument roughly inscribed with the words "Poste de Surveillance, Armée Française, Guerre 39–46" to mark their tour of duty on the lonely hilltop.

Other encounters with spiritually charged objects during the archaeological reconnaissance reinforced a feeling that ancient values and beliefs continued to inform people's interaction with their landscape. Small bundles of traditional medicines in bowls tied up with cloth, for instance, were sometimes found along footpaths and crossroads. These were meant to prevent the passage of people with evil intentions; other objects, often with iron nails hammered into them, were hung over doorways (including the entrance to the Maloango Museum in Diosso) to protect the property. Drawing from the memoirs of Bernardino Ungaro, Pierre Belgarde, and Castellet de Clais, who established a short-lived mission station at Kibota in Loango in 1766, Proyart, an abbé in France, provides an insight into the antiquity of such practices, remarking that in the eighteenth century, "the most determined robber dares not cross the threshold, when he sees it defended by these mysterious signs" (Proyart 1814: 595). Andrew Battell, an English adventurer and small-time trader who lived in Loango between 1607 and 1610, reports similar uses of traditional medicines at the beginning of the seventeenth century:

> They use to set in their fields, and places where Corne or Fruites grow, a Basket with Goatshornes, Parrats feathers, and other trash: This is the Mokisso's [Mokissi] ensigne, or token that it is commended to his custodie; and therefore the people very much addicted to theft, dare not meddle, or take any thing. (Battell in Purchas 1617: 874–875)

Different types of signs were found inscribed or painted onto late-nineteenth and early-twentieth-century tombstones during the archaeological reconnaissance. Dennett (1968: 75) found these and other symbols sewn onto ritual clothing in ways that could be syntactically "read" by their makers. The meanings he records complement the deeply rooted cosmological interpretations of similar symbols found in works such as Robert Farris Thompson and J. Cornet's *The Four Moments of the Sun* and the symbolism of iron smelting described in Eugenia Herbert's *Iron, Gender and Power*. They also resonate more widely with Kongo religious beliefs as explained in André Fu-Kiau's *Le Mukongo et le monde qui l'entourait*, Wyatt MacGaffey's *Religion and Society in Central Africa*, and Karl Laman's four-volume ethnography, *The Kongo*.

The tombstone designs also symbolized the political authority of the last MaLoango or King (Denbow 1999). One, for instance, included a hand with seven stars (Figure 1.3). As with most symbols, such ideograms have multiple layers of meaning embedded in them. The word for "palm of the hand," *kànda*, for instance, is a pun for matrilineal clan or *kanda* (neutral tone) according to Nsondé (1995: 102). Joseph Kimfoko-Maddungou (n.d.: 4), curator of a small museum at the last MaLoango's house near Diosso, provides additional meanings for the palm and star ideogram:

> The king is represented by the palm with seven stars and the arms that direct or guide it include the seven clans of Nkongo. These stars also represent, symbolically, the face of the king: two stars standing for his eyes so that he may oversee his territory, two stars representing his ears so that he may hear the sorrows and desires of his people, two stars representing the king's nostrils so that he may "smell out" or remain sensitive to the troubles of his people, and, finally, one star that stands for the mouth of the king through which he renders justice. It is his voice alone that can be heard throughout the kingdom (Kimfoko-Maddungou n.d.: 4, author's translation from French).

According to Dennett (1968), the stars also signify a cultural landscape – the seven traditional districts or provinces ruled over by Loango kings: (1) Samanu, found along the Luango Luici

Figure 1.3. Early twentieth-century tombstone in Loango with heart, hand, stars, and key motifs that symbolize concepts of the soul, ancestors, and clan.

River south of Pointe Noire near the present Cabinda border; (2) Tchibanga, the northern province which was divided into two sections by the Kouilou River – a region where pretenders to the throne were "never found wanting"; (3) Loanjili, the province that connects the first two provinces, with the exception of an area called Buali fronting Loango Bay; (4) Buali, the strip of land along the coast of Loanjili that connected the traditional capital with the beach near Pointe Indienne where the kings of Loango traditionally lived and where the tomb of the last MaLoango is located (Figure 1.4); (5) Tchikamba, the province directly inland from Buali/Loanjili. It rises toward the forested Mayombe Mountains in the east; (6) Nkonde, another inland province of scattered savannas and gallery forests, lies southeast of Buali and Tchikamba and is the place where the sisters of the MaLoango traditionally resided. The king's successor was chosen from among their sons; and (7) Mbuku, a region northeast of Tchikamba where the Mambuku or guardian of the eastern gateway to the Kingdom resided (Figure 1.5). These region names were still in use during the archaeological reconnaissance.

Gateways composed of two poles supporting a fringe of palm fronds protected the northern, southern, and eastern entrances to the kingdom in the late 19th century (Dennett 1968: 90). These were identical in design to the larger example that straddles the entranceway to the tomb of Moe Poaty III, the last MaLoango. Such structures still occasionally evoke cosmological forces. One afternoon while traveling along a jungle trail leading from one savanna to another, for instance, we came upon one of these gateways – a small one built over the walkway leading to a small thatched house. As we approached, a man I took to be the owner was standing outside. When I stopped and asked him why he had built it, his face erupted in a wide smile.

9

Figure 1.4. Photo of the grave of the last MaLoango or King near Diosso. The gateway of palm fronds under which Romain is walking, called *mabili* in the Vili language, is a type of charm. In the nineteenth century, a similar gateway guarded the eastern entrance to the Kingdom of Loango.

"I am a very lucky man, the father of twins. This is built to honor them," he said.

Although this may seem confusing, unusual events or rare births, such as that of twins or albino children, are thought to be the result of supernatural forces that mark out such individuals as having a special relationship with the supernatural. Albinos, for instance, were believed by the ancient inhabitants of Loango to have spiritual powers far greater than those of ordinary people. As a result, they were often appointed by the MaLoango as advisors or diviners within the kingdom (Battell in Purchase 1617: 875). Proyart (1814: 596) adds that

> [t]his error of nature ... far from being a disgrace to those on whom it falls, conciliates respect and veneration; ... placed above the *ganga* [diviner], they are regarded as extraordinary men and quite divine; so much so, that the missionaries saw one whose hairs were sold as reliques, which, it was said, had the virtue of preserving the bearer from all kinds of accidents.

The gateway to this man's house clearly resonated on many levels with beliefs and traditions that continue to inform people's perspectives of their past and present lives.

The Mayombe Mountains: Guardian of the Eastern Gateway to Loango

Between 1925 and 1932, more than 11,000 lives were lost constructing the rail line through the Mayombe Mountains from Pointe Noire (Andriamirado 1984). And the single-track route through the jungle is still treacherous: a collision between a passenger and a freight train in September 1991 killed more than 100 people; another collision in 2001 killed at least 50 passengers. In July 2010, a derailment due to excessive speed on a curve took 176 lives when the train plunged into a deep ravine.[4]

The Pointe Noire-Brazzaville rail line was built by the French to compete with the Matadi-Kinshasa line built over two decades earlier by King Leopold II of Belgium. A new port at Pointe

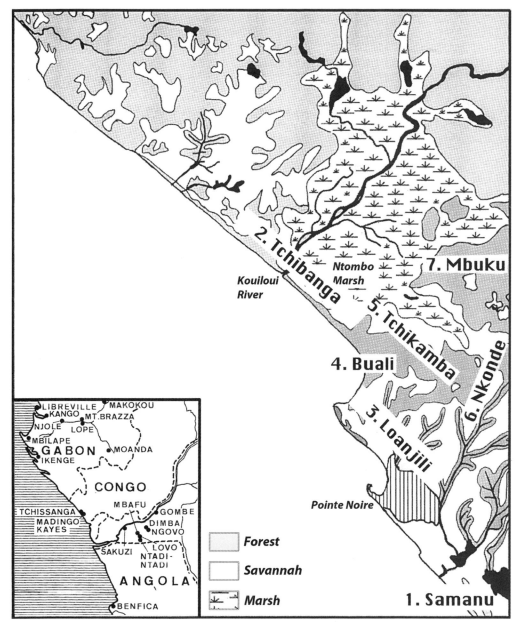

Figure 1.5. Map showing the location of the seven traditional provinces or districts of the Loango kingdom.

Noire was completed in 1939 to avoid the notorious "Indian bar" at Loango Bay and to allow larger ships to dock and connect to the rail line. The twin capital cities of Brazzaville in the Republic of Congo (R. Congo), and Kinshasa in the Democratic Republic of Congo (DRC), developed at the terminus of these lines into the interior. Neither the French nor King Leopold could make use of the river itself to link to the sea because just downstream from these two cities it explodes through a rocky 350 kilometer maelstrom known as the Livingstone Falls. Along this stretch of the river, rapids reach as high as a three-story building as the waters draining from the interior of Central Africa complete their long journey to the sea. Today the sister cities of Brazzaville and Kinshasa face one another across a wide point in the river known as Malebo Pool (formerly Stanley Pool). This is the first navigable point on the river route into the vast interior of equatorial Africa. From here, goods from the outside world are transferred onto barges bound for ports up river; logs and other raw materials from the jungles of Central Africa are, in turn, unloaded from the barges into rail cars to complete their trip to the seaports of Matadi and Pointe Noire. Brazzaville and Kinshasa have a combined population of more than 12 million people – making the Pool region the largest transborder metropolitan area in the world.

Before construction of the rail line, caravans from Loango passed through the Mayombe jungle along routes known to only a few families who guarded and passed down this knowledge from generation to generation (Andriamirado 1984). They were the porters who guided the missionaries, adventurers, and ambitious colonizers such as Savorgnan de Brazza on their journeys into the interior to claim the Congo for their patrons. But different from the "joyful open land" of the coastal savannas, movement through the mountains to the interior savannas where the Niari copper fields lay was treacherous. To those accustomed to the coastal savannas, the jungle was unhealthy, its air, "too rich and redolent with tree sap," and its rugged terrain a natural barrier to movement from the coast to the interior:

> At the turn of the century, the only ones who could survive [in the Mayombe] were the real masters of the terrain: the gorillas and their courtly entourage of creatures, each more dangerous than the other. The gorillas no longer venture along the railway, but their entourage remains in the grass and under the smallest shrubs. The black snake, *Ndouma*, a killer, always a danger, as are spiders hidden in the rocks, and hordes of ants, Magnans, that can turn an unwary sleeper into a skeleton in a few hours. The law of the jungle is the only one that applies. (Andriamirado 1984: 28, author's translation)

In the distant past, the terrain would have also restricted access to the coast for early Bantu-speaking migrants who traversed the tropical forest along inland waterways such as the Sangha, Ogooué, and Congo (Eggart 1987; Lanfranchi, Clist, and de La Croix 1991). This could be why the ceramics used by the earliest "Neolithic"[5] peoples in Loango more than 3,000 years ago seem most closely related to those from the coastal regions of Gabon and the DRC (de Maret 1982a, 1982b; Gosselain 1988; Clist 1989, 2005; Denbow 1990, 2012). These commonalities indicate a coastal route of expansion, perhaps by boat, for these early settlers who may represent the first food producers to arrive in the region at the end of the Later Stone Age (Blench 2006). The archaeological evidence thus suggests that the Mayombe, with its vine-tangled jungle, steep ravines, and cascading rivers was a longstanding barrier to movement between the coast and the interior, one that was rarely challenged until the mid-2nd millennium AD when Europeans arrived to stimulate demand for slaves, copper, and other goods from the interior.

We had our first encounter with traversing this "confusing, uncontrollable forest" of the Mayombe one evening in July 1990. As a weekend break from our excavation routine, we decided to take the train from Pointe Noire to Loubomo on the edge of the copper-rich Niari valley. Our trip was easy when compared with the trials faced by earlier generations. In the 90-kilometer stretch through the Mayombe there are seventeen tunnels, one more than 1.7 kilometers long. Each had to be blasted through a jumbled terrain of ravines, cascading rivers, and matted jungle and vines. Landslides are a common occurrence due to the instability of the alternating layers of micaceous schist and slippery clay. Endemic diseases that include malaria and sleeping sickness compound the dangers of the physical environment.

At the time of our journey, the train station in Pointe Noire was a deteriorating landmark that still retained a few remnants of the neo-Normandy style that it shared with its sister stations in Dauville and Pont-sur-Yonne in France. We had booked rooms at the "Grand Hotel" in Loubomo, a colonial structure of a similar age and style. On arrival, we found the hotel was no longer "grand," and our rooms on the second floor were approached along a cobweb-draped hallway whose tall ceilings echoed our footsteps. Inside, the rooms were damp and dark with narrow, flyspecked windows that were shaded on the outside by green-painted shutters propped open at the bottom to admit the occasional desultory breeze. Little light penetrated the interior. The staff had bravely tried to maintain a semblance of the hotel's earlier grandeur – a task made difficult by the sparse, mismatched furnishings, a nearly empty and undistinguished restaurant, and a broken swimming pool whose dry, cracked bottom was littered with leaves and rubbish that masked its better days.

Our stay was, nonetheless, pleasant until it was ended suddenly when one of our graduate students experienced an epileptic seizure. She had not read the fine print on her antimalarial medication that warned that people with conditions such as epilepsy should not take it. After she recovered, we decided to return to Pointe Noire immediately and phoned Dr. Camus, a friend and medical doctor working for Conoco. He agreed to meet us at the train station in Pointe Noire and take her to his home for a checkup.

Boarding the train late in the afternoon, we met our first difficulty. Due to limited space in the run-down and undoubtedly original wooden coaches, we were told that passengers were limited to two free bags; these were to be stored on overhead shelves. Additional luggage cost extra. Because my wife Josie and I had only one suitcase, we figured that our second piece of luggage would be a basket that she had purchased earlier in the Loubomo market. It was not a tourist basket, but a large, loosely woven type of work basket meant to be suspended by a tumpline from the forehead. Local women used them as they foraged in the forest with their machetes for greens and firewood.

Judging from the response Josie received when she purchased the basket, these were not simply work tools, but items infused with a sense of engendered identity. When she bought it, the women in the market were so surprised that they gathered around her laughing and clapping – pleased that she had chosen this basket, rather than one of the flashier tourist ones on sale. In some small way, the rather plain, tumpline baskets were to them an iconic metaphor of women's work and daily struggles. When we tried to board the train with it, we were stopped by the basket's symbolic counterpoint – the train conductor. Clearly not happy, he raised his hand and asked curtly, "Whose basket it that?"

"Mine," my wife answered.

"You can't take that on the train. You have to pay extra for those kinds of baskets."

"Why?" my wife responded. "We only have one suitcase, and this should count as our second piece of luggage. We are allowed two free suitcases on the train."

"That's not a suitcase. It's a work basket. Tools and work equipment are not free. You have to pay for them. Only tourist baskets are free. That's not a tourist basket, so you must pay for it."

"But I am a tourist and I purchased it as a tourist because I liked it," my wife countered. "I am not going to use it for any work. It should therefore count as a tourist basket and be allowed on free."

A crowd quickly gathered, clearly savoring the growing discomfort of the conductor. They happily followed each verbal blow as the argument went back and forth. Eventually, the basket was allowed on free, to the delight of the women in the crowd, many of whom were doubtless thinking that their baskets should also be allowed on for free. With night falling, we climbed into the dusty coach, sinking with relief into its worn cloth seats to begin the slow overnight journey back to Pointe Noire.

The rail line through the mountains is a "single-rail" system, which means that trains can only pass in opposite directions at designated lay-bys where the track is doubled. When trains approach each other, one must stop at a lay-by and wait for the other train to pass before it can take its turn to travel the next stretch of track. Right-of-way is determined by picking up a "key" at each station. The key gives the train holding it the right to enter the next section of line. At two in the morning, and not long after passing a dim, moth-spattered light that marked a small, jungle station, the train came to a jerking halt in the dark. At first I thought we were at a lay-by. But looking out the window, I could see people walking back and forth in the darkness, their flashlights flickering over the ground. We were in the middle of nowhere, with only the soft light of our carriage to hold back the enveloping darkness of the forest.

As time passed, the passengers grew uneasy. A stop like this was unusual. No one seemed to know what was happening. An hour went by. No word. Finally, a large woman sitting in front stood up and asked the question everyone had been thinking.

"Why have we stopped here?"

"Who knows," someone replied. "Maybe the train has broken down. Or maybe a bridge is washed out. Or maybe people have pulled up a section of the track."

Uneasy laughter followed this last statement. During earlier political clashes, protestors and gangs of youths called "ninjas" had been known to pull up the tracks as a political protest that temporarily severed the economic lifeline of the country. Deaths sometimes occurred.

"Maybe it's the fault of the politicians [*les hommes de politique*]. They always want something," a woman protested.

Everyone was now on edge, as much concerned about the potential consequences that might befall those thought to be stirring up trouble as about the unknown cause of the stoppage. What dangers lurked in the darkness outside? Eventually, a man dressed in a suit ventured out to ask what the men were searching for. After several minutes, he returned and announced, "They have lost the key. The driver picked it up at the last station, but then dropped it. It fell between the tracks and now they are looking for it. We can't go on without it."

A relieved sigh filled the compartment, even though some were still not convinced this was a true statement. Around three in the morning, the train jerked and we started moving again. Evidently the key had been found. As we trundled on through the darkness, the coach's gentle rocking lulled us to sleep as its lazy tube of light – filled with hushed voices, the soft milk-smack of nursing babies, and the high whine of the odd mosquito – passed through the night. Drilling through tunnel after tunnel, we emerged at daybreak onto the sunny plains of Loango.

The Mundane Logistics of Archaeological Fieldwork

When the archaeological project was carried out, Brazzaville had one of the highest costs of living on earth if one was a business traveler dependent on purchasing housing, food, and other necessities rather than producing them as a subsistence farmer might. The typical price for lunch at one of the small restaurants that dotted the beach in Pointe Noire was U.S. $50 for a bowl of soup and a fish entrée; a bottle of Pepsi-Cola cost $5. The food was excellent because local fishermen delivered fresh seafood and oysters daily. The mainly expatriate chefs competed with one another for the business of foreign oil workers with hefty salaries and expense accounts. Culinary standards (and prices) were high because competition for this lucrative business was fierce – most of the chefs were French expatriates hoping to raise a nest egg that would allow them to open a restaurant in their home country. On the upside beer, which only came in 750-milliliter bottles, was the same price as a liter of locally bottled water – CFA 250 or $1 – which led to many lunchtime debates about which to consume. Because we could not afford the cost of accommodation and meals in town, we chose instead to live on an isolated stretch of beach below the archaeological site of Tchissanga, 45 kilometers north of town, where Conoco built us our rough, three-room shack. This eliminated petrol costs and driving time to and from town. It also put us in direct contact with the local fishermen and hunters who supplied the markets of Pointe Noire. Our living expenses gradually became more manageable as we learned where to find the local producers of the food and other products we needed to adapt our living conditions to more local circumstances.

Smoked porcupine, snake, squirrel, fish, and freshwater prawns (*crevettes*) became staples in our camp diet along with manioc, mangoes, and bananas. Smoking is still the most commonly used method of preservation, and a wide variety of smoked "bush meat" or "gibier" was on frequent

Figure 1.6. Henri and Michel, archaeology students from Marien Ngouabi University in Brazzaville, singing the praises of smoked bush meat or *gibier* offered for sale along a rural track. Much of the food for the camp was purchased in this way because it was cheaper than going to the market in Pointe Noire. (Photo courtesy of ConocoPhillips.)

offer at roadside locations as we traveled rural paths during the reconnaissance (Figure 1.6). One day, however, we were offered a freshly killed civet by a local hunter. The animal had not yet been smoked. Casimir, Romain, and the other crew members were excited by the lucky find and insisted I buy it for dinner. Arriving in camp that evening, Casimir and the others went behind the shack to skin and clean the animal. My daughter, Jennifer, who was seven at the time, was quite excited to see the civet – especially its shiny, white canine teeth. My son Jeremy, who is six years older, had already become an expert at trolling the Grande Marché in Pointe Noire on market day. During his journeys he had discovered the section where traditional medicines were sold and over the weeks he had assembled a stash of "panther's teeth" and other oddities that were the envy of my daughter. Seeing the bright teeth peeking out of the civet's mouth, Jennifer ran to Casimir shouting, "Can I have the teeth? Can I have the teeth?"

To my surprise, Casimir brusquely dashed her hopes. "No," he said. "Women cannot touch these animals. Only men."

"Why?" asked Jennifer.

"Because."

"Why?"

"Because if women touch them or eat them, they will get large sores or boils on their hands and arms. These animals are taboo for women, so you can't have the teeth. You can't even touch it."

Depositing the civet on a table, he went around to the other side of the house with the other men to fetch a knife to butcher it.

As soon as they disappeared, Jennifer, as furious as I have ever seen a seven-year-old, ran over and grabbed the civet's fur in both her hands, shaking it vigorously.

"I can too touch this civet cat!" she exclaimed. "So there!" Luckily none of the locals found out – and Jennifer did not break out in sores.

We purchased other foods during weekly visits to the Grand Marché. The market, which covers several city blocks in the center of town, is a haphazardly roofed-over structure constructed of rusted sheets of corrugated iron that present a ramshackle appearance from the outside. Entering through the open sides, one stoops low to pass along narrow pathways that wind over the stained, gritty surface of the uneven concrete floor. As one twists between dark stalls packed side by side, one passes all manner of merchandise and foodstuffs that include everything from brightly colored scarves, soap, cigarettes, and fish to gorilla's hands, dried bats, and whole, smoked monkeys. The only illumination was the occasional fly-specked bulb dangling from loosely strung wires that ran between the low rafters supporting the ceiling. One is soon immersed in the loud sounds of haggling and the myriad smells, mostly unpleasant. As buyers jostle one another along the twisting pathways, an anxious eye is kept out for the pickpockets who also cruise the alleys in groups of two or three, preying on the unwary; nothing is left unattended or unwatched.

The first day I met our cook, Albert, a kindly, somewhat elderly gentleman, I was surprised to learn that he left all his belongings unattended in a gym bag in the back of our open pickup truck in order to dash inside the market to buy some soap and a comb. Although he was gone for only a few minutes, it was long enough for him to find, on his return, that his bag with all his clothing had disappeared. Romain and Casimir were incredulous that someone as old as Albert could be so naïve as to leave his belongings unattended. But that was his trusting nature. Albert was also resilient, and for the rest of the field season he stayed awake far into the night weaving baskets around the campfire while the rest of us slept. Sometimes he accompanied us to collect the grass and other materials he needed for his baskets as we surveyed distant savannas. He then sold the baskets in the Grande Marché for cash to replace his stolen clothing.

Albert later took a job in a nearby gorge with Jane Goodall who, with funds from Conoco, had established a preserve to care for captured chimpanzees that had been kept as pets and then abandoned. The first time we visited him there, Romain was jealous of the new concrete buildings that had been erected for the chimpanzee project. They looked so sturdy and modern when compared with our aging wooden shack, which was slowly collapsing as the corrosive sea air rusted the nails out of the planks.

Driving up, we found Albert caring for a young chimp balanced on his hip like a baby. Romain, perhaps jealous of the money being spent on them rather than on us, muttered, "They are villains, those chimps – troublemakers. Do you really like being around them, Albert?"

Albert, ever the gentleman, simply smiled.

2

Pride and Prejudice: Big Oil, Eucalyptus, and the People without History

Beginnings

"Please hold for Doctor Pitcher," the secretary requested. *"Who is that?"* I wondered as I waited in my office at the University of Texas in the fall of 1987.

"Hello? Doctor James Denbow? This is Max Pitcher, executive vice-president of Conoco Oil in Houston. People at the Smithsonian said you might be someone to call about archaeology in the Congo. Is that right?"

"Well, maybe," I answered. "I'm certainly interested in that region, but I've never worked there, so I can't say I know all that much. In fact, I don't know if anyone has really done much work there – it's sort of a blank area archaeologically. Pierre de Maret in Belgium might be able to help you."

"I have just come back from the Congo, and as I was looking at a borrow pit beside the road, I saw some pieces of old pottery and a few stone chips. Could I send them to you to have a look?"

"Sure," I responded. "Put them in the mail and I'll have a look at them. But I can't promise anything."

A few days later a small package arrived with three or four potsherds and a handful of white, quartzite stone chips inside. The pottery was eroded and tempered with large chunks of rock; none of it was decorated. The stone flakes were also nondescript. Although they were clearly broken off from larger cobbles, they were not formal tools, and none had visible evidence of use or retouch. Sadly, there was not much I could say about them. I picked up the phone to tell Max the bad news.

"Hi, Max," I said. "The package arrived safely, but I'm afraid I can't say very much about the pieces you sent. None of the sherds is decorated, so there is nothing that I can compare them with to get an estimate of age or cultural relationship. The quartzite flakes are interesting, and if they belong to the same time period as the pottery, then they could indicate it is very early. On the other hand, none of the flakes shows obvious evidence for reworking or use, so depending on where you found them, they could even be natural – not artifacts at all."

"I see," said Max. "How would you like to go to the Congo and have a look at the place for yourself?"

I almost fell out of my chair. Was he kidding? Even the air ticket would be more than I could normally afford.

"Sure," I answered, not believing my luck. "I don't have plans yet for this coming summer. I would be happy to go then and have a look."

"No, that's too late. Couldn't you go sooner?"

"How about over the Christmas break, then?" I replied, a little hesitantly.

"Can't you do it before then? Christmas is too late."

I could not figure out what the rush was, but I did not want to lose this chance to see firsthand a region that was practically unexplored. "OK," I said. "If I can get someone to cover my classes, maybe I could squeeze in seven to ten days over the Thanksgiving break. But if I am to go, I want to make sure that if there are any local Congolese archaeologists, they are involved, too – from the beginning."

"That's great," said Max. "I'll have my secretary make all the arrangements."

The Oil Business

At the time, I could not figure out what the rush was about. Those artifacts had been in the ground for a considerable time, and there did not seem to be any imminent danger of the site being destroyed by new digging or construction activity. Why did I have to go before Christmas? I was soon to learn that the oil business is a very competitive venture, particularly when companies are jockeying for exploration rights in an area expected to be productive. What I was to learn was that the Congo had just opened a bidding system for new onshore exploration leases for the first time. For me, the invitation to go to the Congo was a great opportunity to learn something new, but, being naive, I did not stop to wonder where archaeology fit into the picture. All my other work had been carried out either through research grants from Fulbright or the National Science Foundation or as part of my old job as a government employee in Botswana working for the National Museum. In those cases, what mattered was the scientific value of the project, not the political one – or at least not directly so.

The ten-day trip was productive. Along with Aimé Manima-Moubouha and Nicole Sanviti from Marien Ngouabi University in Brazzaville, more pottery was uncovered at the site. We named the site Tchissanga after the historical province in which it was located. Some of the pottery was decorated and came from a prehistoric level about 35 centimeters below the present ground surface (Denbow, Manima-Moubouha, and Sanviti 1988). Stone flakes accompanied the pottery, and it was clear from the stratigraphy and geology that these items had to have been brought to the site through human activity. After collecting radiocarbon samples for dating, we had a few spare days, so I decided to look around to see if we could find other sites. We had the time, a vehicle, and petrol – so why not?

We headed north across Ntombo Marsh, following the heavily potholed tarmac road that led to a bridge over the Kouilou River. Not only was the road in bad shape, but many of the metal telephone poles running alongside it were also so rusted by the sea air that they had holes right through them; some were so weakened that they were bent almost double by their own weight. "Those were put up in the colonial days when things worked," said Aimé – a lecturer in archaeology and a running catalogue of all the things that had once worked in the colonial era and now, through neglect and lack of money, did not.

After crossing the bridge, we passed though a small section of mangrove forest to arrive at a physiographic location similar to that of Tchissanga. Surely we would find another site here, I thought. Near a sharp bend in the road we came upon another borrow pit and got out to have a look. In the side of the bulldozer cut, we could see a pronounced black soil horizon

Figure 2.1. The "beautiful" Ceramic Later Stone Age (CLSA) pot from Madingo-Kayes that eventually found its way into the archaeological display in the presidential palace in Brazzaville.

about 40 centimeters below the present surface. The pottery we collected was completely different from that found at Tchissanga. Whether it was earlier or later in date we had no way of knowing, but its depth below the surface suggested it was old. We had no time to carry out a test excavation. We named the site Madingo-Kayes after the village that overlooked it from a nearby hilltop.

On our way back to the vehicle, it began to rain. As we stumbled through the water that began to gush along the edge of the cut, we came upon fragments of a complete pot washing out of the borrow pit at its western end. I collected the pieces in my raincoat and carried them back to my hotel room in Pointe Noire where I glued them together that evening. This beautiful pot had yet another type of decoration (Figure 2.1). Although we had no radiocarbon dates yet, we were clearly on our way toward constructing a cultural chronology for the region. We just needed more sites and more radiocarbon samples. I wondered what my chances would be of convincing Conoco to pay for a longer field season the next summer.

I was lucky that Max Pitcher was not only a highly placed executive in Conoco but also a scientist with a PhD in geology. My pitch would undoubtedly have been much harder had I had to deal with someone with an accounting or business degree. Of course, there were also those behind-the-scenes considerations of which I was only now becoming aware.

The 500–800 BC dates I subsequently received for Tchissanga were surprisingly early. Indeed, these were among the earliest dates for Ceramic Later Stone Age (CLSA) materials yet obtained in the coastal region of Central Africa. I therefore had some ammunition when I attended the annual Conoco executive meeting in Bandera, Texas, to request funding for further research.

Interested in discussing the findings, Max was also pleased with how successful the work had been and with how scientifically important the site at Tchissanga seemed to be.

"We need a larger scale excavation there to recover more samples and to uncover pits with in situ materials. Pits are a characteristic of similar early sites in Gabon and Cameroon," I said. "If we can find them, we will have a potential link with early settlements up the coast. We might also be able to recover carbonized seeds or other materials." I added that we had also found another site with very different ceramics that should be tested and dated as well. I felt that with more work we would be well on our way toward unveiling the prehistory of a previously poorly known part of the continent.

"How much will it cost?" asked Max.

I had prepared a budget based on the brief knowledge I had of costs in the Congo, which were frightfully high. In fact, at that time Brazzaville was ranked on some lists as the third-most-expensive city in the world in terms of cost of living – right behind Tokyo and Hong Kong. I handed my budget to Max with some trepidation. He looked at it, scowled, and handed it back to me.

"You know what I do when I see a budget like this?" he asked.

"No," I replied with a sinking feeling, thinking the amount was too high.

"Double it," he said.

I almost fell over.

Later I learned that some of their interest in the archaeological project, and the hurried timing of it before Christmas, was driven by deeper currents. At a subsequent meeting in Houston, I was asked about projects that might make a suitable "gift" at a signing and presentation ceremony to be held in June.

"How about making a film about the Congo?" one executive suggested.

I commented that ethnographic films are some of the most difficult to do in a sensitive manner – particularly by a non-Congolese director. "Wild animals are much easier since they can't complain if they feel misrepresented," I added. "A display case exhibiting some of the materials from the archaeological excavation would be easy, however. I have had some experience with that in Botswana where I worked for the National Museum."

As preparations began for the summer field season, Max decided that I should make a display on the project for presentation during the lease-signing ceremony. Since our last talk, Conoco had won an exploration lease for the territory in which it was particularly interested. I discovered that the reason for Conoco's initial rush to carry out the project was so it could be used as a small bargaining chip in the negotiations. Basically, its argument was "We not only search for oil in a cost effective manner, we are also an environmentally concerned company. And that concern extends to archaeology and history." Rumor had it that the wife of the president of the Congo was also from the Madingo-Kayes region, which did not hurt. Drawing on my experience at the National Museum of Botswana, I quickly put together photographs, text, and a few artifacts for the display case. Included among these was the beautiful pot from Madingo-Kayes that I had reconstructed the previous year.

The next season I brought three students from the University of Texas, as well as my family. I expected that Aimé and two other students from Marien Ngouabi would join us at Tchissanga, but they could not because of a change in their school schedule brought about by a student strike earlier in the year. We set up our datum point, laid out a grid across the hilltop, and had just begun excavations when I was asked to fly to Brazzaville to organize the archaeological display in a glass case flown at great expense from the United States. It was to be placed in the minister of energy's office on the seventh floor of one of the more modern buildings in the capital. I was told the minister, Mr. Adada, would be coming in around 8 AM for the signing ceremony. Arrangements had been made to give me access to his office at 6 AM so that I could put the display together. I had just finished when Minister Adada came in unexpectedly early.

"What are you doing in my office?" he asked, puzzled to find a stranger there.

I told him that I had put together a display case containing artifacts excavated near Madingo-Kayes. It was a present from Conoco in honor of the signing celebration that morning.

"Show me," he said.

I spent the next 15 minutes pointing out the artifacts we had uncovered, discussing their age, their possible cultural relationships, and what they could tell us about the early history of the Congo. He became quite interested and asked several questions. Then he said, "You know, I get a lot of presents and presentations from oil companies in my office. Usually they are scale models of oil rigs, or photographic displays, or sometimes computers designed to help with overseeing oil production. But this is about *us*. It's about *our* country and past. The artifacts in this case were made by the hands of *our* ancestors." Then he surprised me by asking, "Can you take it down?"

"Well, yes," I said. "I only put it together this morning."

"I think this is too important to be in my office. I think it should be in the President's Palace. What do you think?"

Nonplussed, I stammered, "I don't know. Whatever you think, I guess. But Conoco wanted it to be here for the signing ceremony."

"Yes," he said. "But afterwards could you take it down for moving? How long would that take?"

"About half an hour," I answered.

"Let me make a phone call." He walked over to his desk and picked up a red telephone. Listening in, I could hear him talking to a "comrade general," asking if he could come to look at something in his office.

The general arrived 15 minutes later in a camouflage field uniform, his trousers tucked neatly into polished boots, a pistol in a patent leather holster at his waist. The minister pointed to the display case, and the general walked over and looked at it quickly, his hands clasped behind his back. Turning to the minister with a quizzical expression he said, "It just looks like a lot of old rubbish to me. Don't you think the president would be upset [*désolé*] to have something like that in his palace?"

The minister then gave the general the same talk that I had given him earlier, and the general was soon convinced. He went to the telephone and called for several soldiers to come immediately after the ceremony to help take down the display case and transport it to the presidential palace. In the meantime, the president of Conoco, Mr. Constantine "Dino" Nicandros, along with several Conoco vice-presidents who had flown in on a private jet for the ceremony, signed the official lease agreement (Figure 2.2). After the signing, an audience with President Sassou-Nguesso had been arranged for the president of Conoco. Some of the Conoco vice-presidents were disappointed that they could not also attend, but it was explained to them that "[t]he president of the Congo only meets with presidents, not with vice-presidents."

Coming back to the minister's office for the presentation of gifts, it was obvious the minister was anxious to get on to the presidential palace. And it soon became apparent that he was taking the display case with him. As the soldiers began lifting it into the elevator, in a surprising turn of events, the minister then turned to me and said, "You ride with me." So I also had an audience with Denis Sassou-Nguesso, then president of the People's Republic of the Congo, and, after several years of civil war, now the current president of the Republic of Congo. It would be nice to know if the beautiful pot from Madingo-Kayes, which captured the interest of Minister Adada in the country's past, still sits in its display case in the cabinet chamber of the presidential palace, thereby transcending the political upheaval that followed the transition to a multiparty state.

During my audience with the president, I began to get a glimmer of how diverse the linkages are between what I had thought were separate corporations. Mr. Nicandros had also brought a gift to present to President Sassou-Nguesso – a beautifully engraved Winchester shotgun. He had learned that the president enjoyed hunting and had brought it as a special gift. "It's from one of

Figure 2.2. The author with oil company executives and the Congolese minister of mines and energy at the signing ceremony for an oil lease. The archaeological display case that later went to the presidential oalace is just visible on the right. (Photo courtesy of ConocoPhillips.)

our sister companies," he said. He was also a vice-president of DuPont, and in the conversation, Seagram's was also mentioned as another related entity. The financial world was a far more intricate and complex entity than I had ever imagined.

The experience also made me aware that the archaeological project was viewed and interpreted on levels that did not always intersect. From Minister Adada's point of view, what made the archaeological project different was that it was deeply interested in Congolese culture and in learning about pasts once thought irretrievable. For Max Pitcher there was a geologist's interest in archaeology and a curiosity about the past. He also saw a possible way to link that curiosity with Conoco's objectives, which were to use the project as a tool to help secure an oil lease while polishing its environmental image on a global rather than a local scale. The local president of Conoco Congo, Roger Simpson, was also vying to win a conservation award given annually by Conoco. And for the Congolese *hommes des politique* or "political class" as they were sometimes referred to, it was an opportunity to show how successful they were at negotiating with the heads of multinational corporations for the benefit of the country.

Back at Camp

Problems had come up in our camp during my absence. The conclusion of the audience with the president was televised on local networks, but before that happened, Mr. Ossoula, the head district official (Sécrétaire Général) in Madingo-Kayes, decided to pay our camp a visit. Unfortunately, he arrived at a time when my wife, who is fluent in French, was away purchasing supplies in Pointe Noire. The U.S. graduate students who had been left behind had little working knowledge of French and did not understand him well; they found his visit threatening. When my wife returned, she found them very upset and ready to pack their bags and flee the camp – by boat, if necessary. Although they had gathered that Mr. Ossoula was upset about something, they did not know what, and, perhaps because they had watched too many bad Hollywood films on Africa, they were sure that something terrible was about to happen.

Unclear about what Mr. Ossoula had come to discuss, my wife Josie rode with Casimir to Madingo-Kayes to find him. The sun was setting by the time they found his house, not far from the district offices. They were shown into a sparsely furnished room where his young children and some of their friends were watching a small black-and-white television in one corner.

It transpired that several villagers had approached Mr. Ossoula, as sécrétaire général of the district, wanting to know why Americans were digging those small, square holes at Tchissanga. They were worried that we intended to bury toxic waste there, a topic that had recently been in the news. It transpired that what Mr. Ossula and the other villagers were concerned about stemmed from a news report a few days earlier about an Italian company that had been caught in Nigeria illegally dumping hazardous waste. The waste was so toxic that many of the workers hired to clean it up had been hospitalized with chemical burns, nausea, and paralysis.[1] Mr. Ossoula, seeing the holes at Tchissanga, wanted to make sure we were not part of a similar scheme.

My wife explained what we were doing and assured him that it had nothing to do with burying toxic waste. In fact, she said, I was presently in Brazzaville and had had an audience with President Sassou-Nguesso. He might be able to see the interview on his television. If he had more questions, I would be back soon and he could talk to me directly then. She added that we would be happy to have him and his family for lunch at our camp. He agreed, and the following Sunday Mr. Ossoula, his wife, and children came for lunch at our camp on the beach. Before lunch, we showed him the artifacts we had excavated, explained the process of radiocarbon dating, and took him on a tour of the site. From that point on I made sure to visit with him each field season, leaving him with updated copies of the archaeological findings and the reconnaissance maps.

A week or so later, when I went to give a talk on archaeology at the Lycée Karl Marx, the local high school in Pointe Noire, I was asked a similar question about toxic waste and radioactivity by a student. It was clearly a sensitive issue. I explained that we were digging up ancient artifacts, and mentioned that archaeologists use the radioactive decay of carbon isotopes or carbon 14 to date their sites.

"Isn't that dangerous?" the student asked. "Aren't you releasing or burying hazardous materials in the Congo with your work, like those we heard about on the news recently? What about this radiocarbon decay you are talking about?"

I reassured the student, just as my wife had reassured Mr. Ossoula, that we were simply carrying out archaeological excavations, adding that there was no danger of us burying hazardous waste or of unleashing dangerous radioactivity by digging at the site.

A second challenge that first season was coordinating the project with Aimé and his students from Marien Ngouabi University. Efforts to incorporate Congolese faculty and students had met with only marginal success because strikes at the university in 1988, 1989, and 1991 forced professors and students to make up missed classroom time during the dry season when the archaeological surveys and excavations took place. As a consequence, Aimé and his students only participated for part of three field seasons in 1987, 1990, and 1992. Instead, the project had to rely on a crew of local laborers hired from the streets of Pointe Noire for its workforce. The local laborers were given on-the-job training in survey and excavation techniques, and despite the difficulties, we were able to open up a series of test pits across the site at Tchissanga to determine its extent, and, if possible, to also determine whether there were different activity areas marked by pits, housing, or other remains. We discovered two areas of occupation with somewhat different sets of ceramics. A prehistoric pit was also found at the base of the hill where it had been bisected by a bulldozer cut.

The logistical snags with Marien Ngouabi University made it apparent that archaeological research was not accorded much prestige in Brazzaville. This impression was reinforced during a visit with Aimé at his home. Because he did not have a PhD, he had little power to influence student schedules so that a joint research project could be carried out. The university did not even provide him a place to store the artifacts he collected. He had to keep them in cardboard boxes stored under his bed in his small, concrete-block house in a run-down section of Brazzaville known as "Poto-Poto" for the sucking sound made by flip-flops as one walked its usually muddy streets.

Nonetheless, as we finished the first field season in 1988 we had high hopes that the following summer, with a larger team, we would be able to carry out a much more extensive excavation at Tchissanga. Sadly, that was not to be.

Eucalyptus and the People without History

The biggest challenge we faced from 1989 onward was how to cope with a massive infusion of capital from the nontraditional business sector of Shell Oil that, in the space of a few years, plowed under almost all of the coastal savanna between Pointe Noire and Lac Ndembo, almost 168,000 acres (Figure 2.3). The first indication I had of this destruction was when I crested the hilltop near the iron tower in 1989 and looked down at the site that we had come to excavate for the third season.

"My God!" I cried out as I looked down to see the entire hillside on both sides of the road tilled and planted in Eucalyptus trees that were already about 40 centimeters high. "What happened? Who is responsible for this?" I just could not believe it. The shallowly buried archaeological deposits had been completely destroyed.

I turned the vehicle around and headed back to Conoco's office in Pointe Noire. Rushing inside I asked, "Does anyone know who plowed over the site at Tchissanga? It must have been done a few months ago because the trees are already knee high."

Everyone was surprised, but no one knew anything about it because at that time they rarely had reason to venture so far north. "Who can I see about this?" I asked, heartsick.

Roger Simpson replied that the eucalyptus company l'Unité d'Afforestation Industrielle du Congo (UAIC) had had small plantations for many years near Pointe Noire. He gave me directions to their offices in another part of the city. On arriving at their cluster of small, one-story offices in a residential area, I went inside and asked to see to the person in charge.

"That would be Mr. LaPlace, the director general," the secretary replied. "Please have a seat."

While waiting, I looked at maps of expanding plantations on the wall and then noticed that much of the furniture had been crafted from eucalyptus wood. I had not known that it was possible to make furniture from it and wondered why anyone would use eucalyptus when so much other hardwood was available. Maybe that was what the plantation is for, I thought, making furniture, or maybe charcoal for local use – large bags of charcoal were commonly seen for sale along the road into Pointe Noire.

After a short wait I was directed to Mr. Laplace's office. He was a neat, well-dressed, and soft-spoken man who rose to greet me. "How can I help you?" he asked in French.

Perhaps it would have gone better if I had been a French archaeologist or had more subtlety or finesse with the language. But I wasn't, and I didn't, so I got straight to the point.

"Your eucalyptus planting at Tchissanga has destroyed one of the most important archaeological sites so far found in the Congo," I began. "How did this happen?"

"What are you talking about?" he asked. "I don't know anything about any archaeological sites there."

"Didn't you hear about the excavation at Tchissanga last year? It was on the television and radio? I even had an audience with President Sassou-Nguesso about it. How could you not know about the site? Didn't anyone recognize from our survey markers and test squares that something was going on there? That it was an archaeological dig?"

"No," he replied as he calmly steepled his fingers. "I know nothing about that. Though now that you mention it, I seem to recall that one of our tractors got stuck in some sort of large hole out there. It took us several days to get it out."

Figure 2.3. A view over a newly planted eucalyptus field in Tchikamba Province. The trees, which are approximately 3 months old, surround an erosional cirque containing a remnant gallery forest. The Mayombe Mountains are faintly visible in the background.

"It was one of our excavation units," I said, slowly burning. "We had come back this season to continue the work begun last year. Our radiocarbon dates indicate this is one of the oldest Neolithic sites so far found in Central Africa. And now it's ruined."

Then I asked why the plantations had expanded so greatly in just a single year when they had earlier been confined to a small area near Pointe Noire.

"The new plantations are not ours," he said. "They belong to Congolaise de Développement Forestier [CDF], a new company related to Shell. They intend to greatly expand the size of the area planted in eucalyptus and they subcontracted with us to do the planting because we have the experience and equipment. It's a shame about the archaeological site, but we didn't know about it and those are not our plantations."

"Maybe you should go see them," he said, giving me directions to their office. Ironically, CDF was just one floor up from Conoco's offices in the center of town.

After arriving back downtown, I climbed the narrow concrete stairs to their office and knocked on the door. The manager, an Englishman named Mr. Mark Callaway, greeted me with a puzzled look as I began to complain about the destruction of the archaeological site at Tchissanga. He was cordial, but guarded.

"I don't know anything about that," he said. "I am new here and this is just an office. Mainly we manage the finances and look after the cloning of the eucalyptus trees. UAIC are the ones doing the planting – you should see them. I haven't even been to Tchissanga." I had hit a catch-22.

"But how can you just plow up an enormous area, over 10,000 hectares [almost 25,000 acres] with no consideration for its impact on archaeological and other resources? Don't you have to account for such things? I know Conoco is concerned to minimize the negative impact of their oil exploration. Doesn't Shell have the same responsibility?"

He was somewhat shocked, but immediately assured me that Shell was "one of the most responsible companies" in this regard.

"We're planting trees, don't you see? Worldwide, rainforests are declining rapidly. This has a significant impact on world climate. Our project is thus very good because we are *planting* trees in these barren savannas. The Congo is a great place for this. The trees, which are clones, grow an average of about 10 centimeters a week here; so they can be harvested in three years. Not only are

25

we putting wasted savanna grasslands to use, we are providing jobs for local people. Shell has an excellent record of environmental stewardship. I don't know anything about archaeological sites, but I don't think anyone thought there were any to be concerned about in the Congo."

Choking on my anger, I replied that archaeological sites can be as endangered as rare species – and once destroyed they could never be brought back. Certainly in the United States part of any environmental impact assessment would have included an archaeological survey and evaluation, especially on a project on the scale of this one.

"I don't know why a survey was not conducted, especially since you intend to plow up tens of thousands of hectares of coastal savanna," I continued. "From my point of view your project is a disaster for the prehistory of the country. Your massive planting campaign has already destroyed many significant sites and seems poised to destroy many times that number. At that rate, much of the cultural heritage of the coastal Congo will be lost in the next few years."

"I don't know anything about that," replied Callaway, "And in any case, we aren't doing the planting. UAIC supplies the tractors and drivers that do the actual work. You should see them. In the meantime, I will bring the matter up with Shell when I am next in London. But I am not sure who is ultimately responsible. It could be Shell in the Bahamas, or in London, or somewhere else."

The destruction of archaeological sites, it seemed, was really no one's responsibility, and no one wanted to assume it unless forced to do so. I had thought there would be some sort of overall agency in the Congo that oversaw the impact of development and industrial projects on the environment. That had been the case when I worked in Botswana, but it was not so here. There was no one to even write to. The Congolese government profited from its share in the plantations, but there was no central agency to oversee the social or environmental impacts of such development projects. Multinational corporations were apparently meant to be self-policing. I went back to camp and wrote letters explaining what had happened to the following Congolese leaders: (1) Mr. Ossoula in Madingo-Kayes; (2) Mr. Tati Loutard, the minister of culture, arts, and tourism; (3) Mr. Adada, the former minister of energy who had been reassigned as minister of secondary and higher education; (4) Mr. Douniam, the minister of scientific research and the environment; and (5) Mr. Noumazalaye, minister of economic forestry. I had hoped that a cooperative effort could be mounted to ensure the future of the country's historical and cultural heritage. That was apparently a radical thought. I received no replies to my letters.

Making the best of the situation that season, because we could no longer excavate at Tchissanga, we carried out excavations at the site of Kayes north of the Kouilou River. We also surveyed unplowed savannas north of the Kouilou, as well as many of the newly planted eucalyptus fields between Pointe Noire and Tchissanga. Although the sites had been ruined from an archaeological perspective by plowing, we could still map them and collect materials from the surface. This would at least allow us to determine how settlement patterns had changed over time. I left that year expecting something would be done to slow the destruction of archaeological sites when Callaway discussed the situation with London. I did not realize that nothing would slow the rate of planting on new savannas. When I returned in 1990, I was horrified at the destruction that had occurred, this time north of the Kouilou River.

The entire hilltop above the site of Kayes had been plowed and planted during my absence, destroying several early sites discovered the previous year. Even worse, the rains that followed the plowing campaign had ripped open the unprotected soil, tearing out gullies that in places were so large that one could walk into them like a tunnel and not see over the top. Along with the precious soil, the cultural patrimony of the country was being torn asunder and washed away. Bulldozers had even plowed through the valley forests separating the savannas, creating gaping holes to allow the tractors to move more freely from one savanna to the next. To be fair, the staff at CDF were also horrified by its own "action first, think later" campaign that had resulted in so much erosion.

The following year CDF modified its planting procedure. As Mr. Bertrand Poirier, the new general manager of CDF, explained, "We no longer need to plow up the entire savanna, removing the grass cover and exposing the soil to massive erosion. We have a new, much better method. Now we spray the savanna with the weed-killer Roundup. This kills the grass, but doesn't harm the eucalyptus seedlings. The dead grass cover prevents erosion until the seedlings are established and their roots can conserve the soil. Then we can plow between the rows to control weeds."

"What about drinking water?" I asked. "Many people get their water from the springs and streams between the hills. They also bathe there. Won't Roundup run off into their drinking water, making it dangerous to drink? Or to wash in? And does it have any impact on the natural forest vegetation, fish, and other animals that live or drink from the springs in the low-lying areas?"

"Oh, no," he assured me. "It's really quite safe."

I wondered how that could be, given what I had already seen in terms of archaeological resources and remained privately skeptical. After all, look what had happened to the archaeological sites in the country. I had not seen any scientists out testing rural water supplies or water-monitoring equipment. How could they be so sure? Or were they simply running on faith?[2] Imagining another year's worth of archaeological sites destroyed, I went to see if Conoco could perhaps help arrange a meeting with Shell in London, hoping it might be more receptive to what was happening on the ground.

The staff at Conoco were very cooperative, and I think they were secretly a little pleased to be able to tweak the tail of a larger tiger. Arrangements were made for me to meet with people in the nontraditional business sector (NTB) in Shell Centre, London. I flew there at the end of the field season in 1990 on my way back to Texas. When I arrived at "the tower" at Shell Centre, I was handed a number of brochures outlining how sensitive Shell was to environmental issues, including archaeological sites. I guessed that these materials were handed out to stockholders. The brochures, however, were all directed at Western, mainly U.K., audiences. There was no mention of programs to protect African heritage, certainly not in the Congo.

Arriving in the NTB area, I was met by Keith Richardson and George Phillips, who greeted me cordially.

"Shell is a very environmentally friendly company. We take such issues seriously and have supported conservation efforts worldwide. Indeed, planting new forests to replace rainforest destroyed by slash and burn farming is a good thing."

I found their practiced glibness galling in view of my experiences on the ground and responded rather shortly: "Well, then, maybe you can explain how you can be so environmentally conscious while at the same time plowing under a good portion the cultural heritage of the Loango coast. Ruining it."

"We don't know how that could have happened. But in all fairness, we didn't know there were any archaeological sites there," said Keith, earnestly. "We are always careful of historic resources, but we never heard about any prehistoric sites in the Congo. So we thought none existed. And besides, before planting we consult with the local authorities. We have meetings, and people give us permission us to plant."

"You never heard about any archaeological sites in the Congo," I said, "because no one has ever looked for them there. And now that I have, I can tell you that you are destroying sites at a frightening pace as you plow up every savanna for a distance of one hundred kilometers around Pointe Noire. In fact, in 1989 you plowed up a site while I was still working on it – the only one of its kind so far known along this part of the coast. Is that how you operate in the U.K.? Why didn't you conduct an environmental survey of the region before plowing it up?"

"Of course not," replied George, handing me yet another brochure, this time featuring some archaeological site in Britain that had been preserved through Shell's efforts.

There were other problems. Returning to the mission at hand, I asked, "In terms of your having local permission to plant, the problem is that all that land is communally held land, not private property."

"Did you pay for that land?" I asked.

"No, but the local authorities all agreed to our using it. It was just lying there in waste, otherwise."

In the Congo, as in most of Africa, people have a right to use communal land, but they do not own it in a Western sense. If someone sees an open patch that is not being used, and no one has expressed any intention of using it in the near future, then permission will almost always be granted by the authorities if someone makes a request to make it productive. To not do so would imply that the authorities held a grudge against that person. Under such circumstances, local authorities would find it difficult *not* to grant permission to use uncultivated ground, especially if one is working in tandem with the government and promises to provide jobs.

There were also other repercussions of Shell's approach.

"The difficulty is that once you have been given rights to use the land, you begin to think of it as if it were private property in a Western sense. In fact, just this year I was threatened by some of your employees who said that if I continued to make trouble I would not be allowed to drive on 'your roads' through your plantations."

"What will happen ten years from now if some villagers ask for some of the land back because their families have grown and they now need more land for their farms?" I continued. "Will you be happy to pull up those trees and remove the stumps so that manioc can once again grow there? Or do you now think you have a higher legal right to it in a Western sense?"

I was clearly angry, and some local people were also becoming so. In a few cases, I had already heard local farmers expressing alarm at the amount of land that was being converted to eucalyptus. They felt like pawns, with their options curtailed. In this sense they were similar to earlier generations who, as domestic slaves, had their rights curtailed because there were no family members to speak out on their behalf (MacGaffey 1977). Indeed, the whole process of land acquisition for eucalyptus planting had disturbing and dark parallels with the ways communally held land had been appropriated during the colonial era a century earlier. As Ekholm (1972: 72–75) writes,

> In both Congo Free State (the Belgian Congo before 1908) and French Congo, all *vacant land* was declared to belong to the state. By "vacant" the colonial administration meant land "not effectively used," a definition which was especially unfavorable for the population in areas using BaKongo's extensive [agricultural] production methods.... Land that was temporarily abandoned could, then, with this interpretation of the word "vacant," pass over into state ownership.... Areas which earlier were used for agriculture, hunting and fishing were closed off, and the people had to do with a less extensive area than they had previously had at their disposal.... [because] neither the Belgian Congo nor the French Congo had had any appreciable white population ... expropriated land was granted to large companies: the mining company UMHK, for example, had an area half the size of Belgium.

"What should be done?" Richardson and Phillips asked somewhat defensively after my outburst.

"On many savannas the sites are buried, not deeply, but enough so that they would be missed in an ordinary walking reconnaissance. One would normally do shovel probes or small test excavations in such a situation, but you are operating on such a large scale that that is not practical. The only way that I can see to locate buried sites before planting is to systematically plow furrows across the savannas in advance of planting in order to bring artifacts to the surface. Any sites located could then be marked for protection. Given the small size of the sites I have seen so far, I think that a plowing interval of one hundred meters would work."

"We could probably do that," Keith replied, "but it will require coordination with UAIC because they actually do the plowing."

"The archaeological plowing would also have to be done enough in advance so that the rains would have a chance to settle the dust and make the artifacts more visible," I added. "Otherwise, the small fragments of pottery or stone tools brought to the surface will be missed in the dust."

Figure 2.4. The author standing next to the signboard erected to protect the Early Iron Age site of Kayes discussed in Chapter 6. My foot is resting on one of the concrete datum points for the excavation. (Photo courtesy of ConocoPhillips.)

They agreed to coordinate the project over the rainy season with UAIC while I returned to Texas for the beginning of the school year. One of my trained field crew, Romain Mougani, was hired by CDF to examine the plow furrows and make collections of the pottery and other artifacts he found. I would return the next year, look at the sites he had located, make decisions about their scientific value, and decide whether they should be conserved or planted. Because the technology for GPS mapping of the sites was not then feasible, wooden signboards would be posted on sites slated for conservation so that the tractor drivers in the field would know to leave a radius of 100 meters around them unplowed (Figure 2.4).

Shell was not happy about leaving open patches of grass in its eucalyptus plantations. "They are a fire hazard," Keith said. But the rest of the program sounded feasible since it was using equipment and personnel already in place. The 4-ft-by-8-ft plywood signs alerted the drivers to the sites, which were then left unplowed. That worked for the first round of planting, but I was disturbed to see that the following year many of the signs had "walked away" because they were seen as good building material by some villagers. In addition, someone had decided that to save money Romain could simply walk in the dust behind the tractors as the fields were being plowed. Then he could just stop the tractors when he found something. When he told me this, we cross-checked a few fields after they had been left to settle with the rains. Sure enough, sites had been missed. It is a story familiar to most archaeologists, who get used to hostile treatment from construction crews. Some of the Congolese workers on the plantation had similar difficulties treating Romain's job seriously, and sometimes teased him. After I went with him to see Mr. Poirier and reiterated that the cut lines had to be done enough in advance so that the rains could settle the dust, Romain revealed his feelings to me.

"I don't like working with people who don't respect the work of others," he grumbled.

By 1992 Conoco was wrapping up their exploration project and its funding for the archaeological project came to an end. Most of their remaining funds were by that time being directed to the

Jane Goodall Institute to care for orphaned chimpanzees in the newly established Tchimpounga Chimpanzee Rehabilitation Center. Our cook, Albert, had already found work there.

Larger Issues of Prejudice

From my discussions with Shell it was quite clear that in Great Britain, any large project, especially one affecting more than 150,000 acres, would have had an archaeological assessment done before the project began. Crews would have been sent out ahead of time to look for sites and decide on excavation or mitigation procedures to preserve the most important ones. Keith and George were nice enough people, but they were not inclined to probe the cultural and political hegemony of colonialism or how it influenced in subtle ways the actions of Shell in the Congo. Such behavior on the part of multinational corporations, in my opinion, is a holdover from times when it was assumed that people in Africa and other "developing" regions lived in "unchanging societies" in which nothing of global historical importance had ever happened before their interaction with Western societies. Sadly, although Wolf (1982) elegantly captured this prejudice over three decades ago in his classic work *Europe and the People without History*, a more recent example is provided by former French president Nicolas Sarkozy, who remarked in an address given in 2007 to university students in Dakar, Senegal, that

> [t]he tragedy of Africa is that the African has not fully entered into history. The African peasant, for thousands of years, lived according to the seasons, following the belief that the ideal life was to live in harmony with nature, knowing only the eternal circle of time's rhythm through the endless repetition of the same gestures and the same words. In this imaginary world where everything repeats over and over again, there is no place for human adventure or for the idea of progress. In this universe where nature orders everything, [such a] man escapes the anguish of history that torments modern man, leaving him immobile in the middle of a static order where everything seems predestined.... Africa's challenge is not to invent for itself a more or less mythical past to help it in the present, but to invent a future using methods it finds suitable. This [traditional African] man never launched himself towards the future. The idea never came to him to get out of this repetitive cycle and make his own destiny.... Africa's challenge is to enter more usefully into history ... to stop the endless repetition, the endless circling, and to free itself from the myth of ... a lost golden age that can never come again because it never existed.... The challenge for Africa is to remain true to itself without standing still.[3]

The operative assumption for Sarkozy and Shell was the illusion that the African past was either an empty, tired, and repetitious circle or simply a fairy tale concocted to be politically correct in the present. It assumes there was nothing of import to learn or to study. In the case of Shell, such attitudes meant that it was unlikely to waste time or money doing a proper archaeological impact assessment because the African past was unlikely to reveal much of interest. As a result, the artifacts that had made the archaeological display case so special to Minister Adada were trivialized and made unimportant – the crude remnants of a timeless and repetitious past.

Contrary to such beliefs, what is circular and repetitive is not the history of a continent still waiting to be fully written, but the tenacity of such prejudiced viewpoints. As Sir Seretse Khama, the first president of Botswana, countered in an address to graduating students at the University of Botswana, Lesotho, and Swaziland in 1970,

> We were taught, sometimes in a very positive way, to despise ourselves and our ways of life. We were made to believe that we had no past to speak of, no history to boast of. The past, so far as we were concerned, was just a blank and nothing more. Only the present mattered

and we had very little control over it.… It should now be our intention to try to retrieve what we can of our past. We should write our own history books, to prove that we did have a past, and that it was a past that was just as worth writing and learning about as any other. We must do this for the simple reason that a nation without a past is a lost nation, and a people without a past is a people without a soul. (Khama, 1970)

The destructive planting practices by eucalyptus plantations resulted in massive soil erosion and a reduction of the biodiversity of the former grasslands. The full impact of this on the overall species diversity may never be known because no detailed baseline studies of pre-plantation bio-diversity were carried out. The widespread spraying of the herbicide Roundup to kill savanna grasses was also questionable. Claims about its environmental safety are disputed, and a report by the Extension Toxicology Network has found that its main ingredient, glyphosate, which in Roundup is combined with tallow amine, is "more toxic to fish than many common surfac-tants."[4] In the absence of detailed records that predate its use in the Congo, the environmental impact of its application in massive eucalyptus planting campaigns is difficult to assess. What is certain is that innumerable archaeological sites were destroyed as collateral damage.

The archaeological resources of the Loango coast were destroyed because Shell, a multina-tional corporation, assumed that there was no history of global significance to be retrieved. Compounding this neglect, there were no local agencies to safeguard such resources and there was no Department of Antiquities to protect the archaeological heritage of the Congo. On a larger scale, the absence of integrated national heritage legislation and conservation infrastruc-ture in the Congo is characteristic of much of Africa and threatens the continent's ability to use scientific data to combat the outmoded colonial and racial prejudices that still trivialize the significance of its past (Schmidt and McIntosh 1996; MacEachern 2001). It should have been Shell's job from the beginning to determine what impact its activities would have on the cul-tural resources of the region. Continent-wide, problems of site destruction have not abated in the intervening years, but have accelerated as the pace of development increases. Despite some improvements such as the recent pipeline survey in Cameroon and Chad (Lavachery et al. 2010), and the programs of predevelopment archaeology and heritage management now well established in Botswana and South Africa (Van Waarden 1996; Scheermeyer 2005), destruction of archaeolog-ical resources is increasing across the continent as the pace of construction, resource extraction, and other developments threatens the continent's archaeological heritage (Arazi 2009).

Finally, historical records indicate that the Loango coast once supported a much more diverse fauna and flora, which has since been greatly reduced by bush-meat hunting and commercial fishing and, now, by the conversion of the once-natural savanna into a vast, monospecific stand of eucalyptus. Species that were once common, such as the hippo and the lion, are now locally extinct. Others, including the leopard, the chimpanzee, the western lowland gorilla, the mana-tee, the dwarf crocodile, and the tree pangolin are endangered, threatened, or rapidly declining. A good deal of the environmental and cultural heritage of the Loango coast has thus been lost through poor or shortsighted environmental and cultural heritage management practices. Rather than dwell on what was lost, however, the remainder of this book details what was learned about the prehistory of this almost unexplored region during the archaeological project.

Bernard Gets the Last Word

The planting stage of the Shell project finished in 1993. As Conoco closed down its oil explora-tion activities, the private funds for archaeology dried up. At the same time, there was increasing unrest as the transition from a Marxist state to a multiparty government unfolded. Increasingly dangerous conditions in the rural areas where the archaeological project was carried out made continuation of the work logistically difficult. A bomb on the scheduled flight from Brazzaville to Paris had exploded over the Sahara in September 1989, killing all onboard. Nationwide strikes in January 1991 closed the international airport in Brazzaville as all towns in the Congo became "villes mortes" with no services for many days. In that instance, a "gift" of U.S. $60 to a Zairian functionaire procured a visa that allowed me to cross the Congo River in a small "navette" to catch a flight home from Kinshasa. I arrived in Brussels the morning the Gulf War began. The situation worsened again in June 1993 when Congo security forces killed the Libyan ambassador at a roadblock between the airport and downtown Brazzaville. My plane, which had left Geneva the same afternoon, was diverted to Douala, Cameroon, so that "we wouldn't have to land in the dark." Swiss Air apparently felt better about depositing us at the Maya-Maya airport in daylight. At the end of that field season, ongoing violence made it impossible to leave using my scheduled flight from Brazzaville. Instead, Shell helped me catch a small, "informally arranged" evening flight directly up the coast to Libreville, Gabon, where an "unofficial" sum of 25,000 CFA helped me to gain an entry visa.

That was my last trip to the Congo. CDF had finished planting and had moved on to production and harvesting. Conoco had also left. It did not find sufficient oil in its exploratory drilling lease to justify a longer commitment. What money was left was given to the chimpanzees that, being cuddly and cute, made for better public relations. A few companies had made reasonable oil strikes; others came up empty. Bernard, the fisherman, put it into perspective one evening as we huddled around a smoking kerosene lantern on the cold veranda at Tchissanga.

"You see," he said, "the sorcerers in the Congo are very powerful. It's too bad about Conoco, but they didn't pay them enough money. Because of that, the sorcerers moved the oil under the ground away from Conoco's drills and over to the pipes of companies that paid them more. That's just how it is here."

3

Natural and Cultural Environment

The land is in general light, and rather sandy. … It is also very fertile; grass grows on it naturally to the height of eight or ten feet. … Notwithstanding six months of continual rain, there are vast plains uncultivated and lying waste for want of water. To whatever depth they dig, neither tuffa nor stone is found. It is a stratum of compact argil [clay], which confines the water to the interior of the earth: it is interrupted in certain places, whence it occurs that the waters subsiding gradually undermine the surface, and often excavate large and deep abysses which open instantaneously during the fall of the rains. The inhabitants of the country flee as far as possible from the vicinity of these moving grounds, which are left uncultivated. (Proyart 1814: 550)

The fine-grained Kalahari sands that blanket the Loango coast extend from South Africa, Namibia, and Botswana northward through Angola and the Republic of Congo to Gabon. Formed during arid episodes in the Late Tertiary or Neocene era between approximately 30 and 2.6 million years ago (Gradstein, Ogg, and Smith 2004), the Kalahari Sand formations have been redistributed and reworked many times (Thomas and Shaw 1991). Most of the early visitors to Loango remarked on them. Battell called them fertile "champaign [sic] ground" (Battell, in Ravenstein 1901:52); for Burton the sands were unusual because of the "holes" or cirques eroded in them, which were visible from the sea, and also because stone of any sort was "as rare as on the Pampas" (Burton 1876: 5). Raw material suitable for Stone Age hunter-gatherers, apart from quartzite cobbles collected from the beach, was therefore scarce. Also absent were the iron and copper ores that are essential for metallurgical production. Perhaps as a result, no direct evidence for smelting of iron or copper was found on the coastal plain, even though tiny fragments of iron appear in the archaeological deposits from as early as the third or fourth century BC. However, iron smelting remains dating to approximately 160 BC have been recovered near the village of Las Saras on the western flanks of the Mayombe Mountains approximately 100 kilometers inland from Pointe Noire (Schwartz, de Foresta, Dechamps, and Lanfranchi 1990). In this more inland area, a variety of rock formations outcrop at the surface.

Because none of the archaeological sites located during the reconnaissance are more than approximately 3,500 years old, the following summary of the modern environment focuses on climatic trends over this shorter period, with an eye to understanding how environmental change affected the opportunities and limitations for human settlement during this period. In the absence of preserved faunal or floral remains at the archaeological sites, particular attention is paid to the variety of plant and animal resources that might have been available for early settlers. Tsetse fly infestation of the coastal forests, for instance, would have inhibited the tending of domestic livestock, especially cattle, on the savanna–forest mosaic of Loango. Palm oil and high protein oil palm nuts (*Elaeis guineensis*), along with a variety of wild game and fresh- and saltwater fish, made up for a likely deficiency in domestic livestock. As settlement density increased during the Later Iron Age, the archaeological reconnaissance also found evidence for the overexploitation of some resources, particularly as the environment was modified during the nineteenth and twentieth centuries under the demands of an increasingly urbanized population.

Geomorphology

The Niari River flows west across interior savannas of central Congo before it cuts a meandering gorge through the uplifted Mayombe Mountains. It emerges west of the mountains as the Kouilou River, which runs through the center of the research area. During the rainy season the Kouilou overflows its banks and empties into the Ntombo Marsh that fringes it to the south. Seasonally inundated swamplands and mangrove forest also line the river from its mouth, where it empties into the Atlantic, to as far inland as Lake Nanga. Swamps also follow the rivulets that link the smaller inland lakes such as Ndembo, Louandjili, and Loufoumbou to the sea.

From the narrow beach that fronts the Atlantic, the coastal plain rises in step-like fashion to the first coastal terrace, approximately 100 meters above sea level at Loango, Tchissanga, and Madingo-Kayes. From this point the littoral rises more gradually to reach a height of 730 meters above sea level near the Cabinda border in the Mayombe Mountains 70 to 80 kilometers inland. The mountains are made up of folded beds of mica schist, quartzite, gneiss, metabasite, rhyolite, and granite (Daines 1991). On the coastal plain, these are buried deeply under deposits of fine, windblown Kalahari sand that has been molded into low, gentle hills cut in places by steep cirques produced by headwater erosion (Figure 3.1). The cirques are particularly spectacular south of the Kouilou River in the vicinity of Tchissanga and Diosso. As early as the sixteenth century, the cirque at Diosso was marked on sailing maps (Soret 1978; Rat Patron 1993; Sitou et al. 1996; La Fleur 2000). Radiocarbon dates from the effluent deposits that drain from Diosso Gorge indicate the cirque has grown in intermittent cycles as wetter periods of erosion were followed by dryer interludes of stability. Today, the cirque is expanding at an average rate of 1.4 meters a year (Sitou et al. 1996: 188), a rate that appears to correlate with a slightly wetter climatic regime that began between 500 and 1,000 years ago. Cirques also occur at more inland locations not visible from the coast, such as along the headwaters of Bimbakassa stream that drains northeast into Ntombo Marsh. In many of these locations, they pose threats to agricultural fields and roads.

Coastal erosion along the beach north of Loango Bay is also significant. At our archaeological camp in Tchissanga a few kilometers north of Diosso, structures built 40 meters from the water's edge in 1988 had washed into the sea by 1992 (Figure 3.2). This strong surf has destroyed almost all prehistoric shell middens and other coastal sites that might once have existed in an area otherwise known today for its productive oyster beds. Earlier sailors described the rough coast between Kilongo in the north and the Kouilou River in the south as "foul ground ... not safe [because] the bottom is sand and rocks, and the shore must not be approached nearer than in 9 fathoms" (Purdy 1855:472). The powerful waves that batter it have also removed all traces of the nineteenth-century European trading posts or "factories" that once lined the beach. These are clearly marked on early-twentieth-century maps, but none could be located during the reconnaissance.

There are no rock outcrops on the sandy plain, so the few polished stone axes, small grinding stones, and chert stone tools recovered at some archaeological sites were most probably

Figure 3.1. A view of a small cirque near Tchissanga.

Figure 3.2. Spring tide eroding the beach as it floods into our camp at Tchissanga.

carried onto the plain from the Mayombe region or beyond. Other rocks such as red scoria and waterworn, white quartzite cobbles are sometimes exposed at the bottoms of cirques or on the beach. Much of the white quartzite found at archaeological sites was not gathered to produce stone tools, however, but was instead smashed into small, angular chunks to temper the coarse pottery made during the early phase of the Ceramic Later Stone Age in the middle of the last millennium BC.

Archaeological remains uncovered in the 1930s during the construction of the deepwater harbor at Pointe Noire suggest that earlier beach lines may now be deeply buried. Archaeological reports from Djindji, for example, illustrate a "hand-axe," a discoid, and numerous retouched stone blades that appear to lie in reworked white beach sands on a terrace 5 meters above sea level (Lombard 1931; Droux and Kelley 1939). The raw materials from which these artifacts were made must have been imported from the Mayombe Mountains more than 100 kilometers inland (Lombard 1931). The artifacts belong to the Middle Stone Age, which dates to more than 30,000 years ago elsewhere in Africa. No material of this age was found during the archaeological reconnaissance, and it is likely that if other Middle Stone Age occurrences exist, they will only be encountered by chance as deeply buried shorelines are exposed. Other sites may now be underwater.

Late Holocene Climate

Archaeological and paleobotanical studies show that climates in the Congo and Ghana underwent significant environmental changes after approximately 2500 BC (Stahl 1993; Schwartz et al. 1996; Vincens et al. 1998; Sowunmi 1999; Delègue et al. 2001; Neumann 2006; Runge, Eisenberg, and Sangen 2006; Kahlheber, Booen, and Neumann 2009; Neumann et al. 2012). Changes in $\delta^{13}C$ soil profiles[1] (Schwartz et al. 1996; Delègue et al. 2001) and evidence from pollen cores (Vincens et al. 1998) from the Republic of Congo indicate that the drier climatic regime established around 3,000 years ago produced new savanna openings in the once-closed forest. For instance, pollen cores from Lake Sinda, one of the driest areas in the Niari valley, found that between 3000 and 2500 BC tree pollen decreased abruptly while grass pollen increased. The fact that the lake was drying up at this time indicates the vegetation changes were related to climatic change rather than to forest clearance by early settlers. Changes in the $\delta^{13}C$ composition of soil organic matter along the Gabon coast around 2000 BC attest to a similar change from closed forest to a more open forest/savanna mosaic north of Loango (Schwartz et al. 1996; Delègue et al. 2001).

Multiple lines of evidence thus suggest that the appearance of savanna openings in what was once-closed tropical forest was related to changes in the annual distribution of rainfall, with more pronounced seasonality between rainy and dry seasons (Maley and Brenac 1998; Maley 2004). Charred grains of cultivated pearl millet recovered from archaeological excavations at Bwanbé-Sommet and Abng Minko'o in southern Cameroon dated between 400 and 200 BC suggest that a more pronounced dry season would have made the cultivation of this savanna crop possible in areas of higher rainfall where it would otherwise not grow (Eggert et al. 2006; Meister 2007; Meister and Eggert 2008; Kahlheber et al. 2009; Neumann et al. 2012).

To the south in the Republic of Congo, botanical evidence for the appearance of similar savanna openings also occurs toward the end of the last millennium BC from excavations at an iron smelting furnace on the now-forested western flanks of the Mayombe. Remains of *Ximenia americana* or sour plum were found with the smelting remains (Schwartz et al. 1990). This shrub grows only in the open savanna, and Schwartz argues that because it has no medicinal or ritual uses that might otherwise account for its transport to the site, the environment around the site 2,000 years ago must have been drier than now. But without more evidence, movements of smelters and smiths between settlements on savanna, where there are no ores to smelt, to locations on the edge of the Mayombe where the ores and hardwoods for smelting are available, could also account for a transfer of dry savanna species to now-forested locations. Although the *Ximenia* does not have medicinal or known ritual uses in the region, its yellow, plum-shaped fruit is widely eaten in eastern and southern Africa. It could, therefore, have been brought for consumption by smelters from the coastal plain. In any case, both the $\delta^{13}C$ evidence from dated soil contexts and the palynological data collected from ancient lake beds indicate that the region from southern Cameroon to the mouth of the Congo River experienced a drying climate with more accentuated seasonality between 2000 BC and AD 1000. This resulted in the appearance of savanna openings in the once-closed tropical forest after 1500 BC that created habitats favorable for the settlement of food-producing communities in the Cameroon, Gabon, the Republic of Congo, and the Democratic Republic of Congo (Schwartz et al. 1996; Vincens et al. 1998; Delègue et al. 2001: 111; Kahlheber et al. 2009; Ngomanda et al. 2009; Neumann et al. 2012). These savanna openings also coincide with an increase in oil palm pollen in soil profiles across the Congo (Vincens et al. 1998; Sowunmi 1999).

Thus, on the coastal plains of Loango, climatic and vegetation changes correlate with the first appearance of archaeological sites containing pottery, flaked stone, and deep pits filled with carbonized oil palm nuts (Denbow 1990, 2012). Evidence from the southern Cameroon indicates that two domesticated plants, pearl millet and perhaps bananas, were consumed by Ceramic Later Stone Age populations as early as 400 BC along with the fruit, oil, and nuts from the oil palm (Vansina 1997; Mbida et al. 2001, 2003; Eggert et al. 2006; Kahlheber et al. 2009; Neumann 2006; Ngomanda et al. 2009: 316).[2] These plants probably facilitated the expansion of Ceramic Later Stone Age populations southward onto the newly opened savannas of the Loango coast (Schwartz 1992). Indeed, given the evidence for early pearl millet cultivation in the southern Cameroon, it is possible that some of the savannas that appear at this time on the Loango coast had anthropogenic as well as climatological causes even though the archaeological excavations recovered no carbonized seeds apart from carbonized oil palm nuts.

The acidic soils and high rainfall in the Congo are not favorable for the preservation of faunal remains that could specify prehistoric hunting or herding practices. The historic records, however, document several transformations in agricultural, hunting, and fishing practices from the sixteenth to nineteenth centuries as Vili farmers and fishermen responded to new opportunities brought about by European contact, modifying their crops and technologies to take advantage of new crops that included maize, manioc, and groundnuts or peanuts and new technologies that included firearms and fishing nets. The new crops, in turn, resulted in the development of new cooking and other utensils, including the clay tobacco pipes found on some sites.

Because no faunal or floral remains were preserved in our excavations apart from the ubiquitous carbonized oil palm nuts, the faunal and floral diversity reported during the historic and modern periods is presented in the following sections. This represents a minimum baseline of the wild plant and animal resources that could have been available to prehistoric populations.

The Cultivated Environment

Agriculture

"I'm a maniac for manioc," Romain often said. He felt no meal was complete unless it had plenty of his favorite starch. And no amount of technical debating around the dinner table in camp ever shook his conviction that manioc had been the food of his ancestors from time immemorial – even when it was pointed out that the plant had been domesticated in the New World and introduced to Africa by slave traders in the sixteenth or seventeenth centuries. After the middle of the eighteenth century, in fact, there is little mention of the earlier African cereals, millet and sorghum, that were the likely earlier staples. These had largely been supplanted by manioc – a crop with higher yields per acre while placing less demand on soil fertility (Von Oppen 1991; Vansina 1997).

Traveling across the grass savannas north of Diosso, we saw little beyond the scattered humps where manioc, taro, or other tubers had been grown. These crops were supplemented by small groves of bananas, mangos, and sometimes oil palms that had been planted behind houses (Figure 3.3, top). Most of the village cultivation in rural areas is still done by hand, using fire and axes to burn clearings in the forest where the soil is then pulled up with hoes to create mounds for cultivation (Figure 3.3, bottom). Although one sometimes comes across old manioc mounds

Figure 3.3. **(top)**. A small village market along the track to Lac Tchitembo. Cooked manioc wrapped in banana leaves (*kwanga*), taro root, and bananas from the trees behind the village are for sale. **(middle)**. Oil palm fruits for sale along the road north of Madingo-Kayes. **(bottom)**. Burning a clearing in the forest for a new manioc field along the track to the archaeological camp at Tchissanga.

in the open savanna, most agriculture takes place in clearings burned into the forest's edge to take advantage of the slightly more fertile soils found there.

Not having our own fields, we generally purchased our manioc from roadside stands where it was laid out like loaves of bread, precooked and wrapped in green banana leaves to produce *kwanga* (Figure 3.3, top). Like today's fast food, it only needs to be reheated at suppertime and served along with side dishes of spiced fish, shrimp, or other foods. Vansina (1997: 265) writes that *kwanga* was probably a coastal innovation in Loango or Soyo that was carried by traders inland to the Pool region where it is recorded as early as 1698. Unwrapped, *kwanga* is an off-white and rather glutinous substance that to me is very bland but to Romain is heavenly. Along with bananas and bread, it is the most popular staple food in the Congo today. This was not always the case, of course, and at the end of the 16th century, Battell (in Ravenstein 1901: 67) does not even mention it in his detailed description of the crops grown in Loango:

> They have four sorts of corn in Longo [Loango]. The first is called *Masanga* [pearl millet], and it groweth upon a straw as big as a reed, and hath an ear a foot long, and is like hemp-seed. The second is called *Masembala* [sorghum]. This is of great increase, for of one kernel there springs four or five canes, which are ten foot high, and they bear half a pint of corn apiece. This grain is as big as tares, and very good. Thirdly, they have another that groweth low like grass, and is very like mustard-seed; and this is the best. They also have the great Guinea wheat, which they call *Mas-impoto* [maize]. This is the least esteemed.

A footnote by Ravenstein incorrectly states that millet "was introduced from abroad," and suggests that the unnamed grain is *Eleusine coracana*, or finger millet, to which he wrongly attributes an Asian origin. Since Battell makes no mention at all of manioc, it may have come in a later wave of imports from Brazil or, more likely, was even less esteemed than maize, which Lopes in 1591 described as "of so little value that they give it to pigs, rice being likewise little thought of" (Lopes et al. 1881: 67).

Manioc took longer for coastal peoples to adopt than maize and from Loango to Luanda it was initially viewed as a crop grown for European rather than African consumption. It took many generations before it became the "pains quotidiens" or daily bread of the Kongo (Vansina 1997: 255–57). African farmers living on the coast may have been slow to take up manioc cultivation because it required a whole new system of production and processing that involved careful preparation of the seedbeds (planting in mounds rather than rows) and soaking the root to remove the poisonous hydrocyanic acid it contains before grinding it into a flour. Furthermore, Von Oppen (1991) argues that the higher productivity of manioc altered local power hierarchies by enabling women, who provided much of the agricultural labor and food-processing labor, to achieve greater bargaining power in their households. In addition, older, more mature households with established fields and more-available agricultural labor used the new surpluses manioc enabled to gain control over younger people and immigrants who had less access to labor and land. By the middle of the eighteenth century, Proyart (1814: 551) writes that manioc, with its higher productivity, was now "the bread of the people, and a constant food which is always in plenty; hence no beggars are to be seen." In the twentieth century, it had become so entwined with female identity that the root played a role in girl's initiation rites in northwestern Zambia (White 1962: 10).

Maize, despite its early disfavor among some coastal peoples, became a plant widely associated with the Europeans who first introduced it from the Americas. Coastal peoples from the Congo to northern Angola used the term *múndèlè*, meaning "maize people," to refer to all Europeans. The same term is found as far south as the Caprivi Strip in Namibia and as far east as Victoria Falls on the Zambezi River (Bostoen 2007b: 21).[3] The crop was ground and boiled in ways similar to indigenous pearl millet and sorghum, and it later became a complement to those crops on the Loango coast. Nsondé (1995: 150), for instance, remarks that the Congo term *mfundi* was used to refer to a dish made from a paste of sorghum or millet flour at the beginning of the eighteenth century, but by the end of that century mission dictionaries describe the same preparation as being prepared with maize flour.

By the middle of the eighteenth century, Proyart found that cultivation of sorghum and millet, both more drought resistant than manioc or maize, had fallen out of favor in Loango; however, both were still grown to the south in the Kingdom of Kakongo, where they were sown "in the midst of the desert [sic] plains where few people bestow any particular culture upon it" (Proyart 1814: 552). When droughts occurred, people suffered, "since they preserve no provisions, nor have they any means of procuring supplies from abroad" (Proyart 1814: 551).

Both "sweet" and "acid" varieties of manioc were grown. The root, soaked in water to detoxify it, was cut into strips and dried on wooden racks before being pounded into flour and steamed. The leaves were also boiled and eaten. Proyart (1814: 551) describes specially made pots for this purpose, "with two bottoms; they put the manioc upon the upper one, which is perforated like a cullender [sic]; the lower bottom is full of water; they close the vessel hermetically, and place it on the fire; the evaporation of the boiling water cooks the manioc." Whether this cooking technique was derived from earlier methods for cooking indigenous yams or tubers, or it was introduced by the Portuguese along with manioc, is not known. No perforated-base pots were recovered from the Congo archaeological project, but colander-like vessels do occur in seventh- to eleventh-century Early Iron Age assemblages at Divuyu and Matlapaneng in northwestern Botswana (Denbow 2011: 82, D37). The ceramics from Divuyu, described in Chapter 8, are related to the Early Iron Age Spaced Curvilinear (SC) wares of the same period from Madingo-Kayes and Lac Ndembo discussed in Chapter 6 (Denbow 2011).

Another plant brought from America was the peanut, known locally as *nguba* or *mpinda*.[4] Proyart writes that the Vili, in addition to expressing oil from it, "bruised" them to make a paste used "as a seasoning for their ragouts" (Proyart 1814: 551). An indigenous ground bean (*Voandzeia subteranea*) and pigeon peas *(Cajanus indicus)* were also grown, along with a variety of nuts and fruits including cola (*Cola acuminata*) and oil palm (*Elaeis* sp.) The sap from the oil palm was also fermented into an alcoholic drink. From the sixteenth and seventeenth centuries, writers describe it simply as an alcoholic "white, milk-like substance," but as the need for a convenient local substitute for grape wine grew, Christian evangelists began referring to it as palm "wine" so they could use it in their liturgy (Nsondé 1995: 144, 146).

In 1617, Batell states that honey was gathered from hollowed out logs placed in the tops of trees; it was harvested once a year by stunning or calming the bees with smoke (Battell, in Ravenstein 1901: 67–68). Proyart (1814: 559), however, denies that the Vili knew how to make bees "labour on their account, by procuring abodes for them." Perhaps because he was French, he did pay more attention to the local cuisine than did most observers, listing among the crops grown in Loango melons, pumpkins (pompion), spinach, and sorrel, along with purslain "quite like ours," and "dog's grass," both with medicinal uses. By the eighteenth century the American domesticate, tobacco, was so common that he saw it as "one of the natural productions of the country; Negros cast the seed of it at random into their courtyards and gardens, where it fructifies without tillage … all of them smoke; and the men and women have their pipes of potter's earth" (Proyart 1814: 552). Most likely referring to mission rather than Congolese gardens, he concludes that cabbages, radishes, "and the greater part of our European table-vegetables … and chicory" can be grown in the Congo "as fine as in France."

To these cultivars, Van den Broecke, writing in the first decade of the seventeenth century (La Fleur 2000: 98), adds beans, sugar cane, Benin pepper, "beautiful ginger," pineapples, sweet potatoes, yams, "Turkish beans," limes, and "arang-apples" or oranges. Although the pineapples and sweet potatoes are American imports, one should perhaps be cautious of the "abundance of limes" and "oranges" he reports because an indigenous species, the "monkey orange" or *Strychnos cocculoides,* superficially resembles those two fruits because it is green before it ripens and then turns to orange.

Although manioc could not have been present before European contact, the history of the banana (*Musa*) is being pushed back dramatically in Africa. Battell mentions the cultivation of "plaintain trees," and new archaeological evidence indicates that the plant, originally an Indonesian domesticate, may have been brought across the Indian Ocean to East Africa more than 5,000 years ago (Leiju, Robertshaw, and Taylor 2006; Robertshaw 2006); however, there are now questions about the validity of the identification of these phytoliths as banana (Neumann and Hildebrand 2009). Distinctive banana phytoliths recovered from prehistoric pits at the site of Nkang in the Cameroon indicate the plant had spread from east to west across Africa by 500 BC (Mbida et al. 2001, 2004). If these identifications are confirmed by future research (see Neumann and Hildebrand 2009), then the earliest ceramic-using settlers arriving on the Loango coast between 1000 and 500 BC could have cultivated them, even though direct evidence for their presence is lacking.

The antiquity of another indigenous domesticate in West-Central Africa, pearl millet, is also undergoing revision (Nsondé 1995). Once thought to be a late introduction to the savannas south of the tropical forest through contact with East African cultivators (Ehret 1974, 1998; Vansina 1990, 2004; Phillipson and Bahuchet 1994/1995), pearl millet has now been dated in the forested regions of southern Cameroon to between 400 and 200 BC (Eggert et al. 2006; Neumann et al. 2012). New linguistic interpretations indicate that a term used for millet in the West Coastal and Southwestern Bantu regions, *-cángú, probably dates back to proto-western Bantu, or perhaps even to proto-Bantu (Bostoen 2007b; Kahlheber et al. 2009). The term *masanga* mentioned by Battell for millet in Loango at the beginning of the seventeenth century clearly places the term there.

Our excavations found vast quantities of carbonized oil palm nuts at Ceramic Later Stone Age (CLSA) and Early Iron Age (EIA) sites on the Loango coast. In modern villages, these trees represent a form of arboriculture because they are commonly transplanted from the forest to line village pathways and roads. The domesticated nature of these trees was even commented on by Battell, who remarked that, "they keep them with watering and cutting every year" (in Ravenstein 1901: 69). The oil palm fruit tastes something like a fig when roasted in the coals (Figure 3.3, middle). Its almond-sized nut is also high in protein. Oil is produced by bruising the fruit, boiling it in water, and skimming off the oil as it floats to the top. Today it is bottled and sold in the local markets. Palm trees are also tapped near their upper leaves to collect the sap, which quickly ferments to become palm wine, the most suitable drink to offer visiting guests or the ancestors.

Domesticated Animals

Historic evidence for cattle (*Bos taurus*) on the Loango coast is ambiguous. Van den Broecke suggests there were large herds present – at least to the south in northern Angola. Battell, on the other hand, describes a situation more similar to that of the present day in Loango where tsetse fly limits their numbers to a few animals. Tsetse flies (*Glossina fuscipes* and *G. palpalis*) are most troublesome during the rainy season when they hover at the edge of the forest waiting for a victim to pass by. During the dry season, they retreat deeper into the forest and do not venture onto the plains. This contemporary practice is paralleled by observations from Battell, who four centuries earlier found that "[i]n this kingdom there is no kind of tame cattle but goats, for none other cattle will live here. Oxen and kine have been brought thither, but they presently die. The hens in this place do so abound that a man may buy thirty for the worth of sixpence in beads" (Ravenstein 1901: 63).

During the archaeological reconnaissance, a small herd of goats (*Capra hircus*) was often observed scrambling along the roadside near the Kouilou River bridge; a small herd of dairy cows was also seen further inland in the southeastern part of the survey area. Apart from the ubiquitous chickens, these were the only domesticated livestock seen in the region. The owners of these animals indicated that as long as the cattle were kept out of the forest, they did not have too many problems with trypanosomaisis or *nagana*; nonetheless, few people keep them because of these difficulties. Just south of Loango in Sonyo, however, Van den Broecke (La Fleur 2000: 60) describes large numbers of domesticated animals, "particularly many oxen, cows, sheep, and goats, which were pastured in flocks of 100 by the herdsmen." Cattle raising was risky not just because of the tsetse fly but also because "officers of the king might at any instance take [them] away" (Proyart 1814: 555).

We do not know whether the first CLSA populations arrived with herds of domesticated goats, but a single proto-Bantu term for these animals in both Eastern and Western Bantu languages has been reconstructed (Ehret 1998: 309). These animals could have come later, perhaps in several waves, as subsequent Iron Age populations took up residence on the coast in the early centuries AD. Although details of the timing and routes followed by early food producers are presently uncertain, the evidence presented in the next chapters indicates that the last millennium BC and first millennium AD were periods of great economic and cultural transformation.

Chickens (*Gallus gallus domesticus*) were very common everywhere according to sixteenth- and seventeenth-century depictions of the region. Although chickens were plentiful, eggs were rarely eaten – at least by common people – because "with a little patience an egg becomes a chicken" (Proyart 1814: 555). Both linguistic and archaeological data from southern Africa indicate that chickens arrived in southern Africa more than 1,000 years ago, where they are present as far inland as the eastern Kalahari by AD 700 (Denbow 1983; Plug 1996). They do not appear to have been present at Early Iron Age sites west of the Okavango in northern Botswana, however, until later. The date of their first appearance along the coasts of Angola and the Congo is therefore open to speculation.

Other domesticated animals recorded by Proyart included ducks, cats, and barkless dogs. He adds that pigs were also raised in Loango in the eighteenth century, but unless these were tamed bush pigs, they were introduced by Europeans.

Hunting and Fishing

Today, animal protein comes mainly from hunted game and fishing. These activities are carried out by the inhabitants of the small hinterland villages who then market the game in Pointe Noire. The range of wild game now present is a much-depleted version of the species described by Proyart (1814: 555–560). He states that no hares or rabbits inhabited the coastal savannas, but a variety of partridges, quails, and larks were found there. Although elephants were common, he argues they were never hunted and claims that the ivory sold to European and American traders came from the tusks collected from animals that had died a natural death. Lions and two varieties of "tygers" were also found: a "grass tiger" the size of a large dog that ate rats and the occasional chicken and a "wood tiger" that consumes larger animals, including buffalo and "deer." Perhaps the wood tyger was a lion (*Panthera leo*) or leopard (*Panthera pardus*); however, it would be unusual for the latter to attack a creature as large as a buffalo. The "grass tyger" could be a jackal (*Canis* sp.), but smaller carnivores such as civets are also found on the grasslands. Lions are now a thing of the past, as are the hippos mentioned by Battell and Van den Broecke. Forest elephants (*Loxodonta cyclotis*) were occasionally encountered during the archaeological project, especially along the edges of the forested areas north of the Kouilou. Smaller antelope were also common, although they were under pressure from hunting. In the past elephants were more common, and Van den Broecke (La Fleur 2000; 98, 101), contradicting Proyart, reports that so many were killed to meet European demand for ivory that local communities were at times awash in a glut of elephant meat.

Van den Broecke, in passing, also provides what may be one of the earliest descriptions of a lowland gorilla (*Gorilla gorilla gorilla*) or chimpanzee (*Pan troglodytes*): "Around the river Cacongo ... is found a certain type of man that the Portuguese call *Salvagis*. They are totally wild, cannot speak, walk naked, and have very shaggy hair over their entire body. On the back above the crack of the ass is a tail, similar in size to a thumb" (La Fleur 2000: 101).

Proyart does not mention the types of hunting equipment used, but it likely included a variety of traps, nets, spears, and bows and arrows. From the seventeenth century on, muskets were also used. A comparison of Battell's and Proyart's writings reveals some interesting changes in fishing technology. Both report fishermen running along the shore following a species of larger fish "like a grampus" (a type of dolphin) that drove smaller fish ashore where they could be clubbed or harpooned. In the rivers and bays, Battell noted that seventeenth century fishermen also used

> mats, which are made of long rushes ... [a] hundred fathoms long. The mats swim upon the water, and have long rushes hanged upon one edge of the mat, and so they draw the mat in compass, as we do our nets. The fishes, fearing the rushes that hang down, spring out of the water and fall upon the mat, that lyeth flat on the water, and so are taken. (Ravenstein 1901: 66)

In the mid-eighteenth century, fishermen also used nets woven from the bark of banana trees. These were so strong that they "would not yield in strength to the best hemp," according to Proyart (1814: 560).

One of the most interesting water creatures encountered during the archaeological reconnaissance lived in the fresh water of Lake Nanga, approximately 30 kilometers up the Kouilou River from the sea. Talking with local fishermen, I was surprised to hear them complaining about a large animal that was destroying their nets. They kept using a word for it in French that I had not encountered before: *le lamantin*.

"What is it?" I asked. "What does it look like?"

"It is big. It has a head like a lion and a body like a shark. It tears up our fishing nets so sometimes we spear it. It tastes good."

I was not expecting such a creature, and it was only when I got back to camp and looked up the name in a French-English dictionary that I found they were talking about a manatee (*Trichechus senegalensis*). I felt foolish, but I had not expected to find such creatures in the Congo, especially so far upstream in fresh water. In some cases Proyart's eighteenth-century descriptions of African animals are equally hard to equate with animals we know today. His identification of "forest tigers" and "grass tigers," for instance, is subject to deductive guesswork. His description of an unusual fish encountered by sailors in Loango Bay could fit either the manatee or the hippopotamus (*Hippopotamus amphibius*), but Proyart would have been familiar with the latter – so perhaps it is the manatee that early sailors described as they harbored in Loango Bay in centuries past:

> On the coasts of Loango there is a species of mischievous fish, which often occasions damage to European captains; it has a head three times as large as that of an ox; it has a great passion for staving barks and canoes; it approaches the places where vessels are at anchor; it raises its neck above the water; and if it perceives a canoe it darts up to it with impetuosity; staves it at the first onset with its head, and takes to flight; it disdains the perogues; and never attacks them. (Proyart 1814: 560)

Although Loango men made salt by evaporating seawater in clay pots, they did not salt their fish or other foods to preserve it. Instead, they dried it in the sun, or "more frequently they smoke it" (Proyart 1814: 560).

Figure 3.4. Our children Jeremy and Jennifer at a small "port" in the mangrove swamp near the Kouilou River where prawns were netted. To save costs, we bought prawns directly from the fishermen here.

The Contemporary Environment

Dense gallery and mangrove forests follow the rivers and streams that meander across the Loango plains (Figure 3.4); other pockets of forest blanket the bottoms of the cirques. Small areas of mangrove swamp are found near the mouth of the Kouilou River and in a few isolated locations up and down the coast. These woodlands are interspersed with dry grassland savannas on the sandy hilltops. South of the Kouilou River, in the center of the research area, is Ntombo Marsh, a flooded grassland dotted with thicket and papyrus. The Loango area today is one of Africa's most endangered ecosystems, and it shelters many endangered or at risk species that include chimpanzees, western lowland gorillas, forest elephants, pangolins, and civets. The impact of at least 3,000 years of human presence along this coast has had an adverse impact on the biodiversity of the region. Today there are far fewer species present than were described by Proyart 250 years ago or by Battell and Van den Broecke a century and a half earlier.

In 1990, Conoco Congo commissioned a baseline environmental study for "Kayes Block C," to which it had been granted oil exploration rights (Dowsett-Lemaire and Dowsett 1991). The area extended along the coast from Diosso Gorge in the south to just north of the mouth of the Kouilou River, and from the coast inland to just east of Lake Nanga. The following summary is based upon that report, supplemented by field observations made during the course of the archaeological survey. The average annual rainfall measured in 1990 at Tchissanga was a little more than 1,200 millimeters per annum, with the greatest amount falling between late September and January; in addition, mist, drizzle, and fog are common, and it is rare to see blue sky even during the two dry seasons. The average mean temperature at Tchissanga ranged from approximately 24°C in August, the coolest month, to 30°C in January, the warmest month (Piton, Pointeau, and Wauthy 1979).

A mixed savanna/forest mosaic covers the coastal plain, with savanna openings decreasing in size as one moves inland. The last small patch of grassland, which covers just 4 km², is found

35 kilometers from the coast. As elevation increases, closed tropical forests envelope the rugged Mayombe Mountains. Rainfall is higher here, and human population density low. The boundary between the forest and savanna is usually distinct and abrupt on the coastal plain, and in many cases the edge of the forest is almost like a wall. Ntombo Marsh covers more than 900 km² in the center of the study area. Around its edges, seasonally flooded forests add an additional 600 km² of wetland, not counting the marshes and gallery forests that fringe Lakes Nanga, Dinga, Kitina, Ndembo, Louandjili, and Loufoumbou. These add an additional 30 km² of wetland. A small area of mangrove forest (15 km²) lies near the mouth of the Kouilou River. Small patches of tropical forest, amounting to approximately 20 km², are also found deep inside the cirques where they are protected from fire and agricultural cutting.

Dryland Savanna

All the coastal savannas are subject to heavy burning, sometimes twice over, during the dry season between May and August. This limits the population of snakes, rodents, and other nuisance species around settlements. It also encourages the growth of new grass, which attracts a variety of antelope at the beginning of the rainy season. The contemporary species makeup is to a certain extent a reflection of the practice of widespread burning during the dry season. The dominant grass species include Natal grass (*Rhynchelytrum repens*), *Ctenium newtonii*, and "Stab grass" (*Andropogon schirensis*), with occasional patches of *Loudetia arundinacea* and *Elyonurus argenteus*. The few low shrubs found on the grasslands are predominately the African custard apple or *Annona senegalensis*. These produce a small, edible, yellow fruit that is commonly eaten as a snack. Nearer the coast, larger woody plants include *Bridelia ferruginea*, the Sicklebush or Bell mimosa (*Dichrostachys cinerea*), the Christmas berry (*Psoropermum febrifugum*) and the cashew (*Anacardiium occidentale*). Disturbed soils contain taller grasses such as *Panicum*, *Hyparrhenia* and *Pennisetum*. Stands of oil palm trees (*Elaeis guineensis*), a plant native to the forest fringes, are often a sign of past human occupation, as are mature guava trees (*Psidium guajava*) which were introduced from South America by European sailors. We found them to be good markers of late-nineteenth- and early-twentieth-century settlements during the archaeological reconnaissance. Because guava trees were never observed away from past or present human settlements, it is likely that annual burning of the savannah during the dry season limits their growth.

Seasonally Flooded Grassland, Forest, and Marsh

The seasonally wet grasslands surrounding Ntombo Marsh support associations of *Anadelphia* and *Andropogon* species. *Jardinea gabonensis* and *Tiliaceae* also occur, along with tall *Hyphaena* palms in the dryer areas. The seasonal flooding of the Kouilou, which begins in November, inundates the grassy edges of the marsh and its adjacent forests and floods the mangrove forest near its mouth. The river recedes to its banks during the dry season in June.

In some places almost pure stands of the Raphia palm (*Raphia hookeri*) line the streams that drain into the marsh from the higher elevations. Floating grass (*Vossia cuspidate*) forms an extensive cover along the perimeter of the marsh, while floating stands of papyrus (*Cyperus papyrus*), interspersed with thickets of *Alchornea cordifolia*, an Euphorbia widely used as a medicinal plant in Africa (Lamikanra, Ogundaini, and Ogungbamila 2006), and *Anthocleista liebrechtsiana*, *Nauclea pobeguini*, and *Ficus trichopoda* (swamp or hippo fig) in the shallower waters. Floating papyrus mats are an attractive habitat for the shy sitatunga (*Tragelaphus spekii*), which can walk across their unstable surfaces using their elongated toes. The swamp fig grows around the mats, which also attract a variety of wildlife including monkeys, antelope, bats, and birds. The hippo fig, by virtue of its name, may once have also sustained these animals. The sap from this fig is used today for birdlime. Because the waters of the marsh are low in oxygen, many of the fish species, for example, *Heterotis niloticus* or African bonytongue or arowana, *Clarias gabonensis* or catfish, and *Parachanna insignis* or Congo snakehead, are types that can come to the surface to breathe (Teugels et al. 1991).

Coastal Thickets, Cirques, and Mangrove Forests

Stands of *Manilkara lacera*, some standing in seawater at high tide, line the coastal beaches. Near the mouth of the Kouilou, these give way to mangrove and flooded forests, the latter containing many of the same species found in the cirques at Diosso and Mpinde: *Manilkara lacera* and *M. welwitchii*, *Chrysobalanus icaco* (the cocoplum), *Canthium* sp., *Cola cabindensis*, *Fegimanra africana*, *Ochna multiflora* (bird's-eye bush), *Rytigynia gracilipetiolata*, and *Syzygium guineense*. *Symphonia gloulifere* is one of the most notable large trees in the deep cirques, along with *Fegimanra africana*, *Macaranga barteri*, and *Maranthes glabra*. Tree heights of greater than 30 meters are not uncommon in these locations because they have been protected from logging, planting, and fire. In the mangrove forests, *Rhizophoro racemose* can also reach heights of up to 40 meters. Thickets of *Phoenix reclinata* (wild date or Senegal palm) and *Avicennia germinans* or black mangrove intrude into the drier locations. Large trees that include *Ctenolophon englerianus*, *Sacoglottis gabonensis* (bitter bark tree), *Vitex doniana* (African black plum), *Uapaca guineensis* (sugar plum), and *Xylopia rubescens* predominate in the flooded forests that fringe Ntombo Marsh and the swampy margins of Lakes Nanga and Dinga.

Rainforest

Although closed rainforest only begins on the higher terrain 40 kilometers from the coast, many of the same species, especially those belonging to the *Irvingianceae* and *Myristicaceae* families, are dispersed in the sublittoral forests. Since the 1950s, the coastal region has been heavily logged, with particular overexploitation of *Aucumea klaineana* (Okoumé or Gabon mahogany) and *Terminalia superba* (Congo walnut or Limba). Logging peaked in 1973 when a combination of overexploitation and a fall in market prices led to a decline in the harvest of these species (Gilbert and Sénéchal 1989). Since the 1980s, logging has aimed at a greater variety of species, with *Staudtia gabonensis* (Niové), *Nauclea diderrichii* (Bilinga), *Tieghemelia africana* (Douka), *Swartzia fistuloides* (Pao rose), *Millettia laurentii* (Wengué), and *Baillonella toxisperma* (Moabi) being among the most important. Bilinga and Niové are also used locally to construct the small dugout canoes used in the region. These boats are generally 4 to 5 meters in length and manned by two or three fishermen. *Pterocarpus soyauxi,* or Tacula or Tukula as it is known locally, is a red dyewood more prevalent in the northern part of the Loango region, especially at Mayumbe in southern Gabon. In the past it was ground into a fine powder, mixed with palm oil, and rubbed on the body as a red cosmetic. It was an organic replacement for the mineral red ochre used in southern Africa for the same purposes (for examples, see Comaroff and Comaroff 1997: 237). In Loango, it was also used during female coming-of-age ceremonies when young women were secluded for a time in what Dennett (1968:68–70) referred to as "Paint Houses." The dyewood was widely traded along the coast of West Africa by the Dutch and Portuguese, where it was in great demand (Van den Broecke in La Fleur 2000: 97, 102). Today the wood is sold commercially as "Padauk," a hardwood prized by wood turners and carvers.

Sacred or Medicinal Trees of the Coastal Savanna

The preceding overview does not include many of the species of cultural significance mentioned by long-term residents such as Dennett (1968) in Loango or Volavka and Thomas (1998) for Ngoyo just to the south. There are many more plants associated with medicinal and cosmological significance and this brief summary is not intended to be exhaustive, but rather to point out a few of the more significant species.

Mbota: Dennett attributes this to *Lonchocarpus* (Bentley) whereas Volavka and Thomas (1998: 70) describe it as *Melletia versicolor*. It is the Congo national tree and is used for house construction and is "associated with the graves of high-ranking chiefs … [and] used for pharmaceutical purposes." It contains compounds effective in the treatment of intestinal parasites (Ekoya et al. 2006). In addition to housing, it is found planted or growing around shrines, sometimes in association with piles of animal horns and marine shells.

Nsanda: This large, spreading tree is known as the "bark cloth fig." In the past it was often found growing near market places. It was thought to have "sacred" properties according to Dennett (1968: 133). He names this tree as a variety of *Ficus religiosa*, but Volavka says that in Ngoyo to the south, it is more likely to be *Ficus thonningii*. The bark from this tree was in the past pounded to produce the bark cloth wraps worn by pregnant women (Volavka and Thomas 1998: 70).

Nkondo: Although these large baobab trees (*Adansonia digitata*) are not common in the area, particularly large examples can be found near Diosso on the road leading to the Maloango Museum. A group of them marks the site where the royal dead were buried in earlier times. Their fruit is a source of cream of tartar and is used locally for a variety of medicinal purposes.

Mfuma. The silk-cotton or kapok tree (*Ceiba pentandra*) grows to be very large and has round, knobby thorns running up the trunk. Burton (1876) reported sighting these trees lining the shore at Loango Bay in the nineteenth century. The tree is used locally to manufacture both medicines and canoes. Its origins are uncertain and it is possible that the species originated in tropical America and spread in recent times to Africa. If it originated in the New World, the mechanisms for its trans-Atlantic spread remain speculative and include scenarios in which seeds were windblown across the Atlantic (Dick et al. 2007). One cannot rule out the possibility that, similar to maize, manioc, and a variety of other plants, it was introduced to African shores by the slave trade. Its preferred habitat is disturbed areas around villages, and it is not found growing wild on the grass savanna. The tree is sacred to both the Maya of Central America and to the Kongo peoples.

Libandji lwa bakwandji (Anonidium mannii or Junglesop): According to Volavka and Thomas (1998: 72) this tree is commonly planted around houses because it is believed to "repel evil spirits." A decoction made from its bark is sprinkled around the house; its leaves may be placed on the roof while a small piece of trunk is buried under the threshold of the house to protect it. Medicines for gastro-intestinal infections are made from it. Lowland gorillas are fond of its sour, fleshy fruit.

Fishing

Marine

At the time of the reconnaissance, there were small fishing communities strung along the coast from Bois de Singes, Holomani, and Tchissanga northward to the mouth of the Kouilou River at Toupou, Boueti, and Bilala. A fishing cooperative also existed at Matombi. Approximately 190 fishermen lived in these locations (Teugels et al. 1991). Most of the boats used were small, nonmotorized dugout canoes, often repaired with tin patches sealed with pitch. Fishing is most productive during the rainy season (November through April), and today it is carried out almost exclusively with stationary gill nets purchased in Pointe Noire. In July when the sea is rough and tides are especially high, long draw nets are pulled-in from shore by Béninois fishermen living on the northern outskirts of Pointe Noire.

A survey of the fish resources along the lower Kouilou in 1990 recorded 103 species, 68 of which were freshwater varieties (Teugels et al. 1991). During the rainy season, Teugels et al. (1991)

found that approximately 65 percent of the species at the mouth of the river were of marine origin; at Lac Nanga, 30 kilometers upstream, 30 percent were saltwater species. Some marine species such as "capitaine blanc" have a tolerance for fresh water and are sometimes caught as far as 70 kilometers up the Kouilou during the rainy season when floods are highest.

Although ocean fishing takes place throughout the year, the catches are poor during the high "spring" tides between May and August. At our camp at Tchissanga, the massive waves at this time of year often swamped the fishing boats as they attempted to land through the pounding surf. The most important fish caught were *Ethmalosa fimbriata* (Mandzi or Shad), *Thunnus obesus* (Karanga or Bigeye tuna), *Galeoides decadactylus* and *Polydactylus quadrifilis* (Capitaine or Lesser and Giant African threadfin), and *Pseudotolithus senegalensis* (Bar, Cassava croaker, or Drum fish). Spiny lobster or langouste (*Panulirus regius*), some of considerable size, were taken only at the Béninois fishing village of Bilala approximately 25 kilometers north of the mouth of the Kouilou. Their harvest required specialized traps. In addition to capitaine, flounder, and rays, the Bilala fishermen specialized in catching sharks, including Great Whites (*Carcharodon carcharias*), drying their fins on racks for export. During the dry season, the archaeological project was regularly able to purchase sole (*Cynoglossus, Citharus*), spiny lobster, capitane blanc (*Polydactylus quadrifilis*), catfish (*Clarias* sp.) and shrimp from this village, even during the dry season when the fishing was poorest.

Freshwater

Freshwater fishing is subject to the same seasonal fluctuations as marine fishing. The best results are obtained during the rainy season between November and April. Catfish (*Heterotis*) and lungfish (*Patachanna* sp.) dominate catches at this time. In the dry season, mullets (*Mugil* sp., *Liza falcipinnis*), tilapia, and large barbel (*Barbus compinei, Barbus* sp.) are more commonly caught. Nets were used on the larger lakes such as Lake Nanga. The smaller lakes such as Ndembo and Louandjili are generally not fished – perhaps because they are unproductive due to overexploitation in the past. Men most commonly fish with nets; women use baskets to trap fish in the shallow waters. Fish poison is also sometimes used. Freshwater shrimp or Missala (*Macrobrochium* sp.) are netted in the mangroves along the Kouilou and Ntoumbi rivers.

In an interesting side note, the maritime fishermen at Tchissanga were often eager to purchase freshwater fish from inland locations if they learned we were traveling to those locations. When I asked Bernard why he would want to buy fish when he already had his own supplies, he replied, "Those fish from Lake Nanga are sweeter." So, even if it's just trading "a fish for a fish," what one does not have always seems sweeter. From the end of the first millennium AD there is also evidence that cockles (*Anadaris senilis/ Senilia senilis*) and oysters were heavily exploited, and in some cases perhaps overexploited.

Hunting

Bush Meat (Gibier)

During the course of the project, we sometimes encountered game that occasionally included endangered species. At the site of BP 113, a small group of resident chimpanzees (*Pan troglodytes*) often screamed at us from the shelter of the nearby trees as we worked. On the plain below the site, forest buffalo (*Syncerus caffer*) were occasionally seen in the early morning after a night's grazing on the savanna. One day near the site of Meningue, near where the closed Mayombe forest begins, two hunters offered to capture for us a baby gorilla (*Gorilla gorilla*); another tried to sell a forest pangolin (*Manis tricuspis*) he had slung over his shoulder. Elephants (*Loxodonta cyclotis*) were sometimes seen in the forest south of the Ntoumbi River, and during the rainy season of 1992 they passed by our camp at Lac Louandjili, 20 kilometers northwest of Madingo-Kayes. Side-

Table 3.1. Game species observed for sale in the market in Pointe Noire on five occasions in 1990

Species Name	Latin name	1	2	3	4	5	6 (medicine market)
Mammals							
Fruit bat	*Eidolon helvum*		36	45		30	
Putty-nosed monkey	*Cercopithecus nictitans*	1					
Moustached monkey	*Cercopithecus cephus*	1					
Indeterminate smoked monkeys			9	6	13		8 dried hands
Mandrill	*Mandrillus sphinx*						1 skull
Chimpanzee	*Pan troglodytes*						2 skulls, several hands & feet
Gorilla	*Gorilla gorilla*						3 skulls, several smoked hands & feet
Potto	*Potto spp.*						5 skins
Galago, Demidoff	*Galago demidoff*	2	5				1 skull, 3 skins
Pangolin	*Manis tricuspis*						
Giant pangolin	*Manis gigantea*						12 scales
Greater cane rat	*Thryonomys swinderianus*	2	12	1	1	6	
Cane rat	*Thryonomys*						6 skulls
African pouched rat	*cricetomys emini*						4 skins, 8 skulls
Brush-tailed porcupine	*Artherurus africanus*	33	42	26	40	28	
Porcupine	*Artherus spp.*						2 skull, numerous quills
Scaly-tailed squirrel	*Zenkerella insignis*						2 tails, 1 skin
Beecroft's flying squirrel	*Anomalurus beecrofti*						3 skins
Green bush squirrel	*Paraxerus poensis*						3 skins
Gambian sun squirrel	*Heliosciurus gambianus*						2 skins
Ribboned Rope Squirrel	*Funisciurus lemniscatus*						2 skins
Jackal, side striped	*Canis adustus*						1 skin
Palm civet	*Nandinia binotata*		1	1	1	2	8 skins
Civet	*Civettictis civetta*	1	1				6 skins
Mongoose, Egyptian	*Herpestes ichneumon*						1 skin, 1 skull
Servaline genet	*Genetta servalina*	2					17 skins
Blotched genet	*Genette tigrine*						16 skins
Leopard	*Panthera pardus*						1 skin & many skin pieces
African golden cat	*Felis aurata*						4 skins
Otter, clawless	*Aonyx congica*						1 skin

(continued)

Table 3.1 *(continued)*

Species Name	Latin name	1	2	3	4	5	6 (medicine market)
Otter, spotted-necked	*Hydrictis maculicollis*						4 skins
Bush pig	*Potamochoerus porcus*	1	5	2	5		
Water chevrotain	*Hyemoschus aquaticus*			1			
Buffalo	*Syncerus caffer*	1			1		
Sitatunga	*Tragelaphus spekei*	1	3	4	4		1 pair horns, 4 feet
Bushbuck	*Tragelaphus scriptus*		2		2		several horns
Waterbuck	*Cobe onctueux*						1 horn
Duiker, blue	*Cephalophus monticola*	54	97	51	43	26	several horns, 45 skins
Duiker, black-fronted	*Cephalophus nigrifrons*	2	2	3	4	2	2 pair horns
Duiker, yellow-backed	*Cephalophus sylvicultor*	1					
Duiker, Peter's	*Cephalophus callipygus*	1					
Duiker, black-backed	*Cephalophus dorsalis*		2	6	3		
Duiker	*Sylvicapra grimmia*						1 pair horns
Giant otter shrew	*Potamogale velox*						5 skins
Reptiles							
Tortoise, forest hinge-backed	*Kinixys erosa*	3	4			11	11 shells, numerous scales
Dwarf crocodile	*Osteolaemus tetraspis*		21	27	2	5	
Nile monitor lizard	*Varanus niloticus*			2			6 skins, 4 heads
Python	*Python sebae*	2				2	3 skins, 2 heads
Forest cobra	*Naja melanoleuca*						4 skins
Gaboon viper	*Bitis gabonica*						6 skins, 4 heads
Cameleon	*Chamaeleo ?dilepis*						2 dried
Birds							
Green pigeon	*Treron australis*	8					
Crowned eagle	*Stephanoaetus coronatus*						2 feet
African Palm Swift	*Cypsiurus parvus*						10 dried specimens
Black-casqued Hornbill	*Ceratogymna atrata*						1 dried head
various							feathers, 20 dried birds
Total		116	238	179	119	112	

Source: Adapted from Dowsett-Lemaire and Dowsett 1991.

striped jackals (*Canis adustus*) were occasionally seen during the day on the more isolated savannas in the northern part of the research area.

All these animals, and indeed almost all species, are under heavy hunting pressure to supply market demand for the urban population of Point Noire. In the case of shark fins, more global tastes were being met. Indeed, demand for bush meat is so high that some species have locally disappeared. At the Bois de Singe (Monkey's Woods) near Tchissanga, for instance, there are no longer any monkeys – they were long ago hunted to extinction. Most species of small antelope were also scarce south of the Kouilou. As a result, the most common types of meat purchased for our camp came from forest porcupine, cane rats, and other rodents. To these can be added the palm civet (*Nandino binotata*) purchased from a hunter near Madingo-Kayes. Judging from the response of the men in our camp, civets were prized culinary items. In the sixteenth century it is possible these animals were semidomesticated because, in 1591, Duarte Lopes, a Portuguese settler, remarked that "some had been tamed by the people of the country for the sake of their perfume, in which they greatly delight. This was before the Portuguese traded in those parts" (Lopes et al. 1881: 53). Fishermen at Lake Nanga also reported eating manatees (*Trichechus senegalensis*).

A study of traditional and commercial hunting in the greater Kouilou region carried out in 1990 as part of the Congo Conoco environmental project documented the game species transported from the countryside into Pointe Noire (Dowsett-Lemaire and Dowsett 1991; Wilson and Wilson 1991). Their results, summarized in Table 3.1, provide an indication of the variety and numbers of animals marketed by hunters in the study area. In addition to fish, the most common bush meat species observed in the Grande Marché in Pointe Noire, in descending order of frequency, were *Cephalophus monticola* or blue duiker (271), *Artherurus africanus* or brush-tailed porcupine (169), *Eidolon helvum* or fruit bat (111), *Osteolaemus tetraspis* or dwarf crocodile (55), indeterminate monkeys (28), *Thryonomys swinderianus* or greater cane rat (22), *Kinixys erosa* or tortoise (18), *Potamochoerus porcus* or bush pig (13), sitatunga (12), *Cephalophus nigrifrons* or black-fronted duiker (11), *Cephalophus dorsalis* or black-backed duiker (11), green pigeon or *Treron calvus* (8), pangolin or *Manis tricuspis* (7), *Nandinia binotata* or palm civet (5), *Tragelaphus scriptus* or bushbuck and *Python sebae* or python (4 each). The most disturbing sights to me were the smoked chimpanzees and monkeys lying stretched out on the seller's tables along with gorilla and chimpanzee skulls, hands, and feet for sale in the medicine market. A variety of carnivore skins, including those of leopards, genets, civets, and otters, could also be purchased. Monkeys, chimpanzees, and gorillas were hunted both for their meat and for medicinal purposes. Sitatunga from the swamps of Ntombo Marsh were also common, along with dwarf crocodiles caught in the Kouilou and its neighboring lakes and flooded forests.

Hunting with traps, snares, nets, and guns is ubiquitous and wire snares were occasionally encountered during reconnaissance in the forests that fringe the coast north of the Kouilou. Although some game was obtained for local village consumption, most was smoked and sent to the markets of Pointe Noire. It was transported on the same lorries that served as "bush taxis." Although we purchased fresh meat on occasion for our camp, most of it was smoked, with the most common species being the forest or brush-tailed porcupine, pythons, cane rats, and various duiker species, particularly "antelope bleu" and "antelope rouge" (*Cephalophus* sp.). Occasionally, fruit bats and a variety of unidentified, medium-sized rodents were also consumed.

4

Preservation: Heritage and Reconnaissance

Nsi, often translated as "earth," … not only expands in space, but extends in time. … [It] encloses the human past, of which it preserves a visible record … the imprints of the organizing principle. The roads and paths follow distinct patterns tested and codified by the past. The vegetation reveals the history of the region for those who know the logic of its planting. Groups of particular kinds of trees still give evidence of old villages or towns which might have been displaced or destroyed a long time ago. The necropolis is marked with a small, planted forest in which special kinds of trees [i.e., *Mbota*] divulge the status of the buried generations. "No trespassing" signs in the form of planted fields of blooming *makuna*, whose adhesive flowers cause a high fever, may still protect a shrine or the peace of the ancestors, although their descendants have moved. The *nsi* … is a symbiosis of the material testimony of ideology and lives past with present human content. It results in a profound aesthetic effect. The means are not architectural monuments, but a monumental environmental design, realized through time, in which myth and history merge. As the organizing principle is optically more perceivable in the savanna, it might be one of the reasons for the covert yet firm disdain which most of the Bakongo have maintained for the Mayombe and its inhabitants living in the confusing, uncontrollable forest. (Volavka and Thomas 1998: 130)

To the Vili in Loango, and related Kongo peoples living along the coast in the Democratic Republic of Congo and Angola, the concept of land, or *nsi*, encompasses not only a community's geographical space but also the connection of a people with their past. These include legends of genesis and spiritual belief in ancestral guardianship and oversight. Through time, the interplay of economic, social, and political forces has been inscribed on the land in the form of settlement distributions, field and hunting-ground locations, cemeteries, sacred groves, and the routes and social memories that link them and give them meaning. Archaeological surveys, by design, attempt to identify and transcribe the historical trajectory of such places by locating and mapping their physical residues – the actual prehistoric artifacts, settlement remains, roads, and monuments that are testimony to social and historical transformations over time. If detailed enough, surveys can even provide information through lacunae in expected features: "black holes" in material and spatial distributions that may point to contested borders or other inconsistencies or contradictions between oral traditions and archaeological phenomena. Archaeological investigations may reaffirm existing traditions, but may also in some cases surprise when contradictions force us to redefine, reinterpret, or shift the coordinates where "myth and history merge" (Volavka and Thomas 1998: 130).

One such contradiction between tradition and archaeology in the Loango region is the near absence of evidence for iron smelting on the coastal plain. Founding myths for Loango and Ngoyo attribute the founding of these kingdoms to a "brotherhood of blacksmiths," the *buwandji* or *buvandji,* who conquered an indigenous population, presumably the "pygmies" or Bongo, sometime in the eleventh century (Hagenbucher-Sacripanti 1973; Denbow 1999: 414–416; Kimfoko-Madoungou n.d.: 2). Volavka and Thomas (1998: 111) aptly summarize the traditions:

> The existence of a brotherhood strong enough to found a state in Ngoyo and to extend its hegemony to Loango presupposes, first, a considerable agglomeration of blacksmiths and, second, their developed organization. No doubt the blacksmiths' profession, which provided important commodities and was vested with a number of exclusive religious responsibilities, was a precondition of this hegemony. But it was the organization which made it possible.

Later, in the thirteenth century, the Vili are said to have invaded the coast, overcoming the Loandjili brotherhood of smiths and introducing the leopard, or "*ngo,*" as the totem of a new (Loa)ngo kingdom. Thus, even the name of the kingdom resonates widely with Central African traditions that associate social power with the leopard. As Vansina (1990: 104) sums it up, "[t]he trail of the leopard is the trail of power. Among all the peoples of the rainforests, without exception, the leopard was a major emblem of political power ... [and] the disposition of the spoils of the leopard, from hunter to highest authority, is the best indicator of the political structure." As the symbiotic relationship between iron smiths and kings developed, a new *buvandji* state, called Loandjili, combined the word *loa,* referring to clan, with *ndjili,* a species of red-tailed squirrel taken by the Buvandji as their totemic symbol – a symbol still found well into the twentieth century on some Loango tombstones (Denbow 1999).[1] Cement models of these squirrels, models of iron-working bellows, depictions of the sun, moon, and other cosmograms were all inscribed on early-twentieth-century tombstones in Loango as an expression of the linkages between the land of the living, the land of the dead, and iron smelting.

The continuing relationship between smiths and kingship is used by Volavka to explain the presence of iron-smithing tools and related objects in the Lusunsi shrine in Cabinda, where Ngoyo kings were once crowned. The remains of the shrine, discovered in the 1930s, contained a giant, hatlike crown and a woven neckpiece of hammered copper wire. Each item was more than 1 meter in diameter, an exaggerated size that Volavka suggests was intended to symbolize the power and authority of kingship as an institution (Herbert 1984). The colors of the metal: "red" copper and "white" iron, were also important (Jacobson-Widding 1979; Denbow and Miller 2007). The red color of the copper links it symbolically to blood – a commodity of spiritual importance. It is also a metaphor for the red "Kalunga line" where day meets night, the place where ancestors and their descendants interact (Thompson and Cornet 1981; Denbow 1999; Fennell 2007). White evokes both the liminal status of initiation and the world of the ancestors. The hammers, iron bars, and other iron-working tools recovered at Lusunsi suggest that the grove was a pivotal place in the coronation process, and also a sacred place of the blacksmith brotherhood (Volavka and Thomas 1998: 106–107). This ritual importance of smiths, and their ritual position with respect to kingship, is expanded on by MacGaffey (1986: 178–179):

> Smiths were sufficiently like the chiefs, in Kongo eyes, that it was necessary to impose ritual distinctions. Chiefs and smiths had a special respect for one another, the latter calling themselves the "parents" (*bamama, bambuta*). Smiths were initiated in circumstances similar to those calling for the initiation of a chief. And whereas the chief was mystically linked

with his predecessors in office, the smith was connected with local spirits. His own initiation required that a large stone be brought from the river ... usually such stones are *simbi* [spiritual] objects.

Although blacksmiths played key roles in the coronation and divination rites within Kongo society (Hagenbucher-Sacripanti 1973: 36), they were in an ambivalent position with respect to power because their ability to control the physical and spiritual forces of metal production also made them a threat to traditional authority structures. They were, in effect, perpetual "outsiders." Perhaps because of this, the legends indicate that smiths were itinerant, with an uneasy relationship with clan-based political authority:

> The blacksmith in the Kongoland was associated with an undivided space. The space divided by kin challenged the hegemonic impact of the [blacksmith] brotherhood by imposing a control upon their movements from one existential space into another. ... [T]he tradition emphatically refers to the otherness of the blacksmiths and describes them as subjects of eviction. (Volavka and Thomas 1988: 219)

Where Legend and Archaeology Intersect

The archaeological reconnaissance outlined in the next section, and the excavation results presented in subsequent chapters, problematize inherited traditions that posit a simple and recent transition from Stone Age hunter-gatherers to Iron Age kingdoms at the beginning of the second millennium AD. It is now clear that ironworkers and pot makers have inhabited the coast for more than 2,000 years. Iron smelting leaves behind durable and visible remains of its practice. These include deposits of slag, a smelting by-product, the fired clay pipes or tuyères used to direct blasts of air into the furnace, and occasionally even the fired and sometimes vitrified walls of the furnaces themselves. For early metallurgists, as well as for later blacksmiths, access to key supplies of ore, charcoal, furnace clay, and labor were key concerns. Spiritual resources were also important. For example, in some parts of Mali and Cameroon (Huysecom and Agustoni 1998; Lavachery et al. 2010) old furnaces were reused by successive generations of smelters who called on their ancestors and associated spirits for blessings to ensure success.

During the archaeological reconnaissance only one site, number 176 (Table A.1 in the Appendix), contained sufficient slag to suggest it might have been an iron smelting location. Situated northeast of Ntombo Marsh on the eastern edge of the present coastal savanna, the site also produced ceramics different from those found at other sites in the region. At seven additional sites, iron ornaments and tools, along with small quantities of slag that likely accompanied village smithing activities rather than smelting, were recovered from surface collections. Excavations at seven sites (Madingo-Kayes, Kayes, BP 113, Gray Sand, Tchissanga, Mvindou, and Lamba) dated from the fourth or third century BC to the eighth century AD also produced isolated iron objects that indicate access to iron, if not its actual production, on the coastal plain.

Geologically, the closest source of iron ore in the Loango region was likely on the western flanks of the Mayombe Mountains. The deep Kalahari sands that blanket the coastal plain have no ore deposits or even rock exposures. The only iron smelting furnace, dated to the last century BC, lies even farther east on the edge of the Mayombe not far from site 176 (Schwartz et al. 1990). Thus, although a brotherhood of Later Iron Age smiths could have invaded Loango at the beginning of the second millennium AD, they were clearly not the first metalworkers there. Earlier generations of smiths and smelters had preceded them by more than a 1,000 years, leaving behind finished artifacts but little direct evidence for smelting.

Archaeological evidence for copper working is even later. Only three copper objects were recovered from surface collections at two sites (75 and 84). Both had multiple occupations, including nineteenth-century horizons that make it difficult to attribute a confident date to these materials. The third surface find came from the site of Loubanzi (site 166). Excavations there produced two more copper fragments dated to the fifteenth or sixteenth centuries (Table 7.2). No European trade goods were recovered. The location of Loubanzi places it near the traditional site of Bouali, the historic capital of the Loango Kingdom.

Such late dates for copper were not expected before the reconnaissance began. Both iron and copper smelting are of much greater antiquity in West Africa, and in southern Africa the two technologies appear together at the beginning of the Early Iron Age in the second to the fifth centuries AD (Herbert 1984; Volavka and Thomas 1998; Bisson 2000). Because of the geographic proximity of Loango to the copper-rich Niari Valley just east of the Mayombe Mountains, it was initially thought that copper would be present from the beginning of the Iron Age. Historical sources, for instance, indicate that after AD 1500 trade in copper from the Niari Valley was one of the important activities controlled by the Loango elite (Martin 1972). But this was apparently not the case earlier. In hindsight, it appears that the rugged jungle terrain of the Mayombe formed a barrier between the Loango coast and the copper-rich interior that was not traversed in any substantive way until European demand stimulated it in the second half of the second millennium AD. The appearance of copper on the Loango coast was thus late and correlates with the formation of a larger Loango kingdom that could support the logistical and technical demands needed to carry out trade over the arduous Mayombe Mountains. Oral traditions support this conclusion and Volavka suggests that the Vili only reached the Niari valley "upon the arrival of Europeans" (Volavka and Thomas 1998: 218). Once there, they exchanged salt, cloth, and European commodities for copper goods and ore. But by the seventeenth century, copper was in great enough supply that the storehouses of the MaLoango and other elite were filled with copper, palm cloth, and ivory (Martin 1972).

Archaeological Surveys

Initial Discoveries

In the 1920s and 1930s, French administrators and civil servants working on the rail and port facilities made the first archaeological finds in what was to become the Republic of the Congo (Lombard 1931; Droux and Kelley 1939). Although most of their attention was drawn to Middle and Later Stone Age (Tumbian) materials because of their great antiquity and physical similarity to Paleolithic materials in Europe, Lombard did illustrate a few Iron Age ceramics from sites on the inland savanna near Brazzaville. Some of these share shapes and decoration motifs with the Later Iron Age wares from Condé and Loubanzi discussed in Chapter 7. Apart from these occasional finds, however, no systematic archaeological reconnaissance had been conducted on the coast prior to the present project.

Reconnaissance of the Eucalyptus Plantations

The rapid expansion of eucalyptus plantations in 1988 created an urgent need for archaeological conservation in order to locate as many sites as possible before planting destroyed them. Through negotiations with Shell and CDF in 1990, an intensive program of archaeological reconnaissance was undertaken. Because the savannas were covered with tall grass and shrubs, archaeological visibility was poor, and many sites would continue to be destroyed unless a methodology could be devised to locate them. Because tractors were available, it was decided that systematic transects of cut lines 2 meters wide and 100 meters apart would be sufficient to locate buried sites in advance of planting. The archaeological transects were plowed during the rainy season so that the rains could settle the dust and improve artifact visibility (Figure 4.1). Our excavations at Tchissanga,

Table 4.1. Radiocarbon dates from excavated sites

Date No.	Lab No.	Site	Unit	Depth cm	Date BP	2 σ cal BC/AD	Area under curve	Material	Association	Ceramic group
I	Tx-7021	Gray Sand	Unit 2	80–100	2,950 ± 80	1392–973 BC 958–938 BC	98.40% 1.60%	c	lithics	LSA
2	Tx-7018	Gray Sand	Unit 1	70–80	2,250 ± 60	511–197 BC	100%	c	pottery, lithics, iron	H
3	Tx-5956	Tchissanga West	Unit 1	30–40	2,880 ± 90	1367–1363 BC 1313–838 BC	0.10% 99.90%	c+o	pottery, lithics	CLSA1
4	Uga-5720	Tchissanga West	exposed pit	surface	2,525 ± 85	806–411 BC	100%	c		CLSA1
5	Tx-6184	Tchissanga West	Unit N55W3	20–30	2,450 ± 70	767–404 BC	100%	c	pottery, lithics	CLSA1
6	Tx-6185	Tchissanga West	Unit N55W1.5	20–30	2,530 ± 60	804–500 BC 495–486 BC 463–449 BC 442–417 BC	98.80% 1.00% 1.50% 2.70%	c	pottery, lithics	CLSA1
7	Tx-6186	Tchissanga East	Unit N1.5E130	35–45	2,250 ± 60	405–171 BC	100%	c+o	pottery, iron	CLSA2
8	Tx-6187	Tchissanga East	Unit N1.5E140	42–50	2,520 ± 60	800–485 BC 463–448 BC 443–416 BC	94.80% 1.80% 3.40%	c+o	pottery	CLSA2
9	Tx-6256	Tchissanga East	Unit N3E140	40–50	2,280 ± 70	701–698 BC 538–164 BC 129–120 BC	0.10% 99.60% 0.30%	c+o	pottery, iron	CLSA2
10	Tx-6188	Tchissanga Base	Feature 1	70–90	2,300 ± 80	749–687 BC 666–643 BC 591–577 BC 567–165 BC 127–123 BC	4.40% 1.30% 0.60% 93.50% 0.20%	c+o	pottery, lithics, iron	CLSA2
11	Tx-7020	Lamba	Pit 1	80–90	2,790 ± 70	1127–807 BC	100%	o	pottery, lithics	CLSA1
12	Tx-7015	Lamba	Pit 1A	100–150	2,220 ± 80	404–54 BC	100%	c	pottery, lithics, iron	CLSA2
13	Tx-7359	Mvindou	Feature 1	20–40	2,270 ± 60	483–466 BC 416–169 BC	0.70% 99.30%	c+o	pottery, lithics, iron	CLSA2
14	Tx-7365	Mvindou	Feature 1	20–100	2,220 ± 60	398–157 BC 135–115 BC	98.20% 1.80%	o	pottery, lithics, iron	CLSA2
15	Tx-7361	Mvindou	Feature 2	40–190	2,250 ± 60	405–171 BC	100%	c	pottery, lithics	CLSA2

#	Lab no.	Site	Feature/Unit	Depth	Date BP	Calibrated date	%		Materials	Class
16	Tx-7366	Mvindou	Feature 2	40–190	2,200 ± 70	401–97 BC	100%	o	pottery, lithics	CLSA2
17	Tx-7360	Mvindou	Feature 3	40–50	2,190 ± 70	392–89 BC / 75–57 BC	97.80% / 2.20%	o	pottery	CLSA2
18	Tx-6183	Tandou-Youmbi	Pit Fill	30–55	2,110 ± 60	358–279 BC / 258–242BC / 236 BC–AD 8 / AD 10–17	14.70% / 1.40% / 83.30% / 0.60%	c	pottery, polished stone axe	H
19	Tx-7016	BP113	Unit 70–80E; 3–4S	40–50	2,060 ± 60	345–322 BC / 205 BC–AD 69	1.90% / 98.10%	c	pottery, lithics	H
20	Tx-7729	BP113	Unit 78–79e;14s	pit 1	1,930 ± 50	64 BC–AD 260 / AD 282–324	94.40% / 5.60%	c	pottery, iron, slag	H
21	Tx-7728	BP113	Unit 49–50e,21n	50–60	1,940 ± 50	46 BC–AD176 / AD 191–212	97.70% / 2.30%	c	pottery	H
22	Tx-7730	BP113	Unit 49–50e;19n	pit 6	1,930 ± 50	41 BC–AD 179 / AD 188–213	96.10% / 3.90%	c	pottery	H
23	Tx-7014	BP113	Unit N5	Fea.1	1,820 ± 60	AD 66–348 / AD370–377	99.40% / 0.60%	c+o	pottery	H
24	Tx-7727	BP113	Unit 48–49e;21n	40–50	1,640 ± 70	AD 245–564	100%	c	pottery	CBG
25	Tx-5958	Madingo-Kayes	West unit 1	30–40	1,810 ± 60	AD 74–352 / AD 367–380	98.70% / 1.30%	c+o	pottery, iron	H+SC
26	Tx-5957	Madingo-Kayes	East unit 1	22–40	1,720 ± 80	AD 128–466 / AD 480–533	94.6% / 5.40%	c+o	pottery, iron	H+SC
27	Tx-6189	Meningue	Feature 1	40–60	1,740 ± 70	AD 88–102 / AD 122–433 / AD 494–505 / AD 524–525	0.80% / 98.7% / 0.50% / 0.04%	c+o	pottery	H
28	Tx-7362	Fignou 4	Romain Feature	70–90	1,730 ± 70	AD 79–397	100%	o	pottery	?
29	Tx-7363	Fignou 4	Romain Feature	70–90	1,790 ± 70	AD 126–437 / AD 489–511 / AD 516–530	97.90% / 1.40% / 0.80%	c	pottery	?
30	Tx-6690	Kayes	Unit 0N,10W	50–60	2,310 ± 70	742–689 BC / 663–647 BC / 549–180 BC	4.10% / 1.00% / 94.90%	c	lithics	—

(continued)

Table 4.1 (continued)

Date No.	Lab No.	Site	Unit	Depth cm	Date BP	2 σ cal BC/AD	Area under curve	Material	Association	Ceramic group
31	Tx-6689	Kayes	Unit 10N,0	80–90	1,550 ± 80	AD 344–649	100%	c	pottery, iron	H
32	Tx-6692	Kayes	Unit 9N,0	70–80	1,440±60	AD 436–489	5.70%	c+o	pottery, iron	H
						AD 511–516	0.50%			
						AD 530–682	93.80%			
33	Tx-6691	Kayes	Unit 19S,0	30–40	1,720 ± 70	AD 130–438	96.60%	c	pottery, iron	H
						AD 487–531	3.40%			
34	Tx-7364	Fignou 1	Pangoud Feature	0–20	1,410 ± 100	AD 421–784	96.30%	c	pottery	?
						AD 787–824	2.80%			
						AD 841–861	1.20%			
35	Tx-6751	Tchitembo	Test pit 1	0–15	1,420 ± 80	AD 794–1164	100%	MS	pottery, lithics	?
36	Beta 292442	Lac Ndembo	Unit 20N40W	30–40	1,610 ± 40	AD 418–597	100%	o	pottery	CBG
37	Beta 292440	Lac Ndembo	Unit 20N17E	30–40	1,340 ± 30	AD 659–780	98.20%	o	pottery, iron	SC
						AD 780–792	1.80%			
38	Beta 292441	Lac Ndembo	Unit 20N19E	40–50	1,250 ± 30	AD 713–745	5.40%	o	pottery, iron	SC
						AD 797–898	91.00%			
						AD 921–943	3.60%			
39	Tx-7019	Conde	Unit 2	10–20	810 ± 70	AD 1040–1112	19.40%	c+o	pottery	Woven
						AD 1115–1281	80.60%			
40	Tx-7017	Loubanzi	Unit 0,10S	20–30	420 ± 50	AD 1415–1527	73.80%	c+o	pottery, iron, copper	Woven
						AD 1554–1633	26.20%			

c = charcoal; o = oil palm nuts; MS = marine shell; CLSA = Ceramic Later Stone Age, phase 1 or 2; H = Herringbone ware; SC = Spaced Curvilinear ware; CBG = Carinated Broadly Grooved ware; Woven = Early Later Iron Age ware.

58

Figure 4.1. Romain walking a cutline plowed to increase the visibility of archaeological sites. More than 400 kilometers of cut lines were walked during the survey.

Madingo-Kayes, and Mvindou had found that furrows 30 to 50 centimeters deep were sufficient to bring to the surface most materials dating within the past 3,000 years. Older sites such as the Middle Stone Age sites exposed in the 1930s during port construction, or those situated at bases of hills where hilltop erosion had covered them over with sediment, were too deeply buried to be disturbed by planting.

Methodology

During the reconnaissance, almost every savanna from Diosso 40 kilometers south of the Kouilou to Lac Loandjili 25 kilometers north was examined. There were no comprehensive topographic or road maps at the time the project was carried out. The maps that were available generally covered only small portions of the coast near the city of Pointe Noire. In addition, I had access to proprietary maps made for oil exploration and for the CDF eucalyptus plantations. None showed the topographic features or tree lines that were needed to accurately plot archaeological site locations in the absence of GPS technology. The project therefore developed its own base maps using aerial side-scan radar images of the coast provided by Conoco. The radar images were particularly useful for Central African conditions because, unlike traditional air photos, they do not show cloud cover that obscures ground features. Dr. Anne Molineux, a former cartographer, traced the radar images to produce the detailed archaeological maps used to plot site locations (Figure 4.2). These were sufficiently detailed that off-road tracks and even small groves of trees could be used to accurately map site locations. The site map was updated annually as new sites were discovered; updated copies were then deposited each year with the district officials in Madingo-Kayes and CDF in Pointe Noire.

On the coastal terraces where erosion was common, the reconnaissance walked all the terrace edges, road cuts, borrow pits, and other eroded or exposed locations in order to locate materials indicative of subsurface deposits. Unplowed hilltops were also walked using approximate

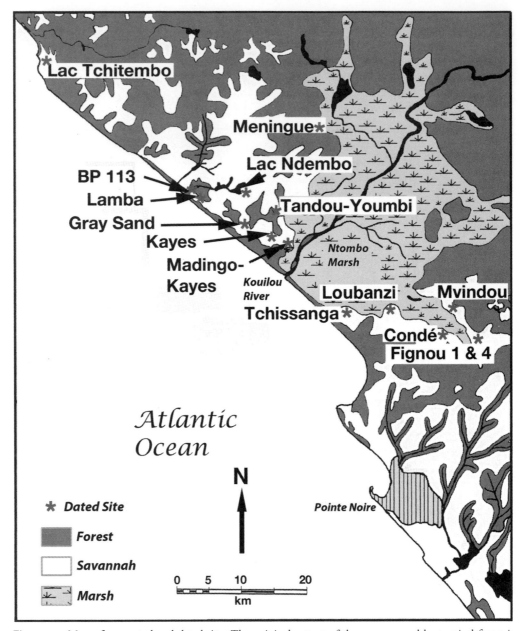

Figure 4.2. Map of excavated and dated sites. The original extent of the area covered by tropical forest is shaded, with the savanna grasslands prior to eucalyptus planting shown in white.

50-meter transect intervals. On inland savannas away from the coast where detection of buried sites from surface indications was less reliable because there had been little natural erosion to expose buried artifacts, cut lines 2 meters wide and 40 to 50 centimeters deep were plowed at 100-meter intervals across each savanna designated for planting. These were walked after the rains had settled the dust and improved artifact visibility.

Between 1990 and 1993 approximately 400 kilometers of transect was walked. Where visibility was good in the newly planted CDF plantations south of the Kouilou, these were also walked to expand the archaeological database. After discussions, CDF agreed to stop planting along the archaeologically sensitive 100-meter terrace overlooking the ocean because site density in this physiographic zone was found to be especially high. Estimates of a site's significance were based upon the site's age, its ability to contribute new or valuable information to the emerging cultural chronology, its artifact density, and the likelihood that important features or activity areas such as pits, houses, or smelting remains were present. Decisions about site preservation rather than planting were biased toward site protection, and those thought to be significant enough for conservation were signposted. Those of less scientific or cultural value were surface collected, recorded on the master site map, and returned to the planting campaign.

Romain, hired as part of the excavation project in 1989, was trained to carry out the day-to-day reconnaissance of CDF plantations. Although he had no formal training in archaeology, he quickly became familiar with the stone tools, ceramics, and other artifacts that were indicators of prehistoric occupation. He walked cut lines during the rainy season, collecting artifact samples and noting their locations. Because he had no formal training that would enable him to evaluate the scientific importance of sites, this was done during the dry season when I came to the Congo to conduct new excavations and to locate each site on the master site map.

Results

During the reconnaissance, twenty-eight unplowed sites worthy of protection were located (Table A.1). Two more could only be partially conserved because planting had already started when they were discovered. Another 154 sites were either too ephemeral or lacked sufficient scientific or historical materials to be able to persuade CDF that they merited preservation. Others had already been destroyed by planting before the reconnaissance began. One site, Diosso, lay within a large village and its spatial extent could not be determined without disturbing the residents. An additional fifteen sites situated on the densely occupied 100-meter terrace overlooking the ocean were not signboarded because CDF had agreed not to plant in this physiographic zone. Their fate is unknown, and it is possible that later road building or other development activities may have had an impact on some of them.

Table A.1 breaks down the sites by number, year of discovery, site or region name when available, whether the site was planted or marked for conservation, and the approximate ages of the cultural materials recovered. For sites with historic components, the presence or absence of specific imported materials is noted by a "1" on the table. For middle- to late-nineteenth-century imports, approximate dates for maker's marks are recorded in the Notes column when possible. Because many of the sites were occupied multiple times, the 204 sites recorded contained a total of 295 cultural components.

Pre-Ceramic Later Stone Components (1300–100 BC)

Ten sites produced only lithic debris and have been designated as Pre-Ceramic Later Stone Age (LSA). Most of these sites were very small and contained concentrations of chert flakes and fragments that covered areas ranging from 2 to 20 meters in diameter. Given their small size, some may have been activity areas where stone was briefly flaked by the inhabitants of nearby CLSA or Iron Age sites. The lithic concentrations at Gray Sand and sites 36, 83 and 146 were located in distinctive white-sand formations that could be the remnants of beach lines associated with slightly elevated sea levels in the past. Excavations at Gray Sand revealed a pre-CLSA level beneath Early Iron Age materials that produced a calibrated radiocarbon date of 1392–938 BC (Table 4.1, date 1). A pre-ceramic lithic horizon below Early Iron Age materials at the site of Kayes on the northern terrace of the Koulou River was dated to 742–180 BC (Table 4.1, date 30). This is comparable to dates from phase 2 of the CLSA discussed in Chapter 5.

Ceramic Later Stone (1300–50 BC)

In this presentation the term *Ceramic Later Stone Age* is used because there is no direct evidence for food production, even though the term Neolithic to describe such sites remains current in the French literature (Clist 2005). Differing systems of ceramic classification characterize archaeological descriptions in the regions north and south of the Equator in West and southern Africa. With some exceptions (Clist 2005), ceramic descriptions that emphasize tool and motor action are often preferred in West Africa (Gosselain 2002; Lavachery et al. 2010) to the system in common use in southern Africa (Huffman 2007), which focuses more on decoration motif and placement on the vessel and less on tool type.

Although there is no direct evidence for food production, the appearance after 1000 BC of ceramics along with deep, organic-rich pits filled with carbonized oil palm nuts (*Elaeis guineensis*) mark CLSA sites off from the more ephemeral Later Stone Age occurrences described earlier. Together the pottery, pits, and small, flat grinding stones made of micaceous schist suggest that sedentary populations now occupied the coast. The ubiquitous carbonized oil palm nuts in the pit fill suggest the possibility of arboriculture, and perhaps even cultivation of pearl millet and bananas given recent botanical and linguistic evidence for this to the north in southern Cameroon (Kahlheber et al. 2009; Neumann and Hildebrand 2009; Neumann 2012).

Phase 1 (1300–500 BC)

Radiocarbon dates for phase 1 CLSA sites range between 1300 BC and 400 BC (Table 4.1, dates 4, 5, 6, and 11). Only three sites with ceramics belonging to the earliest phase of the CLSA were located. These ceramics were distinguished from those of the later phase by the presence of rocker-stamping or comb-wrapped stick impressions extending from the shoulder to the base of the vessel. Pots were generally small and globular in shape with flat bases. Tempering was very coarse and composed of angular fragments of smashed quartzite or volcanic scoria 2 to 4 millimeters in size. Decoration was usually done with a rounded stick to produce broadly grooved cross-hatching or pendant arcades (Figure 4.3); other ceramics had coarsely comb-stamped bands on the neck.

Phase 2 (500–50 BC)

During the surface reconnaissance, twenty-one sites belonging to the second phase of the CLSA were located. These generally produced few or no lithics. Ceramics included flat-based pots, but less coarse sand temper, more sharply everted rims, and more finely incised panels of cross-hatching than were found in phase 1.

The CLSA ceramics share some shape and decoration similarities with a subset of ceramics of similar age belonging to the Okala Tradition in Gabon (Clist 2005: 269). The bowl and pot forms with flat bases, channeled lips, occasional rocker-stamping, and broadly grooved motifs are all characteristic of Okala. Absent from the Congo materials, however, are the bilobial and carinated vessels associated with the later phase of Okala (Clist 2005: 418). More similarities occur with the slightly later Ngovo Tradition ceramics found south of the Congo River (de Maret 1986; Gosselain 1988; Clist 2005: annex 5, tableau 3). These similarities suggest that new populations expanded southward from Gabon along the coast during the last millennium BC. These communities would have likely encountered indigenous hunter-gatherers represented by the earlier Later Stone Age traces, overlapping with them in the use of some resources while introducing new adaptations that included intensive use of the oil palm (Vansina 1995). Recent finds of pearl millet dating between 400 and 200 BC from the coastal forests of southern Cameroon (Eggert

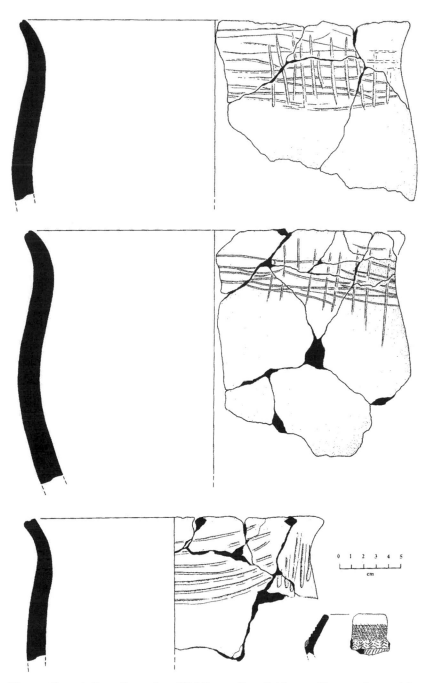

Figure 4.3 Phase 1 Ceramic Later Stone Age (CLSA) pots from Tchissanga illustrate the crudely grooved crosshatching and pendant arcades that characterize this group. Typically, such vessels also have a grooved line running along the top of the lip.

et al. 2006; Kahlheber et al. 2009) along with a reassessment of linguistic terms for this plant (Vansina 1995; Bostoen 2006/2007; Kahlheber et al. 2009; Neumann et al. 2012) suggest the strong possibility that the makers of CLSA phase 2 and subsequent Herringbone wares cultivated this cereal on the Loango coast in the last centuries BC.

Early Iron Age (150 BC–AD 800)

After ca. 200 BC the ceramic sequence from Loango bears little stylistic resemblance to the Early Iron Age materials of the Oveng tradition from coastal Gabon, with which it is partially coterminous in time. There is even less stylistic correspondence with materials from the interior of Gabon belonging to the Okanda and Otumbi traditions (Clist 2005: 555, 559, 619–628). The new settlements that appeared on the coast during the last two centuries BC contain very different ceramics characterized by everted-neck, shouldered jars decorated predominately with comb-stamped or incised herringbone motifs. The necked shapes and the predominance of comb-stamping distinguish them from the earlier Ceramic Later Stone Age phase 1 and 2 vessels. In addition, the Congo Early Iron Age wares have rounded rather than flattened bases, and the earliest Herringbone wares also have thickened, beveled rims. At two sites, Tandou-Youmbi and Kayes, surface reconnaissance found polished stone axes or hoes in association with the Herringbone ware.

Herringbone Ware Sites (150 BC–AD 650)

The surface reconnaissance identified 26 EIA Herringbone ware sites. These were characterized by jars decorated with comb-stamped herringbone motifs on the neck; decoration was rarely observed below the neck-shoulder junction. Bowl forms were not found at any of these sites during the reconnaissance, and they were rare in excavated contexts. The earliest dated Herringbone ware site is Tandou-Youmbi, dated to the last centuries BC, which overlaps with the end of the CLSA (Table 4.1, date 18). At BP 113 distinctive thickened and beveled-rim jars follow (Figure 4.4), with dates between approximately 50 BC and AD 400 (Table 4.1, dates 19–23). The Herringbone wares appear stylistically distant from those of the second phase of the CLSA and probably represent an intrusion of new peoples onto the coastal plain. Related materials from the sites of Meningue and Kayes extend the potential range of these wares into the seventh century. Five sites with Herringbone ware also produced iron fragments during the surface survey; six also had iron slag. Because all these sites had multiple occupations, the association between iron working and Herringbone ware settlements was not definitive from surface collections. Excavations at BP 113 and Kayes, however, produced definite associations with iron working.

The Herringbone sites were concentrated on the coastal terraces overlooking the Atlantic Ocean north and south of the Kouilou River, but examples were also located farther inland at Meningue. At this stage, the origins of this ware are uncertain. A few examples of ceramics decorated with herringbone designs are dated to the second century AD at Benfica 17 kilometers south of Luanda, Angola and the nearby site of Quibaxe (dos Santos Júnior and Ervedosa 1970: 49, and their figures 50a, 50b, 52c, 58, and 60; Ervedosa 1980: 204; Martins 1976; Clist and Lanfranchi 1992). The radiocarbon dates fit well with the Herringbone ware dates from the Loango, but, at present, the Iron Age cultural chronology of northern Angola is practically unknown, and other ceramics from Benfica appear to belong to cultural traditions not found in the Loango survey.

Carinated Broadly Grooved Ware (AD 400–600)

Twenty-nine sites produced very different EIA ceramics not related stylistically to the Herringbone ware discussed earlier. The term *Carinated Broadly Grooved* (CBG) ware is used to describe these

Figure 4.4. Phase 1 Early Iron Age (EIA) Herringbone ware pot with a thickened, beveled rim recovered from a pit at BP 113.

materials. Jars of this type have unique, very sharp carinations on the shoulder. They are decorated with horizontal bands of broad grooves just below the rim and below the carination. Curvilinear designs also occur below the carinated shoulder on some jars. Two bowl shapes have been found: tall, barrel-shaped vessels, sometimes with applied lugs, and shallower hemispherical bowls usually decorated with bands of grooving below the rim; these also have button-like lugs applied just below the rim (Figure 4.5). At some sites north of the Kouilou, these wares were also distinguished by the use of talc as a temper. This gives the vessels a very "slippery" feeling and would have made them very useful as cooking vessels because of their resistance to thermal shock (Rice 1987: 150).

CBG wares are presently very insecurely dated in Loango: a single calibrated date of AD 245–564 comes from BP 113 (Table 4.1, date 24); a nearly identical result of AD 418–597 (Table 4.1, date 36) was also received for levels containing CBG wares in area B on the west side of the Lac Ndembo site. Desmond Clark (1968; see also Ervedosa 1980: 201) illustrated nearly identical wares from Dundo in NE Angola where they were dated to between the eighth and eleventh centuries AD. However, other ceramics from Dundo are more closely related to later Naviundu wares from the Democratic Republic of Congo (Van Noten et al. 1982; Anciaux de Faveaux and de Maret 1984; Huffman 1989), so it is possible that earlier CGB wares will be found at Dundo. On the Loango coast, CBG wares represent a second intrusion of a new population, which either replaced or was assimilated by the makers of earlier Herringbone wares. The relationship with

Figure 4.5. A phase 2 Early Iron Age (EIA) lugged Carinated Broadly Grooved (CBG) ware bowl discovered during the reconnaissance.

Dundo suggests this migration came from the southeast. Its presence on the Loango coast was short-lived, however, because another Naviundu-inspired ceramic tradition, spaced curvilinear (SC) wares, appeared in Loango a few centuries later.

Spaced Curvilinear Ware (AD 600–900)

Twenty-five EIA sites contained ceramics that appear related to the intrusion of a new cultural tradition into the area in the seventh century AD. Distinguishing characteristics of the SC wares include necked vessels decorated with spaced horizontal bands of oblique incision and comb-stamping (Denbow 1990: 154). In some cases, the spaces between the bands are either empty or filled with curvilinear or interwoven motifs in a wide variety of guilloche, triangular, and undulating forms (Figure 4.6). As discussed in Chapter 6, whereas SC wares were first dated at Madingo-Kayes to between AD 74 and 533 (Denbow 1990; Table 4.1, dates 25, 26), with subsequent excavations we found that this date goes with an earlier Herringbone occupation at this multicomponent site. Subsequent excavations at the SC ware site of Lac Ndembo produced dates in the seventh to ninth centuries for SC ware. This corrects the misleading early dates for SC ware from Madingo-Kayes and indicates that SC ware represents a third intrusion onto the coast, this time related to the wider Naviundu Complex (Anciaux de Faveaux and de Maret 1984; Huffman 1989, 2007).

Later Iron Age

In both the excavation and survey data there appears to be a hiatus between the EIA populations that made SC wares and Later Iron Age (LIA) settlements. Only one site, Lac Tchitembo – a

Figure 4.6. Examples of phase 3 EIA Spaced Curvilinear (SC) ware recovered from the surface of the Madingo-Kayes site.

shell midden with no decorated ceramics – belongs to this period. A calibrated radiocarbon date from shells at the site, when corrected for marine carbon, places it between AD 794 and 1164 (Table 4.1, date 35). The shellfish, principally oysters and cockles, was likely procured from the adjacent saltwater lagoon rather than from the open ocean. This is the only shell midden found during the reconnaissance. Its preservation from the effects of the prodigious waves that pound the Loango coast is due to its inland location connected by a small stream to the ocean 500 meters away.

The systematic nature of the surface reconnaissance makes it unlikely that the hiatus in occupation in the ninth to eleventh centuries is a product of spotty reconnaissance methodologies or poor site visibility. This suggests two possibilities, the first of which is that for some unknown reason population densities declined during the last quarter of the first millennium AD. Although the correlation could be spurious, this would coincide with tentative evidence for slightly wetter conditions and a reduction in savanna grasslands as forests expanded in the Congo and Gabon (Sitou et al. 1996; Delègue et al. 2001). Alternatively, a restructuring of settlement occurred, with populations coalescing into a few large, centralized villages after AD 900. This would have left the hinterland thinly populated, with few archaeological sites. Even large centers could have been missed by the reconnaissance if they happened to lie in the densely populated areas around Pointe Noire and Diosso that were not covered during the survey.

Figure 4.7. Examples of "woven" decorated ceramics from excavations at the Later Iron Age site of Loubanzi.

LIA sites discovered during the reconnaissance can be grouped into two broad categories based on vessel shape, decoration, and presence or absence of European trade goods. The first set of pre-European contact sites consists of twenty-three surface sites with no European trade goods. These likely date to between approximately AD 1000 and 1600. A second set of ninety-eight sites is associated with European imports and date between AD 1600 and 1900. Test excavations carried out at two of the earlier sites, Condé and Loubanzi, are described in Chapter 7.

Precontact LIA (AD 1100–1500)

Twenty-three sites were identified as belonging to the pre-contact period. These sites contained everted-neck jars – a shape also common to the EIA. But the vessels were decorated in the neck with lozenges or diamond-shaped "woven" patterns made by roulette or incision (Figure 4.7). This combination of jar shape, decoration placement, and motif is dated between AD 1100 and 1500 at Condé and Loubanzi; neither site had European goods associated with it. In a recent summary of the ceramics of the Kongo kingdom south of the Congo River, Clist (2012a: 202) presents a new typology that groups wares formerly known as Group II (Mortelmans 1959, 1962; de Maret 1982b) into a redefined Mbafu Tradition. He argues that the decoration motifs on these ceramics share a widespread cultural "esthétique" represented in diverse Kongo art forms that include rock art. The LIA ceramics collected in the Loango reconnaissance, particularly those dated after AD 1500, represent a separate facies of this tradition.

Although iron objects were recovered from the excavations at sites dating as early as the fourth century BC, the reconnaissance and excavations only found copper fragments at three sites: site 75, with LIA materials and post-1500 European trade goods; site 84, which produced a wide range of ceramics that ranged from CLSA phase 2 wares and lithics to woven ware and historic materials; and site 166, Loubanzi, which produced a calibrated radiocarbon date of AD 1415 to 1633 (Table 4.1 date 40).

The relative scarcity of copper was surprising given the proximity of the copper ores of the Niari Valley east of the Mayombe. Being less subject to corrosion than iron, copper was expected to be a more common find in the reconnaissance and excavations. For instance, thirteen fragments

Figure 4.8. Historic period "chamber pot" shape with decoration produced by pressing the ridged edge of a cockleshell into the wet clay.

of iron were recovered during the reconnaissance; however, the corrosive conditions of the salt air on the seacoast mitigated against its preservation. No slag heaps, iron smelting furnaces, or other direct indications of iron smelting were encountered during the reconnaissance even though by the third century AD iron was in common use on the coastal plain.

Historic Period (AD 1500–1900)

The archaeological reconnaissance found the coastal plains of the Congo scattered with detritus left from over four centuries of European trade. Ninety-eight sites produced European crockery, wine and rum bottles, and the occasional tobacco pipe along with indigenously manufactured pottery. Cloth, one of the most important items mentioned in trade records, was not preserved.

Although surface collections produced large quantities of European goods, especially earthenware, glass bottles, and tobacco pipes, indigenous ceramics were also recovered in large numbers. The impact of the Atlantic trade on these later assemblages is suggested by changes in the shape and design of indigenous ceramics. After the fifteenth century, flared-rim "chamber-pot" shapes replaced the necked jars that were the principal vessel shape during the EIA and first phase of the LIA. Few indigenous bowls were recovered from historic sites, perhaps because they were replaced by earthenware and metal ones from Europe. Incised, woven patterns were still a favored motif on some vessels, but because the new shapes had sharply-flared necks, these designs were placed lower on the shoulder. Indigenous potters did not attempt to reproduce the naturalistic scenes and painted flowers found on most European wares, but a variety of new motifs occur on indigenous pottery that included stamps using the notched edge of a cockleshell (Figure 4.8). Other potters included copies of cowry shells, which were molded onto the decorative borders of the woven designs.

The new chamber-pot shape would have been well suited for cooking the single-pot Congolese "ragouts" mentioned by Proyart (1814: 551). In the sixteenth century, Congolese cuisine appears to have consisted of sorghum or millet "bread," or manioc "loaves," made to be dipped into the stew (Lopes et al. 1881: 66). Whether similar "stews" were eaten in the EIA is unknown. The small diameter of the Congolese vessels in all periods suggests that meals were cooked and eaten in small groups. It is unclear whether these were composed of men eating separately from their wives and children, as is sometimes the case today, or together in nuclear family groups.

Some of the lozenge designs found on the indigenous LIA wares from Loango are similar to those illustrated by Van Noten et al. (1982) from the western Congo and northern Angola, where they are also associated with European trade goods that date from the eighteenth to early twentieth centuries. Such a wide geographic spread for a ceramic style and shape, grouped by Clist into the Mbafu Tradition in the Democratic Republic of Congo, suggests that the design preferences found during the LIA encompassed more than one ethnic or political division.

European Imports

Some of the most distinctive European imports found during the reconnaissance were Westerwald salt-glazed jugs from Germany that were recovered at twenty-three sites. These were usually decorated with raised folate motifs painted in cobalt blue and manganese purple (Figure 4.9). All the fragments recovered included manganese purple paint, which is an indication they were made after 1650, not earlier. Although Westerwald wares have a very long period of manufacture, their foliate designs and necks decorated with grooved blue rings are consistent with wares dating to the first half of the eighteenth century. However, because such vessels were likely to have been curated for decades by their owners, they are not particularly useful as a precise dating tool.

Twenty-three sites contained clay tobacco pipes of both indigenous and European manufacture. Only one European pipe had an identifiable maker's mark, an "SD" that could tentatively refer to Samuel Decon, a British pipe manufacturer working in the first half of the eighteenth century (Browne 1898: 15). By the middle of the nineteenth century, many European porcelain manufacturers applied maker's marks to their vessels, allowing them to be assigned to a particular country and date (Table A.1, notes). A gray gunflint of European manufacture was also recovered from the surface near Diosso.

Shell Middens

Whereas the Loango coast is known today for its abundant seafood and shellfish, only one prehistoric coastal shell midden was identified at Lac Tchitembo north of the main survey area (Figure 4.2). Much smaller household-size shell middens 1 to 2 meters in diameter were commonly observed during the reconnaissance of LIA sites dating after AD 1500, however (Figure 4.10). Cockles (*Anadaris senilis/ Senilia senilis*) are the most common shellfish in these middens, but they are no longer commonly eaten and were not observed in the market at Pointe Noire. Interviews with local fishermen found that most had not eaten them for more than twenty years; younger informants were not familiar with them at all. This suggests that this resource may have been overexploited. Dennett (1968: 157) found them more common at the end of the nineteenth century and commented that "[m]any women and children are drowned each year by forgetting that when the tide begins to rise it is time to cease digging for cockles. A mound of these shells is found in the Xibila [sacred place or grove]."

Figure 4.9. Rhenish Westerwald salt-glazed stoneware vessel recovered from the surface near Lac Loandjili. Very early wares were blue and gray. The addition of purple color in this example, produced by applying manganese dioxide, indicates it postdates AD 1650.

Spatial and Cultural Chronology

The reconnaissance results indicate that CLSA sites, particularly those associated with the second phase between 500 and 200 BC, were concentrated around inland, freshwater marsh environments. Tchissanga East and Lamba, although situated near the coast, are also adjacent to freshwater streams and marshes where freshwater fish and game could have been obtained. Although these sites are generally small, the deep pits filled with carbonized oil palm nut fragments, broken pottery, and occasional grinding stones and lithics found at them suggest they represent small, sedentary populations who intensively exploited the oil palm and were perhaps incipient food producers.

During the EIA, the coastal terraces immediately overlooking the ocean were a particularly favored habitat between 100 BC and AD 500. Fewer EIA Herringbone ware sites were located on the more inland savannas along the southeast side of Ntombo Marsh – places where several CLSA sites and sites containing CGB ware were found. Sites belonging to a different and as yet poorly known EIA tradition were also found at Fignou 1 and 4 and at Pangoud. Unfortunately,

Figure 4.10. Romain examining a small historic shell midden exposed in an archaeological cut line. These cockles (*Andaris senilis*) were common on eighteenth- and nineteenth-century sites.

the decorated ceramics from the latter are too small to assign a cultural affiliation; however, in the case of one large fragment decorated with fine cross-hatching on the rim, there is some resemblance to wares from Benfica and Quibaxe in Angola. Radiocarbon samples from Fignou 4 date it to between AD 126 and 437 (Table 4.1, dates 28 and 29), coterminous with the Herringbone ware sites north of the Kouilou. The single date from a pit at Fignou 1 (Figure 4.11) is slightly later (AD 421–784), but the few ceramics recovered were too fragmented and too few in number to permit an assessment of cultural affiliation (Table 4.1, date 34).

The EIA Herringbone ware sites often cover 0.25 to 0.50 hectare in area, which is larger than the CLSA sites. This suggests that larger populations now occupied the coast. Surface collections found polished stone hoes or axes at two of these sites; however, lithics were otherwise uncommon. Iron fragments were recovered at some Herringbone sites, indicating that metalworking was now taking place in the wider region, if not directly on the coastal plain. Some of the pits associated with the EIA appear to have had functions different from those of the CLSA. At Tandou-Youmbi, for instance, a shallow pit found eroding from a road cut (Figure 4.12) had little organic fill but contained the remains of three whole or nearly whole pots, a phallus-like object, and a polished stone axe (Denbow 1990: 156).

Several sites, especially south of the Kouilou River, produced CBG ware. North of the Kouilou, some of these wares were tempered with large fragments of talc 1 to 2 mm in diameter. These were the only vessels found with this temper during the reconnaissance. At BP 113 and Lac Ndembo, these wares were dated to between AD 245 and 597 (Table 4.1, dates 24 and 36).

Very few sites that could be placed in the period from approximately AD 900 and 1600 were located during the reconnaissance. The most likely explanation is that villagers living in the hinterland coalesced into a few large villages or towns centered on the present locations of Diosso and Pointe Noire that were not examined by the survey. The centralization is likely related to the increased power and wealth of the Loango elite and their new fiscal abilities to command obedience and respect; fear of slave raiding could have been another incentive. From about 1820 onward, as the economic benefits of the slave trade to the local elite tailed off, the archaeological

Figure 4.11. A typical Early Iron Age pit with organic fill containing carbonized oil palm nuts from the site of Fignou 1 south of the Kouilou River.

Figure 4.12. A prehistoric pit discovered eroding from the side of a borrow pit at Tandou–Youmbi. It contained the remains of several phase 1 EIA Herringbone ware pots, a polished stone axe, and a clay figurine.

Figure 4.13. Examples of eighteenth-century string-lipped case gin and brandy bottles.

reconnaissance found that a more dispersed settlement pattern more similar to that found during the EIA developed. The "legitimate" trade followed this trend and maps of the Loango coast from the late nineteenth century indicate that European trading centers or "factories" were also decentralized and spread out along the coastline (Rouvier and Geisendörfer 1887). The age and country of origin of some of the ceramics recovered from the nineteenth-century sites could be determined from maker's marks. Of these, seven were from the Netherlands, two from Germany, and one each from the United Kingdom and France (Table A.1, notes). These findings are in general agreement with those of Mortelmans (Van Noten et al. 1982: 423), who wrote of the materials excavated at the sites of Dimba and Ngovo in the Democratic Republic of Congo that "all the imported ceramics begin in the 18th or even 19th century. ... They are from Maastricht [the Netherlands], perhaps from Great Britain" (author's translation).

In North America the types of transfer ware, sponged ware, and annular ware recovered in the Congo were of styles targeted to the lower classes and export market (Hume 1970: 129, 131). The most common were sponge-decorated wares, "a crude, easily recognized, peasant style of decoration achieved by free-painting and dabbing the ware with a sponge impregnated with pigment" (Mankowitz 1957: 208). In addition, the coast is littered with the remains of case gin and brandy bottles, most with eighteenth- and nineteenth-century dates (Figure 4.13). The intoxicating effects of imported brandy, rum, and gin were much sought after because it was believed the rapidly inebriating effects of their high alcohol content facilitated communication with the ancestors.

After the initial archaeological reconnaissance, thirteen sites were chosen for test excavations. Their locations are indicated on Figure 4.2. The sites were selected based on differences in ceramic style, which, in turn, was expected to relate to differences in chronology and cultural forms over time. Part II of this book presents a detailed summary of the archaeological excavations, beginning with the LSA and CLSA in Chapter 5. Chapter 6 discusses excavations at EIA sites, and

Chapter 7 reports on LIA and historic materials. Chapter 8 carries the analysis across Angola to the northern fringes of the Kalahari in Nambia and northwestern Botswana.

The Serendipity of Beautiful Objects

During my first visit to the site of Madingo-Kayes in 1987, I discovered fragments of a small pot eroding in the rain from the side of a borrow pit. As I glued the pot together later that night, I realized that it was visually striking. Small in size and with a flat bottom, every part of its varicolored surface was decorated – even the base (Figure 2.1). Later, as I became more familiar with the pottery styles of the coast, I realized the vessel belonged to a late phase of the "Neolithic" dated between the fourth and second centuries BC (Denbow 1990). The body decoration that gave the pot such a tactile feeling was made by rolling a thickly knotted string across the wet clay before it was fired (Soper 1985). This was an unusual technique, but one consistent with a few of the ceramics from Tchissanga and other early sites.

The colors and texture made it visually striking, a factor that I suspect played a decisive role in the minister of energy's decision to move the archaeology case from its location in his high-rise office in downtown Brazzaville to the Presidential Palace described in Chapter 2. If it had been just a few broken potsherds, or even a complete pot of similar age but "plainer," the comrade general's assessment that the archaeological collection looked like "just a lot of old rubbish" might have prevailed. But the pot was beautiful – something one could be proud to associate with one's ancestors. So it was swept into the Presidential Palace along with the archaeologist who picked it up.

Archaeological lore is full of such stories about the appeal of one-of-a-kind objects, often finely crafted of gold, jade, and other valuable or exotic materials. And they drive most of us "dirt archaeologists" nuts. Our daily work usually consists of sitting in dusty university or museum labs, which for some deep psychological reasons seem to be relegated to underground, basement locations. Here we pore over drab assemblages of shattered bone, poorly fabricated and fragmented household artifacts, and other assorted rubbish discarded in ancient times. Few of us get to peer into the golden visage of King Tut, or touch the jade mask of Lord Pacal. Instead, we conduct statistical analyses of artifact attributes, examine spatial correlations between features and artifacts, and scrutinize tedious and mind-numbing Excel spreadsheets that summarize the stratigraphic results of our excavations. But there is no doubt that the occasional serendipitous discovery can open doors otherwise closed.

Despite its interpretive and theoretical emptiness, the beautiful Congolese pot created a portal through which, however fleetingly, archaeological concerns gained access to the Presidential Palace in Brazzaville. Unfortunately, access does not necessarily translate directly into the power to change conditions. The destruction of the coastal savanna by eucalyptus plantations that began the following year was never connected in most people's minds with the need to conserve the fragile archaeological resources contained in the Loango soil. The ubiquitous Euro-American myth that there still exist places and peoples with no history, and so are in no need of conservation measures, is still too strong to be broken by a few glancing blows. Civil war erupted a few years after the pot was placed in the presidential palace. I can only hope that it has survived, safely nestled among the other artifacts in its glass case. Although rare and visually pleasing artifacts can draw people to archaeology, it is only through careful survey, excavation, and analysis that the more usual and mundane detritus of daily life can be coaxed into giving up its secrets, thereby permitting a more detailed reconstruction of the ancient past.

5

Ceramic Later Stone Age Excavations

In ... crafts and arts, the Bakongo see a chronological order in which their own ancestors proceeded from one stage to another ... they do not see themselves firing their pots in a past more remote than when fire was used for smithing. Nor do they admit a relationship between their ancestors and lithic tools found in their country, although their blacksmiths used some stone instruments until the past century. The Bakongo apparently date their ancestry from the start of the age of metalworking. By picturing their god as an occasional ceramist, they presumably indicate that the pre-iron period was still the godly stage preceding the creation of the Mukongo. (Volavka and Thomas 1998: 144)

The Ceramic Later Stone Age or "Neolithic"

The archaeological assemblages from the Congo coast discussed in the remainder of this book belong to the very end of the prehistoric era dating between approximately 1500 BC and AD 1900. This covers the period from the end of the Later Stone Age (LSA) and the first manufacture of pottery (Ceramic Later Stone Age, or CLSA) to the origins of metallurgy and the first contact with European traders, missionaries, and adventurers. Although the Later Stone Age and Iron Age are defined on the basis of tool-making technology, use of the term *Neolithic* in Central Africa is more problematic. In many parts of Europe, the Middle East, and Africa, the term was developed to refer to the period at the end of the Upper Paleolithic or Later Stone Age when some communities began to take up farming and herding (Childe 1925). The term literally means "New Stone Age," indicating that the transition from hunting and gathering to food production took place before the dawn of metallurgy. The timing of this innovation varied greatly from region to region depending on local economic and ecological circumstances. Any community that tended domesticated animals and/or plants, but had no knowledge of, or contact with, metallurgy, could be referred to as "Neolithic."

In Central Africa the term *Neolithic* is often still used to refer to the period between approximately 4,000 and 400 BC when pottery first appeared across the region in association with LSA tools (Clist 2005). The problem is that in Central Africa high rainfall, acidic tropical soils, and

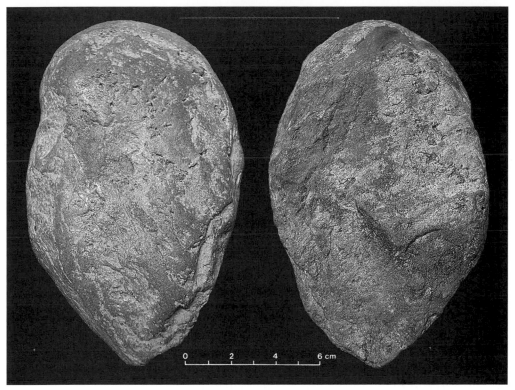

Figure 5.1. A polished stone axe or hoe recovered from the surface of Kayes. On the left-hand view, the underside of the axe retains its polish along the working edge. The right-hand view was facing up and was corroded by the effects of rainfall and sea air over the centuries.

agricultural systems based on hard-to-preserve root crops work against preservation of plant and animal remains; direct evidence for domestication is usually absent.[1] Archaeologists have, therefore, come to rely on more indirect indicators. The presence of pottery, for instance, because it is heavy, fragile, and difficult to transport, has often been taken as indirect evidence for sedentism at Stone Age sites. Features such as deep pits filled with organic-rich soils are also assumed to correlate with sedentism and, therefore, Neolithic economies – even if the remains of domesticated plants or animals are not preserved. A new type of stone tool also makes its appearance: the polished stone "axe" or "hoe." Their use as hoes rather than axes is suggested because the working edge is usually polished and smooth, without the telltale chipping, crushing, or other wear that would result from chopping the hardwoods common to the tropical forest (Figure 5.1). Alternatively, they could have been used to cut relatively soft material such as the stalk that attaches the cluster of palm nuts to the tree. Taken together, the pottery, pits, and ground-stone hoes or axes imply the appearance of more sedentary, food-producing communities at the end of the Late Stone Age and before the beginning of metalworking, which on the Loango coast begins around 400 BC.[2] Although not perfect, the term *Ceramic Later Stone Age* rather than *Neolithic* is used throughout the discussion that follows because no direct evidence for agriculture or animal husbandry in the form of carbonized seeds, pollen grains, phytoliths, or bones has yet been found in the Congo.

Archaeology and Cultural Classifications

Most regions of the earth have had more than a century of archaeological work as early pioneers developed the basic artifact and cultural chronologies that modern practitioners now rely on. As a result, in many parts of the world there is usually little need to develop from scratch the basic sequences of cultural phases and radiocarbon dates that are still needed in many parts of Africa. The 1927 Pecos conference, for instance, established the "Pecos Classification System" that outlined the ceramic and cultural chronology for the southwestern United States; the "McKern Midwest Taxonomic System" was developed at about the same time (Swartz 1996). François Bordes helped develop the basic lithic sequences of France in the middle of the twentieth century, whereas Louis Leakey, J. Desmond Clark, A. J. H. Goodwin, C. van Riet Lowe, Neville Jones, and others laid the groundwork for Stone Age studies in eastern and southern Africa (see for example, Clark 1970; Bordes 1979). African Iron Age studies are a more recent development and effectively began with the move toward independence from colonial powers in the 1960s, although some archaeologists such as Thurston Shaw in Nigeria and Merrick Posnansky in Uganda were instrumental in developing Iron Age research programs in West and East Africa before then. In southern Africa, P. W. Laidler (1929, 1938) and John Schofield (1948) produced the first ceramic typologies that formed the basis for later Iron Age chronologies (Huffman 2007).

In Central Africa, such groundwork studies are still in their infancy (Van Noten 1964; Lanfranchi et al. 1991; Wotzka 1995; Mercader, Garcia-Heras, and Gonzalez-Alvarez 2000; Clist 2005). Many more excavations and radiocarbon sequences are needed before firm cultural and chronological frameworks can be developed. In addition, differing systems of ceramic classification characterize archaeological work in the regions north and south of the equator in West and southern Africa. With some exceptions (Clist 2005, 2012b), analyses that emphasize tool and motor action are often preferred in West Africa (Gosselain 2002; Lavachery et al. 2010) to the system in common use in southern Africa that focuses more on decoration motif and placement on the vessel and less on tool type (Huffman 1989, 2007). The ceramic descriptions in the following sections pay heed to both systems by numerically annotating the types of tools and techniques used, the motifs produced, and their position on particular vessel shapes. Clist (2012a) proposes a similar methodology for ceramic classification of the Later Iron Age in Central Africa.

The fine-grained, yellow Kalahari sands of the Congo littoral are an archaeologist's dream. Their light color forms a perfect background against which the dark, organically enriched soils found in prehistoric pits and rubbish dumps easily stand out (Figure 5.2). The sand also retains just enough moisture through the short dry seasons to give it structure – it does not collapse as dry sand would when excavated. "It is like cutting cake," Romain often said as he excavated yet another "perfect" unit with precise 90-degree corners and impressively straight walls. Of course, the soft, fine nature of the sand also makes it extremely vulnerable to erosion if the capping vegetation cover is destroyed, a serious problem during the initial years of eucalyptus planting.

Later Stone Age Occupations: Gray Sand, Kayes, and BP 113

Later Stone Age horizons were identified in excavations at three sites: Gray Sand, BP 113, and Kayes. In each case, these layers were found stratigraphically below Iron Age occupations. In two cases, Gray Sand and the unexcavated Site 40 located on the edge of a mangrove forest on the north bank of the Kouilou (Table A.1), the bleached white color of the sand suggests that, at some point in the past, higher sea levels had oxidized the sands in these locations, removing the iron and other minerals that give the sand its yellow color. Lombard (1931) as well as Droux and Kelley (1939) also recovered LSA materials from reworked white beach sands approximately 5 meters above current sea level at Pointe Noire.

Gray Sand

The Gray Sand site is situated approximately 10 kilometers north of the mouth of the Kouilou at the base of the 100-meter coastal terrace. From this point, a level plain spotted with patches

Figure 5.2. Romain and Gislain exposing the outline of a prehistoric phase 2 Ceramic Later Stone Age pit uncovered by a bulldozer at the site of Mvindou.

of forest and savanna runs to the sea approximately 2 kilometers west (Figure 4.2). Two 1-by-1-meter units separated by a 1-meter balk were excavated at the base of the terrace near the edge of a newly planted eucalyptus field. The stratigraphic distribution of the cultural remains is presented in Table 5.1.

In Unit 2A, a 2-sigma calibrated date of 1392 to 938 BC (Table 4.1, date 1) was obtained for the non-ceramic LSA levels between 80 and 100 centimeters below the surface. The lithics included 42 chert and 265 quartzite flakes and fragments; no formal stone tools such as backed crescents, scrapers, or cores were recovered. Although quartzite is readily available on the coastal plain, the chert must have been carried to the site from a greater distance – perhaps from the Mayombe Mountains more than 50 kilometers to the east. Because chert made up approximately 14 percent of the lithics at Gray Sand, it is possible that early-LSA territories or interactions covered areas that extended to the edge of the Mayombe Mountains. Later sites have more quartzite and less chert, indicating a preference for higher-quality chert material in earlier times.

Above the LSA horizon, EIA ceramics and iron fragments were recovered in small quantities. These were associated with a 2-sigma calibrated date of 511 to 197 BC (Table 4.1, date 2).

Kayes

The site of Kayes lies approximately 10 kilometers southeast of Gray Sand at the base of a bluff overlooking the mangrove swamps on the north bank of the Kouilou River. As at Gray Sand, the LSA deposits underlay an Early Iron Age occupation that was subsequently buried by slope wash from the hilltop. Lithics were not seen eroding from the gully that forms the western edge of the site (Figure 5.3), nor were they found in levels beneath the Iron Age horizon in the other units. Of the 181 quartzite flakes and fragments recovered from the site as a whole, 131, or 72 percent, came from a single unit and level (Table 5.2). All the stone tools were fashioned from quartzite, the most readily obtainable stone on the coastal savanna. Similar to Gray Sand, no formal tools

Table 5.1. Provenience of excavated Later Stone Age (LSA) materials from Gray Sands

Unit	Level	Depth (cm)	Early Iron Age		Indeterminate Early	Undecorated sherds	Iron	Copper	Quartzite	Chert	Sand stone	Other
			rim	body								
1	1	0–10				7						
1	2	10–20				2						
1	3	20–30				1						
1	4	30–40				4						
1	5	40–50				1			1			
1	6	50–60				12			2			1 pebble
1	7	60–70	2	5		13	1		11	1		1 pebble
1	8	70–80	2	11		21	3		16	1		2 stones; 6 pebbles
1	9	80–90				6			30	3		
1	10	90–100			1				15	4	1	
1	11	100–110							4			
1	12	110–120							14			
2	1	0–20				4						
2	2	20–40			2	19			2	1		
2	3	40–60							4		2	
2	4	60–70	5	17		33			53	4		1 slag;
2	5	70–80				1			114	7		
2	6	80–100							76	22		1 stone
2	7	100–120							6	5		
Total			9	33	3	124	4	0	348	48	3	

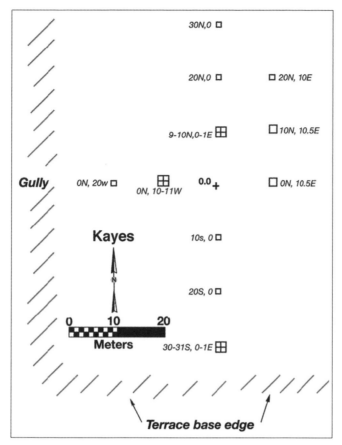

Figure 5.3. Layout of the excavation units at Kayes. The Later Stone Age horizon was exposed below the Iron Age levels in Unit 0N, 10–11 W. An Early Iron Age phase 1 midden with herringbone ware was encountered in units 9–10N, 0–1 E.

such as backed blades, choppers, or scrapers were identified. In addition, no iron or pottery was recovered in the pre-ceramic levels.

The circumscribed area of the lithic scatter at Kayes suggests it formed a small activity area where stone was worked. There are no indications from the other units that this was part of a larger LSA occupation at the site. A 2-sigma calibrated date of 742 to 180 BC (Table 4.1, date 30) was obtained for the pre-ceramic lithic horizon. A few stone flakes were also found in the overlying Iron Age deposits in most units. These were accompanied by iron bangles and tools dated to the fifth and sixth centuries AD. The presence of small numbers of quartzite flakes in the later levels indicates that stone tool use did not cease abruptly when iron became available.

BP 113

The site of BP 113 is named after a British Petroleum survey marker found at the site (Figure 5.4), which is located 20 kilometers north of Gray Sand on top of the 100-m coastal terrace overlooking the sea approximately 1 kilometer to the west. A small stream draining the inland lakes of Loufoumbou, Loandjili, and Ndembo cuts across the north side of the terrace on its way to the ocean. Evidence for a pre-Iron Age LSA occupation was found in only one unit, 79–80E, 4S on Figure 5.5. Between 80 and 100 centimeters below surface in this 1-meter square, more than

Table 5.2. Provenience of excavated LSA and EIA materials from Kayes

Unit	Depth (cm)	Decorated & rim sherds	Quartzite flakes & fragments	Stone object	Copal	Tuyere	Iron slag	Iron artifact
0N, 10W	40–50	4	2				2	1 rod
0N, 10W	50–70		131					
0N, 10E	70–90		1					1
0N, 10E	90–100	3				1	4	1 wire
0N, 20W	50–60	1						
0N, 20W	60–70		2					
10N, 0	50–70	8	15			1	9	
10N, 0	70–80	14	9	1 stone bead			6	3 + 1 bangle
10N, 0	80–90	5	7				3	
10N, 0	90–100	2				1	2	
20N, 0	70–80	2						
20S, 0	30–40							1
20S, 0	50–60	6	1					
20S, 0	60–70	9	1					
20S, 0	80–90	1						
30S, 0	30–40	13	3				1	
30S, 0	40–50	21	7	1 grind stone				1 bangle
30S, 0	50–60	14	2		15			
Total		103	181	2	15	3	27	9

Figure 5.4. The survey beacon BP 113 that was erected by British Petroleum over an Early Iron Age (EIA) site later named after the beacon. The site contains stratified horizons belonging to the Later Stone Age, phases 1 and 2 of the Early Iron Age, and the historic period.

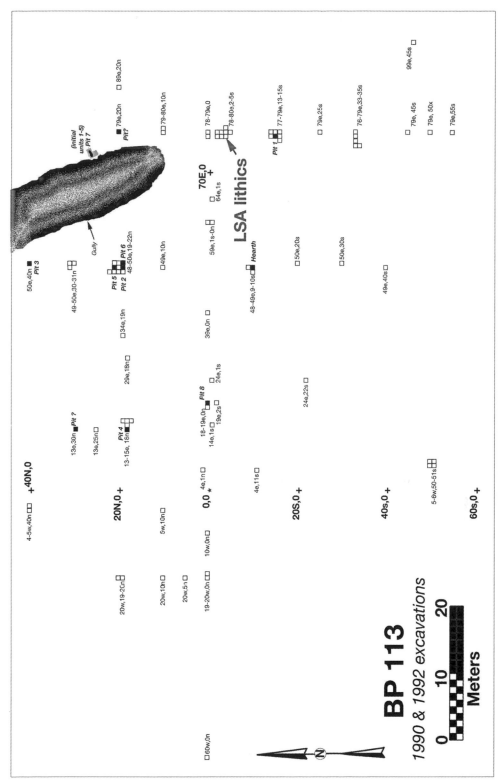

Figure 5.5. Map of the excavation units at BP 113. The black squares indicate the location of phase 1 Early Iron Age pits. The Later Stone Age horizon was confined to the area indicated in gray lettering at 78–80E, 2–5S. The metal survey beacon datum point is marked 0, o.

400 quartzite and 23 chert flakes were recovered; these make up 74 percent of the quartzite and 72 percent of the chert from the site as a whole. Chert makes up slightly more than 8 percent of the lithics from this horizon and roughly 6 percent of all the chipped-stone from the site. This is less than the 14 percent chert found in the LSA levels at Gray Sand, but more than at Kayes, where no chert was recovered. The CLSA levels from Tchissanga, Lamba, and Mvindou, which date between 400 and 200 BC, also contain small quantities of chert along with quartzite, suggesting that the change in lithic preference may have occurred gradually over the course of the last millennium BC. The units surrounding the lithic concentration at BP 113 were not taken down as deep, so the areal extent of the lithic scatter is not known. Other nearby units produced no lithics at this depth, however, suggesting that, similar to Kayes, the lithic scatter was a small, well-defined activity area rather than part of a larger, longer-term occupation horizon. The findings thus suggest that stone tool production was carried out only on a sporadic basis by small numbers of individuals working for short periods.

Ceramic LSA Sites: Tchissanga, Mvindou, and Lamba

Phase 1 CLSA: 1300–400 BC

Tchissanga

The Tchissanga site is situated on a high coastal terrace overlooking Ntombo Marsh to the north and the Atlantic Ocean to the west. The initial inspection of the site in 1987 found small concentrations of thick, coarsely tempered pottery, fragmented quartzite, and charcoal in a bulldozer cutting near the top of the hill (Figure 5.6). No formal stone tools were observed, but some of the flakes bore evidence of use as informal tools. The scattered quartzite chunks could also have resulted from stone tool manufacture, or, alternatively, from smashing quartzite cobbles for use as tempering in the pottery. Conoco had obtained an uncalibrated radiocarbon date of 575 ± 85 BC for charcoal collected from the surface of the bulldozer cutting (Table 4.1, date 4). But because the charcoal was not from an excavated context, its association with the cultural materials was not secure.

In 1987 two 1-by-1-meter test pits were excavated in the undisturbed soil approximately 10 meters south of the edge of the borrow pit. This area was labeled "Tchissanga West." Another set of five test pits was excavated in the undisturbed soil near the eastern side of the borrow pit and labeled "Tchissanga East." At Tchissanga West decorated ceramics were uncovered in situ on a prehistoric surface or horizon approximately 35 centimeters below the surface. These occurred along with fragments of flaked quartzite. The globular-shaped vessels were decorated with broadly incised pendant arcades and cross-hatching (Figure 4.3). A more extensive description of the ceramics from these sites can be found in Denbow (1990). Figures 5.7 and 5.8, reproduced from that publication, illustrate the range of vessel shapes and the frequency of decoration motifs recovered; many of these motifs are also found on ceramics of similar age from coastal Gabon (Clist 1987, 1995, 2005; Lanfranchi et al. 1991). Large, angular chunks of shattered quartzite and volcanic scoria were used to temper these thick, often poorly fired vessels. Charcoal associated with these finds produced a 2-sigma calibrated date of 1367–838 BC (Table 4.1, date 3). This makes Tchissanga West one of the earliest CLSA sites known along the Atlantic coast (Denbow et al. 1988; Denbow 1990).

More-extensive excavations were carried out at Tchissanga in 1988 with funding from Conoco and the National Geographic Society. The excavations in Tchissanga West, Tchissanga East, and an exposed prehistoric pit in Tchissanga Base (Figure 5.9), produced a series of calibrated 2-sigma radiocarbon dates that ranged from 804 to 417 BC for Tchissanga West and from 800 to 120 BC at Tchissanga East (Table 4.1, dates 3, 5, and 6). A single date for the pit at Tchissanga Base produced a calibrated date of 749 to 123 BC. The unfortunately wide temporal

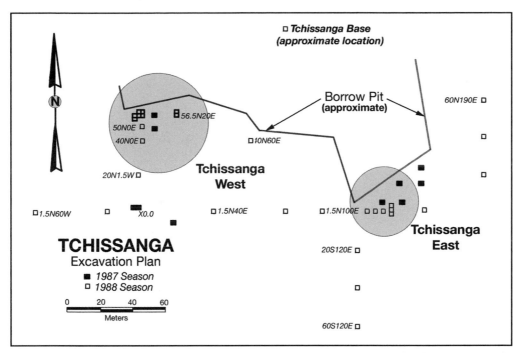

Figure 5.6. Map of the excavations units at Tchissanga West, Tchissanga East, and Tchissanga Base. The modern borrow pit exposed the remains of several phase 1 Ceramic Later Stone Age pits at the site.

range of these dates is because the radiocarbon calibration curve used to correct for variations in the proportion of carbon 14 in the atmosphere is nearly flat in the period between 750 and 400 BC (Michczynski 2004), producing a very wide margin of error for dates falling into this period.

The ceramics from the slightly later deposit at Tchissanga East were characterized by finer grooving and less-coarse tempering. The decoration motifs were also more varied and included some vessels with occasional lugs and handles applied to their exterior. The slightly later radiocarbon dates for Tchissanga East indicate that two culturally related groups occupied the site at slightly different times. The ceramics from the pit excavated at Tchissanga Base were similar in style and age to those from Tchissanga East.

Table A.2 summarizes the results for the excavation. Almost 1,800 stone flakes and fragments were recovered from the site, almost all of it quartzite; only one chert tool, a backed segment, was recovered at Tchissanga East. Overall, the lithics were most highly concentrated in the Tchissanga West units, but significant numbers were also recovered from Tchissanga East and Tchissanga Base, indicating that stone use continued during these later periods. At the site, twenty-five iron fragments were found. In Tchissanga West, most of these were found in the levels above the CLSA horizon and postdate it. This was not the case at Tchissanga East and Tchissanga Base, each of which produced three iron fragments. Although the calibrated dates for these units cover a wide spread, the context of the iron fragments indicates that iron was being produced in the region at some point in the last four to five centuries BC.

The Tchissanga excavations provided evidence that sites dating between 1000 BC and AD 200 are not necessarily deeply buried. The occupation horizons on the hilltop were only 30 to 40 centimeters below the surface, a depth that made them particularly vulnerable to erosion or destruction if the site was cleared of grass cover or plowed for eucalyptus planting. Cultural deposits at the base of hills and terraces, such as those at Kayes and Gray Sand, were less vulnerable because they were more deeply buried by slope wash.

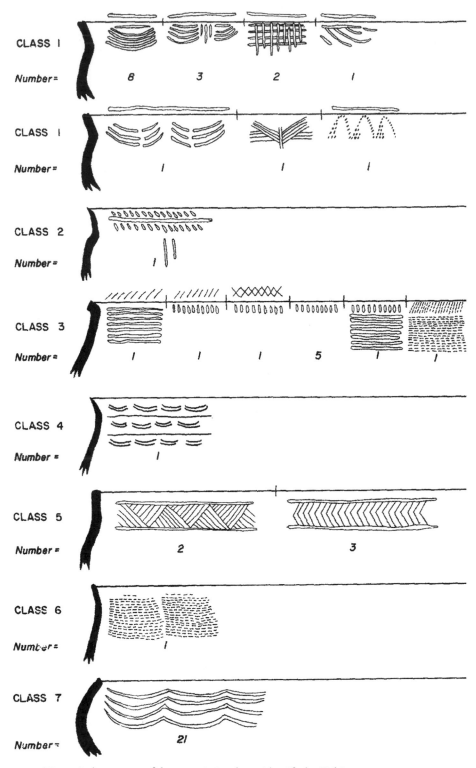

Figures 5.7. Numerical summary of the ceramic jar classes identified at Tchissanga.

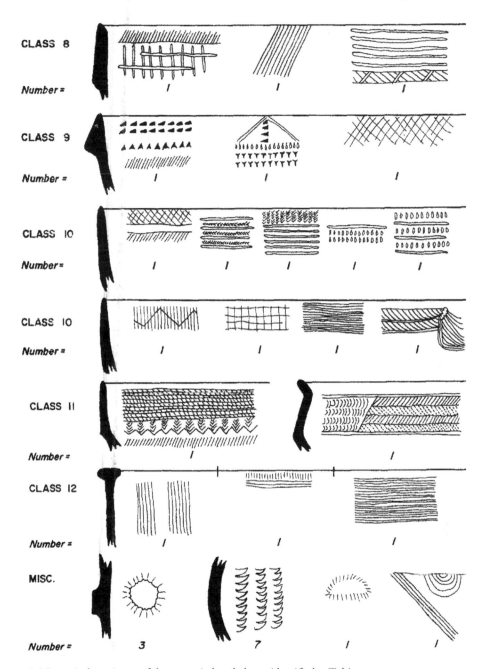

Figure 5.8. Numerical summary of the ceramic bowl classes identified at Tchissanga.

The excavations at Tchissanga West produced the earliest dates for ceramics so far obtained for the Congo littoral. No other sites with stylistically comparable ceramics were identified during the reconnaissance; however, a few of the materials from Lamba, described in the following section, had early dates associated with stylistic attributes such as rocker-stamping or waffle-like impressions on the lower body that appear to be characteristic of phase 1 CLSA materials on the Congo coast. Apart from a few grinding stones that could have been used for processing plant foods or grinding pigment, there was no evidence for agriculture or animal husbandry preserved at phase 1 sites.

Figure 5.9. Casimir and Bob measuring a pit exposed by the bulldozer cutting at Tchissanga Base.

Lamba

Lamba is located approximately 150 meters southeast of BP 113 on the same coastal terrace. Fresh water is available from the Loandjili stream, which ponds into a small marsh on the east side of the site. Two erosion gullies that empty into the Loandjili mark the north and south sides of the site. No artifacts were observed on the flat surface of the terrace between the gullies, but numerous potsherds and a few stone flakes were found eroding from the northern gully at a depth of approximately 50 centimeters below the surface.

In order to determine the site's areal extent, four 1-by-1-meter test squares were excavated on an east-west line 20 meters south of the northern gully. Running from the top of the terrace, the 1-meter squares were placed at 30-meter intervals down the back slope of the terrace to within 20 meters of marsh. In the first three squares from the top of the terrace, Early Iron Age materials were recovered between 40 and 60 centimeters below the surface. In the easternmost unit, Test square 4, 30 meters from the edge of the marsh, CLSA material was found stratified below the Early Iron Age levels. At 50 centimeters below the surface, a prehistoric pit containing CLSA material was exposed. The test pit was expanded into a 2-by-2-meter unit to encompass the feature. These units are labeled "Test 4, ext. 1, 2 and 3" in Table 5.3, which provides a stratigraphic summary of the materials recovered. At its top, the feature was oval in shape and measured approximately 1.5 by 1.2 meters in width. The base of the pit, however, bifurcated into two depressions labeled Pit 1A and Pit 1B (Figure 5.10). Although differences in soil texture were not readily discernible during excavation, differences in content suggest that there were two overlapping pits of somewhat different ages.

Two radiocarbon dates were obtained from the feature: a calibrated 2-sigma date of 1127 to 807 BC from the top of the feature at 80 to 90 centimeters below surface and a 2-sigma date of 404 to 54 BC from charcoal collected from deeper in the fill in pit 1A. Several factors could account for the difference in dates. First, some of the ceramics, particularly those from the pit labeled Feature 1B, have "waffle-like" impressed decoration on the lower body (Figure 5.11) that is similar to

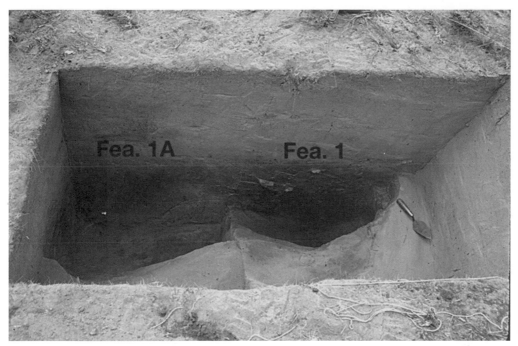

Figure 5.10. View of the excavation at Lamba showing two overlapping pits (1 and 1A). Feature 1 produced ceramics and a radiocarbon date associating it with Phase 1 of the Ceramic Later Stone Age (CLSA); the overlapping pit, Feature 1A, dates to Phase 2 of the CLSA.

some materials from Tchissanga West, which also has earlier dates. A high frequency of grooved, flat lips on many of the Lamba vessels (72 percent) is another characteristic of the Tchissanga West ceramics (Figure 5.11c). These similarities could argue for an earlier date for Pit 1A. A second possibility is that the carbonized oil palm nuts that made up the charcoal sample were in fact associated with the natural land surface just outside the pit, and so dated the surrounding natural soil matrix rather than the pit itself. The second, later date from Lamba falls in the range of those from Tchissanga East (Denbow 1990) and indicates this pit should be placed in Phase 2 of the CLSA; most of the ceramics from Pit 1A support this later affiliation.

Ceramics

The ceramics from Lamba, and indeed from all the sites excavated during the project, were examined along several dimensions that included overall vessel shape and size, tempering material, and the placement and layout of design motifs on the vessel.

Shape. More than 800 potsherds were recovered at Lamba, but only 39, representing 26 vessels, were decorated and of sufficient size to be included the ceramic analysis. Three vessel shapes were identified: wide-mouthed jars (Figures 5.11a, c), hemispherical bowls (Figure 5.11d), and round-shouldered bowls (Figures 5.11e, f). Table 5.4 summarizes the sizes and rim forms recorded for each shape.

Temper. Quartzite and volcanic scoria were the two most common tempering materials used, occurring in fifteen of the twenty-six vessels (58 percent). Two unique tempers were also recorded: a jar with talc as a temper and another with charcoal inclusions. Table 5.5 summarizes the tempering materials identified for each shape.

The single vessel with talc is interesting because this unusual material was also the primary tempering material used for the Carinated Broadly Grooved (CBG) wares found in the nearby site of BP 113, where they date to the sixth century AD. No other talc-tempered vessels were

Table 5.3 Provenience of excavated materials from the Ceramic Later Stone Age site of Lamba

Unit	Level	Depth (cm)	Decorated rim	Decorated body	Undecorated rim & body sherds	Iron	Quartzite	Chert	Ochre	Stones	Other
Test 1	1	0–10									
Test 1	2	10–20									
Test 1	3	20–30									
Test 1	4	30–40									
Test 1	5	40–50			7					2	
Test 1	6	50–60			9			2			
Test 1	7	60–70			11			1			
Test 1	8	70–80									
Test 2	2	20–30			1						
Test 2	3	30–40			1						Pieces of copal
Test 2	4	40–50			9			1			
Test 2	5	50–60			2			3			
Test 3	1	0–10			1						
Test 3	2	10–30			1						
Test 3	3	30–40						1			
Test 3	4	40–50			1						
Test 3	5	50–60			3		1				
Test 3	6	60–70			1		1	6		1	
Test 4	2	10–20			1		1				
Test 4		50–60			2						
Test 4		60–70	2				7			2	1 piece kaolin
Test 4, Feature 1		70–80	1	1	12		7			3	Down to top of pit
Test 4, ext. 1	1	80–		3	17		7				Pit fill
Test 4, ext. 1	2	0–10									
Test 4, ext. 1	3	10–20									
Test 4, ext. 1		20–30			3		1				

Unit	Lvl	Depth									Notes
Test 4, ext. 1	4	30–40					1	1			
Test 4, ext. 1	5	40–50			15		1				
Test 4, ext. 1	6	50–60			25		1	2			Top of pit
Test 4, ext. 1	7	60–68	3?		27		1				Pit fill
Test 4, ext. 1	8	68–base	3	7	37		1	1		3	Yellow sand just above pit
Test 4, ext. 2		40–50	3	4	94	4	3				
Test 4, ext. 2		50–54			3		1				
Test 4, ext. 2		54–60	3	5	93		5			1	1 stone;
Test 4, ext. 2		60–70	2	9	63		4			2	Pit fill
Test 4, ext. 2		70–80		9	60		1	1			1 stone;
Test 4, ext. 2		80–90		8	29		2			2	Lower and upper grindstone
Test 4, ext. 2		90–160	2	10	94		6	2	4	3	Yellow sand above pit
Test 4, ext. 3		40–50			3		1				
Test 4, ext. 3		50–60			4						
Test 4, ext. 3		60–70		15	67		2				Top of pit
Test 4, ext. 3		70–80	1	9	44		1				
Test 4, ext. 3		80–90			15		1		1		
Test 4, ext. 3		90–100			3						Possible area of overlap between pits A & B
Test 4, ext. 3		90–100			12	1	1	1	1	4	
Test 4, ext. 3		100–150		2	38		3	1		3	
Total			**17**	**82**	**807**	**5**	**51**	**22**	**6**	**27**	

Table 5.4. Lamba vessel shape by size and rim form

	No. of vessels	Rim diameter range (cm)	Average rim diameter (cm)	Round lip	Round thickened	Round grooved	Flat grooved
Wide-mouth jar	19	9–38	27	1		1	8
Hemispherical bowl	3	14	14		1		2
Round-shouldered bowl	4	17	17	1			

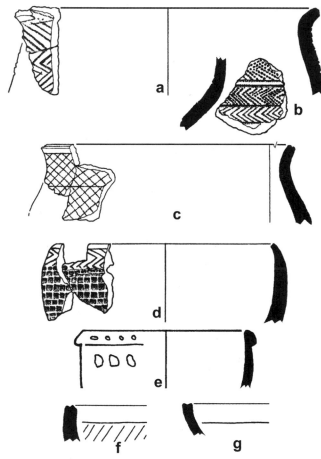

Figure 5.11. Illustration of the vessel types recovered from Lamba. Pots a and c share the incised line along the lip characteristic of Ceramic Later Stone Age (CLSA) Phase 1. Bowl d illustrates the waffle-like impressions also most common in CLSA Phase 1, but not later.

encountered during the Congo project and, given that this temper was found in two quite differ-ent wares in terms of time and culture, it is possible that a talc source may exist in the vicinity of these sites. Talc tempering would have prevented these vessels from cracking at high temperatures (Rice 1987:150). Similar to other early CLSA sites, most of the temper in the larger jars was com-posed of very coarse materials (>6 mm in diameter). These were not natural inclusions from the

Table 5.5. Lamba temper type by vessel shape

	Quartzite	Scoria	Limestone	Talc	Charcoal	Grain size	
						Coarse	Fine
Wide-mouth jar	13	18	1	1		11	8
Hemispherical bowl	0	4	0	0	0	0	4
Round-shouldered bowl	2	3	0	0	1	0	3

Table 5.6. Lamba decoration motif by vessel shape

	Grooving	Grooving & comb-stamping	Grooving & punctates	Grooving & cord-wrapped stick impressions
Wide-mouth jar	16	1	2	
Hemispherical bowl	2	0	1	0
Round-shouldered bowl	0	0	2	4

Table 5.7. Lamba ceramic classes

	Class 1	Class 2	Class 3
Wide-mouth jar	2	17	0
Hemispherical bowl	0	0	3
Round-shouldered bowl	4	1	1
Total	6 (23%)	17 (66%)	3 (11%)

clay source, but rather angular fragments produced by crushing the quartzite or scoria and then adding it to the clay during manufacture.

Firing and Surface Finish. The dark gray color of many of the sherds indicates they were fired at low temperatures in a reducing atmosphere, most likely a bonfire. Experiments with reheating the potsherds found that the firing temperatures used were a relatively low 600°C to 700°C (Hargus 1997). Evidence of burnishing was found on the exterior surface of all the sherds. Decorated vessels used a variety of techniques and tools that included comb-stamping, grooving, cord-wrapped stick impressions, and punctates. Table 5.6 quantifies these techniques by vessel shape. Motifs on wide-mouthed jars were mainly produced by grooving the wet clay with a rounded stick; they often also have a thinner grooved line running along the top of the lip. Round-shouldered bowls often had cord-wrapped stick texturing over the body below a decorated panel of incision or comb-stamping.

Vessel typology. The same ceramic types found at Tchissanga East were identified at Lamba (Table 5.7).

Class 1 vessels decorated with incised or combstamped herringbone motifs.
Class 2 vessels with incised cross-hatching on the neck as the main decorative element.
Class 3 vessels decorated with a single horizontal band or grooved line.
Of the vessels, 69 percent were decorated with shallow grooving whereas 12 percent were decorated with grooving and punctates. Nine of nineteen wide-mouth jars (48 percent) had

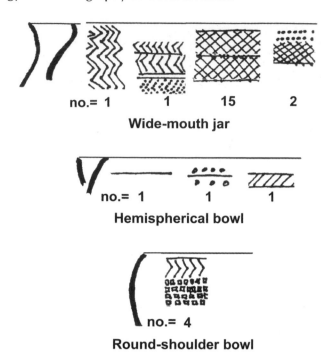

no.= 1   1   15   2

Wide-mouth jar

no.= 1   1   1

Hemispherical bowl

no.= 4

Round-shoulder bowl

Figure 5.12. Numerical summary of the shapes and decoration motifs recorded at Lamba.

a groove running along the top of the lip. Cord-wrapped stick impressions or rocker-stamping was found only on the lower body of round-shouldered bowls. The cord-wrapped stick impressions produced neatly aligned waffle-like indentations on the body (Figure 5.11d). The beautiful pot found eroding from the borrow pit at Madingo-Kayes provides another illustration of this technique and indicates that it was also used on globular shaped jars (Figure 2.1). Figure 5.12 provides a numerical summary of the decoration motifs by vessel shape.

Non-Ceramic Materials

Table 5.3 summarizes the distribution of the cultural materials recovered from the Lamba test squares. Although the upper 30 to 40 centimeters in all units consisted of sterile slope wash devoid of artifacts, test squares 1, 2, and 3 were closer to the top of the hill and contained ceramics and small numbers of chert and quartzite flakes between 30 and 70 centimeters below the surface. Test pit 4 was sterile down to 30 to 40 centimeters below the surface when small quantities of ceramics began to appear. At 70 centimeters, the dark brown stain marking Pits 1A and 1B appeared.

The pit fill produced fifty-one quartzite and twenty-two chert flakes and fragments. None of these was a core or had been fashioned into more formal tools. The twenty-three rounded quartzite cobbles found were intentionally collected since they are not natural inclusions in the soil. They may have been gathered for crushing as pottery temper or for flaking into tools. A possible lower grinding stone made of imported sandstone, and six fragments of red ochre, were also recovered.

Five small (<10 mm) fragments of very corroded iron, four from the yellow sand immediately above the pit in extension 2, and one from the fill of Pit 1B, indicate that iron was manufactured somewhere in the region during the last half of the last millennium BC. There is no evidence for smelting at the site, and no slag was recovered, indicating that the iron smelting took place at another location – possibly on the western edge of the Mayombe 50 kilometers to the east.

Figure 5.13. View of the excavation units next to the gulley at Mvindou.

Phase 2 CLSA: 500–100 BC

Mvindou

Mvindou, discovered in 1991, is the third CLSA site dated by the Congo archaeological project. Situated approximately 20 kilometers inland, the site was found as CDF/UAIC bulldozers were preparing the area for eucalyptus planting. The bulldozer, which had begun to level a small gully prior to planting, exposed the mouth of a prehistoric pit (Feature 1) along with several large fragments of pottery (Figure 5.2). Twenty-two additional 1-by-1-meter units were laid out on the undisturbed ground to the east and west of the gully in order to determine the areal extent of the site (Figure 5.13). Units were labeled by their distance in meters from a central datum point marked 0, 0 on Figure 5.14. In Unit 20N, 0E, the top of a second pit (Feature 2) was exposed at 40 centimeters below the surface (Figure 5.15). A third feature, exposed at 40 centimeters below the surface in units 5–6S, 0E–1W, contained the scattered remains of two nearly complete broken pots, and the remains of several others, lying on a prehistoric occupation surface (Figure 5.16).

Table 5.8 summarizes the excavation results by unit and level. More than 177 decorated sherds were recovered, along with 23 chert flakes and fragments, 85 quartzite flakes and chunks, 9 rhyolite fragments (possibly for use as temper), 10 pieces of sandstone, and 8 small chunks of ferricrete. None of the chert or quartzite flakes was fashioned into formal tools. The relatively high proportion of chert at the site is unusual given its scarcity at the other LSA and CLSA horizons discussed

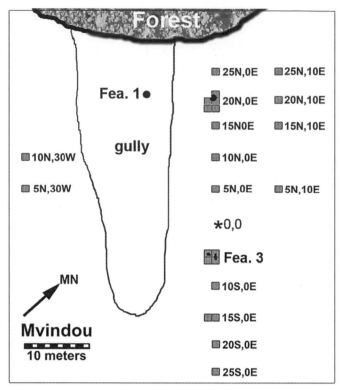

Figure 5.14. Map of the excavation units at Mvindou. The forest at the top of the map is situated in a steep drop-off into Ntombo Marsh. Locations of pits and features are indicated in black.

Figure 5.15. A view of Pit 2 exposed at the Ceramic Later Stone Age site of Mvindou.

Figure 5.16. Bernard the younger uncovering the remains of two broken Ceramic Later Stone Age phase 2 pots on a prehistoric living surface uncovered in units at 5S,0E at Mvindou.

earlier. The site's closer proximity to the Mayombe Mountains, where chert could be procured, might be responsible for this finding. Seven small iron fragments were also recovered, five from Feature 1, one from Unit 5N, 30W, and one from Unit 25N, 0E.

The stratigraphy and artifact distributions in the test squares indicate the presence of a single occupation horizon approximately 45 centimeters below the present surface. Apart from the pits, there is no cultural material above or below this level. Both the shallow occupation horizon and the narrow range of the radiocarbon dates suggest the site was occupied for only a brief time. The four radiocarbon dates, which come from paired samples of wood and carbonized oil palm nuts, support the proposition of a single, short term occupation that falls into a narrow calibrated 2-sigma range of 483 to 57 BC (Table 4.1, dates 13–17). These dates are comparable with the phase 2 date from Lamba and support the proposition that iron manufacture began on the Loango coast in the second half of the last millennium BC – a date consistent with those from Gabon and the Democratic Republic of Congo (de Maret 1982a, 1982b; Digombe et al. 1988; Lanfranchi et al. 1991; Clist 1995, 2012b).

Feature Descriptions

When excavated, the pit found in the bulldozer cutting (Feature 1) was 1 meter in diameter and 1.2 meters deep. Narrow gouges in the side of the pit suggest it was excavated using a digging stick 4 to 5 centimeters in width. Because the top of the feature had been cut away by the bull-dozer, it is not known what the original depth may have been. The pit was excavated in two halves using 20-centimeter increments in order to determine whether there was any internal stratigraphy, but none was observed. The fill, composed of dark, organic-rich soil, was peppered with the carbonized remains of cracked oil palm nuts and wood charcoal. Two radiocarbon samples, one from wood charcoal and the other from charred oil palm nuts, produced 2-sigma calibrated dates between 483 and 115 BC (Table 4.1, dates 13 and 14). Both are similar to those from Tchissanga East and Lamba.

Table 5.8. Provenience of excavated materials recovered from Mvindou

Unit/Feature	Level (cm)	Decorated sherds	Iron fragments	Hematite	Quartzite flakes	quartzite cobbles	Chert flakes	Sandstone	Ferricrete
10N,0E	0–40	0	0	0	0	10	0	0	0
10N,0E	0–50	1	0	0	1	0	0	0	0
10N,0E	50–60	0	0	0	0	0	0	0	0
10N,30W	20–30	0	0	0	1	1	0	0	0
10N,30W	30–40	0	0	0	0	1	0	0	0
10S,0E	0–40	1	0	0	0	0	0	0	0
10S,0E	40–50	2	0	0	2	0	0	0	0
10S,0E	50–60	0	0	0	0	0	0	0	0
15N,0E	35–50	7	0	0	0	0	0	0	0
15N,0E	45–55	0	0	0	0	0	0	0	2
15N,10E	30–40	0	0	0	1	0	2	0	0
15S,0E	30–40	4	0	0	0	0	0	0	0
18N,0E	20–30	6	0	0	0	0	0	0	0
18N,0E	30–40	3	0	0	0	0	2	1	0
18N,0E	40–50	2	0	0	1	0	0	0	0
18N,1W	20–30	2	0	0	1	0	0	0	0
18N,1W	40–50	7	0	0	0	0	0	0	0
19N,0E	30–40	1	0	0	8	1	0	0	6
19N,1W	30–40	22	0	0	1	0	0	0	0
20N,0	0–30	0	0	0	0	3	0	2	0
20N,0	20–30	0	0	0	0	0	1	0	0
20N,0	30–40	13	0	0	1	0	0	0	0
20N,0	40–50	4	0	0	3	6	0	0	0
20N,0–Feature 2	40–190	12	0	0	0	0	0	0	0
20N,10E	40–50	0	0	0	1	0	0	0	0
20N,10E	50–60	1	0	0	5	0	2	0	0
20N,1W	30–40	3	0	0	2	1	6	0	0
20S,0E	30–40	1	0	0	0	0	0	0	0
20S,0E	40–50	4	0	0	0	0	0	0	0

Location	Depth								
25N,0E	10,70	0	0	0	0	0	0	1	0
25N,10E	40–50	0	0	0	0	0	0	0	0
25N,10E	50–60	0	0	0	0	0	0	0	1
25S,0	20–30	0	0	0	0	0	0	0	6
25S,0	30–40	0	0	3	1	1	0	0	0
5N,10E	20–30	0	0	0	0	0	0	0	0
5N,10E	30–40	0	0	0	0	0	0	0	1
5N,30W	20–30	0	0	0	0	0	0	1	7
5N,50W	20–30	0	3	1	0	1	0	0	0
5S,0E	50–60	0	0	0	0	1	0	0	0
5S,0E	60–70	0	0	0	0	0	0	0	2
5S,0E-Feature 3	40–50	0	0	1	0	1	0	0	1
5S,0E-Feature 3	40–50	0	0	0	0	2	0	0	7
5S,0E-Feature 3	40–50	0	0	0	1	0	0	0	0
5S,1W	20–30	0	0	0	0	0	0	0	0
6S,0E	0–40	0	0	0	1	2	0	0	3
6S,1W	30–40	0	3	0	0	0	0	1	20
Feature 1	0–20	0	0	4	1	3	0	3	14
Feature 1	20–40	0	0	0	3	0	3	1	5
Feature 1	40–60	0	1	0	7	4	0	0	1
Feature 1	60–80	0	0	0	7	7	0	0	7
Feature 1	80–100	0	0	1	3	2	2	0	4
Feature 1	100–120	0	0	0	0	0	0	0	4
Feature 1	surface	0	0	0	0	0	0	0	4
Total		8	10	23	30	55	9	7	177

The second pit, Feature 2, was encountered at 40 centimeters below the surface in Unit 20N, 0. When excavated, the pit reached a depth of 1.9 meters below the surface and measured 1.1 meters in diameter and 1.5 meters in depth from its lip to its base. Its dark, organic fill had no discernible internal layering or strata. Charcoal, separated into paired wood charcoal and carbonized oil palm nut samples, produced calibrated 2-sigma radiocarbon dates between 405 and 97 BC (Table 4.1, dates 15 and 16). These are nearly identical with those from Feature 1. The location of both pits on the downhill side of the site adjacent to a wooded drop-off into Ntombo Marsh suggests this zone could have served as a refuse disposal area for an occupation higher on the hill. Alternatively, the pits could have been used for storage of root crops or other foods that have not been preserved. Apart from a highly organic fill rich in carbonized oil palm nuts, there is no evidence of function.

Feature 3 was an occupation horizon exposed in a 2-by-2-meter square at 6–7N, 0–1W of the datum. Although the upper 40 centimeters produced almost no cultural remains (Table 5.8), between 40 to 45 centimeters below the surface, large fragments from at least two broken pots were exposed lying flat on an occupation surface. Three quartzite flakes and one chert flake accompanied these remains. The large pottery fragments suggest this area may have served as a living area distinct from the pit-field downslope.

Ceramics

Attributes measured on the Mvindou ceramics are summarized in Tables 5.9 through 5.12.

Shape. Of the 266 pottery fragments recovered from the excavations, 177, or 67 percent, were decorated and/or rim sherds – a fairly high percentage. After exclusion of sherds too fragmentary or small for the vessel shape to be determined, fifty-four sherds representing twenty vessels were analyzed. The following vessel types were identified: (a) wide-mouthed jars (Figure 5.17), (b) round-shouldered bowls (Figure 5.18), and (c) slightly necked bowls (Figure 5.19). Table 5.9 presents the size range and rim form for each vessel category. Fifteen of the twenty Mvindou vessels had preserved lips; both round and flat thickened lips occurred on all vessel shapes, but flattened lips were found exclusively on the round-shouldered or hemispherical bowls.

Temper. Table 5.10 summarizes the temper type and size by vessel form. The most common tempering material consisted of coarse fragments of limestone, quartzite, or red volcanic scoria. Angular quartzite temper was found in all twenty vessels; this was combined with red scoria in another eleven. Most vessels had more than one type of tempering material added to the clay.

The grain size of the temper was further subdivided into fine (<6 mm) and coarse (>6 mm) fractions. The angularity of the inclusions indicates that the tempering materials were not a natural part of the clay, but were purposefully collected, crushed, and added to the clay to increase its strength. If they had been naturally occurring inclusions in the clay source, more weathering or rounding of the particles would be expected.

Firing and Surface Finish. The dark, friable nature of most of the sherds indicates they were fired at low temperatures in a reducing atmosphere. Sample potsherds subjected to kiln firing experiments found that most had been fired at temperatures in the range of 600°C to 700°C (Hargus 1997). These characteristics suggest the pottery was fired in the open or in shallow pits covered over with brush or wood, which was used as fuel. All the sherds showed evidence of polishing or burnishing on their exterior surfaces. The smooth, waterworn quartzite cobbles would have been perfect for this task. Decoration techniques included comb-stamping, grooving, and, less frequently, combinations that utilized both techniques. Table 5.11 summarizes the decorative techniques utilized for each vessel shape.

Vessel Typology. Overall, wide mouth jars and slightly necked bowls had the greatest variety of decoration types. The main typological subdivisions of the Mvindou pottery are summarized numerically in Table 5.12.

Table 5.9. Mvindou vessel shape by size and rim form

	No. of vessels	Rim diameter range (cm)	Average rim diameter (cm)	Round lip	Flat lip	Flat, thickened lip
Wide-mouth jar	9	22–26	24 (*n* = 3)	3	0	1
Round-shouldered bowl	8	8–14	12 (*n* = 5)	4	4	0
Slightly necked bowl	3	14–16	15 (*n* = 3)	1	0	2

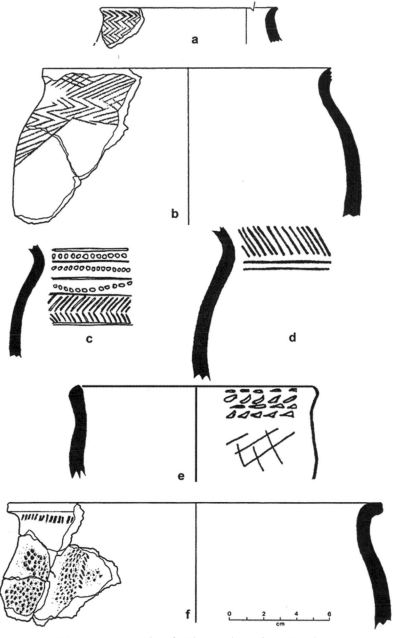

Figure 5.17. Examples of wide-mouth jars from Mvindou.

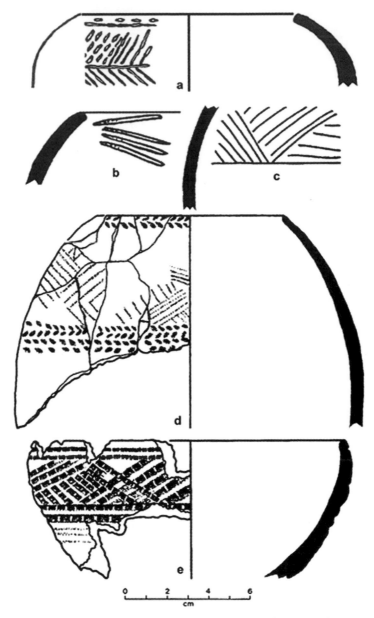

Figure 5.18. Examples of round-shouldered bowls from Mvindou.

Class 1 vessels decorated with incised or comb-stamped herringbone patterns. The vast majority of these vessels, including one with a pendant triangle descending from a herringbone band, are wide-mouthed jars (Figures 5.17a, b).

Class 2 vessels with grooved, crosshatched bands. These vessels include both wide-mouth jars and slightly necked bowls (Figure 5.17e; Figure 5.19a).

Class 3 vessels with horizontal bands of oblique hatching. This motif was found on all vessel shapes (Figure 5.17d; Figure 5.18b; Figures 5.19a, b).

Class 4 vessels with bands of incised or comb-stamped alternating triangles. This motif was found primarily on round-shouldered bowls, with the band of interlocking triangles bounded by bands of punctates or horizontal comb-stamping.

Table 5.10. Mvindou temper by vessel shape

	No. of vessels	Limestone	Quartzite	Red Scoria	Grain size	Coarse Fine
Wide-mouth jar	9	3	8	5	6	3
Round-shouldered bowl	8	1	8	4	2	6
Slightly necked bowl	3	1	3	2	1	2

Table 5.11. Mvindou decoration technique by vessel shape

	Grooving	Comb-stamping	Grooving & comb-stamping	Grooving & rocker-stamping
Wide-mouth jar	6	0	2	1
Round-shouldered bowl	1	6	1	0
Slightly necked bowl	1	0	2	0

Table 5.12. Mvindou shape by decoration class

	Class 1	Class 2	Class 3	Class 4
Wide-mouth jar	6	1	2	0
Round-shouldered bowl	1	0	1	6
Slightly necked bowl	0	1	1	1
	7 (35%)	2 (10%)	4 (20%)	7 (35%)

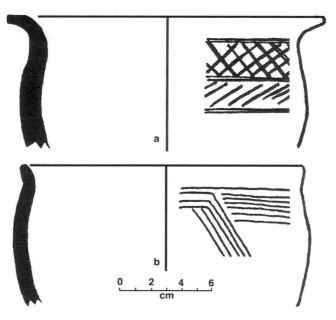

Figure 5.19. Slightly necked bowls from Mvindou.

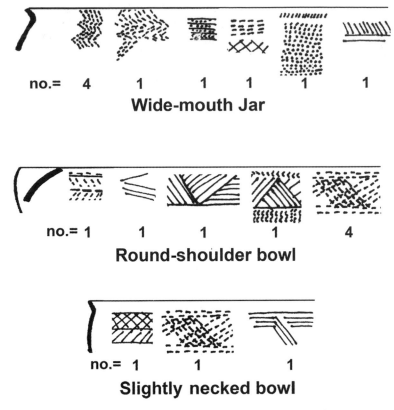

Figure 5.20 Numerical summary of decoration motifs by vessel shape at Mvindou.

Figure 5.20 presents the frequency distribution of decoration motifs by vessel shape. Both wide-mouth jars and slightly necked bowls share similar motifs, with comb-stamped herringbone patterns in the neck being the most common. Round-shouldered bowls were usually decorated with incised or comb-stamped alternating triangles bordered by bands of punctates or incised lines.

Conclusion

Although there is no direct evidence for food production, the appearance after 1000 BC of ceramics along with deep pits filled with carbonized oil palm nuts (*Elaeis guineensis*) marks the CLSA sites off from the ephemeral Later Stone Age occurrences found at Gray Sand, BP 113, and Kayes. The combination of pottery, pits, and small, flat grinding stones made of micaceous schist imported from the Mayombe Mountains suggest that sedentary populations now occupied the coast. The ubiquitous oil palm nuts in the pit fill suggest the possibility of arboriculture. The appearance of these settlements coincides approximately with dates for a change from forest to a more open forest-savanna vegetation cover on the Loango coast. This suggests that some of the savanna openings could be anthropogenic in origin and are perhaps related to the use of fire to clear the forest for settlements or crops.

During phase 2 of the CLSA, small fragments of iron make their appearance at Tchissanga East, Tchissanga Base, Lamba, and Mvindou. These in situ finds come from secure pit contexts at most of these sites and indicate that iron was in use on the Congo coast between the fourth and second centuries BC. No direct evidence for smelting in the form of furnace remains or slag deposits was found on the coastal plain, however, and iron ore outcrops are absent there. But a late first millennium BC date for an iron smelting furnace on the forested flanks of the Mayombe, 50 kilometers east, suggests that iron may have been smelted at more inland locations and then traded to the coast. Schwartz et al. (1990) also suggest that climatic conditions at this time could have been slightly drier, producing savanna openings where there once had been closed forest. A subsequent return to wetter conditions at the beginning of the second millennium AD has since reduced or closed these openings in the forest.

More broadly, the Ceramic Later Stone Age ceramics recovered share some shape and decoration similarities with a subset of ceramics of similar age belonging to the Okala Tradition in Gabon (Clist 2005: 269). The bowl and pot forms with flat bases, pots with channeled lips, occasional rocker-stamping, and broadly grooved motifs are all characteristic of Okala. Absent from the Congo materials, however, are the bilobial and carinated vessels associated with the later phase of Okala (Clist 2005: 418). More similarities, including globular pots with grooved rims decorated in the neck with broadly grooved pendant arcades, occur with the slightly later Ngovo Tradition ceramics found south of the Congo River (de Maret 1986; Gosselain 1988; Clist 2005: annex 5, tableau 3). These similarities suggest that new populations expanded southward following coastal routes from Gabon during the last millennium BC. These communities likely encountered indigenous hunter-gatherers represented by the earlier LSA traces, overlapping with them in the use of some resources while introducing new adaptations that included intensive use of the oil palm.

6

The Early Iron Age

Prior to the existence of the Loango kingdom, the country reportedly had been ruled by a government organized by the buwandji, a brotherhood of blacksmiths. Loango tradition sees them as Bawoyo who invaded Loango, imposing a centralized organization upon the local population. It is remembered that nine suzerains of the buwandji were inhumed in the old graveyard of Loandjili. ... Founded and led by an organized caste of blacksmiths, it had a non-elective government. Hagenbucher-Sacripanti's informants in Loango were specific about the non-elective leadership in the state of the buwandji ... [which] leads to the conjecture that the rulers were heads of the family of master blacksmiths within which the leadership was hereditary. (Volavka and Thomas 1998: 106)

Introduction

The oral traditions collected from Loango and Ngoyo are clear in tying the beginnings of political centralization on the Loango coast to an invasion of a brotherhood of blacksmiths that provided a foundation for political hegemony (Volavka and Thomas 1998: 111). Nonetheless, as we have seen, the Loango plain is geologically unsuited to iron production because it contains no ores. Indeed, apart from the rounded quartzite found on the beach there are no stones at all until one arrives on the slopes of the Mayombe Mountains 60 kilometers inland. It is, therefore, not surprising that the archaeological reconnaissance found no evidence for iron smelting on the sandy coastal plain. As we have seen, however, iron smelting is attested as early as the second century BC farther inland (Schwartz et al. 1990). Although the distances to potential sources of iron ore are not great, on the order of 50 to 60 kilometers, locating villages in closed forest would have increased the cost of clearing agricultural and household land. Apart from the furnace reported earlier, no Iron Age settlements have been recorded in this environmental zone. Although one cannot at this stage rule out the possibility of such settlements, with a trade in finished iron goods being carried out with agricultural communities on the savanna, no archaeological surveys have been conducted to locate such sites. It is also possible that iron smelting was conducted in the forests by parties of smelters who made periodic trips there from communities on the coastal plain.

The date for the Mayombe furnace coincides with the earliest appearance of a new style of ceramics on the coastal plain characterized by necked jars with comb-stamped or incised herringbone decoration on their necks. The earliest date for this material comes from the small cache of broken pots found eroding from the prehistoric pit at Tandou-Youmbi (Figure 4.12). The pit also contained two molded clay objects and a polished stone hoe or axe (Denbow 1990). No iron objects were found in the pit, which produced a single, calibrated 2-sigma date of 358 BC to 17 AD (Table 4.1, date 18). More extensive excavations at the site of BP 113, situated 20 kilometers east of Tandou-Youmbi, provide the best glimpse into this new Early Iron Age tradition.

Early Iron Age (EIA) Phases 1 and 2: Excavations at BP 113 and Kayes

BP 113

The site of BP 113 (UTM coordinates: 0786978; 9517663)[1] is situated approximately 20 kilometers north of the mouth of the Kouilou River; it straddles the summit of a coastal terrace approximately 1 kilometer west of the Atlantic Ocean (Figure 4.2). The site is approximately 150 meters northwest of Lamba on the same terrace. The Louandjili stream flows below the site to the northeast, where it ponds into a small marsh before cutting through the terrace north of the site on its way to the Atlantic. No surface ceramics were found on the level crest of the hill during the initial reconnaissance but numerous potsherds were observed eroding from a gully that slopes down to the Louandjiri on the eastern side of the site.

Over two field sessions in 1990 and 1992, 84 m² was excavated at the site. The 1990 excavations were directed by Denbow and were carried out with the assistance of graduate students from the University of Texas at Austin and a local field crew. The second season, in 1992, was directed by Denbow with the assistance of Professor Manima-Moubouha and two students from the University of Marien Ngouabi in Brazzaville. The metal pipe set in concrete by British Petroleum was used as the 0, 0 datum point for the excavation grid, which was laid out along an E-W magnetic axis. Figure 5.5 records the location of excavation units from both years, and includes the locations of features and pits identified during both field seasons. The ceramics and other materials from the 1992 excavations were left in the Congo with Manima-Moubouha for analysis. Table A.3 consolidates the provenience of the cultural materials from both sets of excavations. While the table presents the stratigraphic distribution of artifacts from both field seasons, the ceramic analyses below reflect only the materials from the 1990 excavation analyzed at the University of Texas.

Excavation units near the head of the gully next to several old guava trees revealed evidence of four phases of occupation: (1) an undated Later Stone Age (LSA) horizon isolated between 80 to 100 centimeters below the surface in a set of units centered around 77E, 15S; (2) an EIA Phase 1 occupation level exposed between 50 and 80 centimeters below surface in units 78–80E, 0–5S. Ceramics from this phase are characterized by herringbone decoration. A calibrated 2-sigma date places this horizon between 345 BC and AD 69 (Table 4.1, date 19). (3) Ten centimeters above the Phase 1 occupation at 40 to 50 centimeters below the surface was a very different ceramic assemblage with Phase 2 Carinated Broadly Grooved (CBG) wares. These are labeled Phase 2 in Table A.3. Ceramics from this phase were tempered with talc, had distinctive carinated jar shapes, and were decorated with broadly grooved horizontal bands and loops (Figure 6.1). The Phase 2 material is very tentatively dated at BP 113 by a single 2-sigma date of AD 245 to 564 (Table 4.1, date 24). The CBG wares are not related stylistically to the Phase 1 EIA herringbone wares; however, their dating overlaps with the end of Phase 1. They represent a new cultural intrusion onto the coast, perhaps from the region of northern or northeastern Angola. In the 78–80E, 0–5S units, the Phase 2 horizon is overlain by 20 centimeters of sterile yellow sand that separates it from the most recent occupation; (4) a late-nineteenth-century horizon exposed in the upper 20 centimeters of

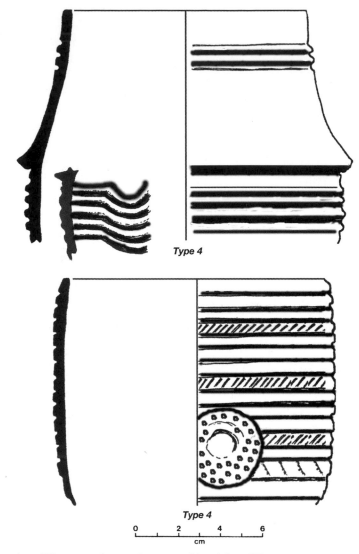

Type 4

Type 4

Figure 6.1. Examples of Phase 2 Early Iron Age pot and bowl from BP 113.

the deposit. This horizon contained imported porcelain wares, glass beads, copper and iron artifacts, and indigenous pottery decorated with panels of broad line incision. One piece of stoneware labeled "Luneville France" dates this occupation to the end of the nineteenth century.

Features

Pits

Eight pits were identified and excavated during the two field seasons. Their locations are indicated on Figure 5.5. All are associated with the Phase 1 EIA occupation; none contained Phase 2 ceramics. The pits fall into two different types: (1) oblong, shallow features with light, less organic fill. Two pits of this type, numbers 7 and 8, contained almost complete pots (Figure 6.2); The near absence of organic matter and their shallow depth distinguish these pits from the organic-rich CLSA pits discussed in the last chapter. Although their function is unknown, they were clearly different. (2) The other type of pit (Figure 6.3) is deep and circular and has a dark, organic fill containing the remains of carbonized oil palm nuts and fragmentary ceramics from many

Figure 6.2. A nearly complete Phase 1 Early Iron Age Herringbone ware pot found in situ in Pit 7 at BP 113.

Figure 6.3. Excavated Phase 1 pits 2, 5, and 6 at BP 113.

different vessels. In two cases, pits 1 and 4, corroded iron objects and, in Pit 1, several tuyère fragments from iron smithing, were recovered. The second type of pit, with its richer organic content, may have been used for storage or refuse. Most of the pits were found on the eastern slope of the terrace facing the marsh.

Hearth

The remains of a small hearth containing large amounts of charcoal and underlain by a red, oxidized layer were exposed between 12 and 17 centimeters below the surface in units 48–50E, 8–10S. The hearth belongs to the final, historic occupation of the site. Three adjacent 1-by-1-meter squares were excavated to a depth of 90 centimeters below the surface, but no other features were encountered.

Iron and Copper

Thirty-four highly corroded iron objects and a fragment of a tanged projectile point were recovered in association with the Phase 1 ceramics. Iron artifacts, small tuyère fragments, and pieces of slag were found scattered in many units east of the datum. Seven tuyère fragments in units at 77–78E, 13–15S suggest that iron smithing may have taken place in this locality.

Several fragments of an ivory-handled pocketknife belonging to the nineteenth-century occupation were recovered in the 76–80E, 25–33S units at 10 to 20 centimeters below surface along with two fragments of copper and a nineteenth-century blue-and-white annular glass trade bead.

Lithics

Small numbers of chert and quartzite flakes and fragments along with unmodified, water-rounded quartzite cobbles were recovered from several units in association with Phase 1 ceramics. A total of 31 chert and 569 quartzite flakes and fragments were recovered from the site as a whole, but the vast majority came from a set of units at 77–80E, 2–15S at a depth below the Iron Age levels. The few stone flakes recovered from the EIA levels indicate that lithic use continued into the first millennium AD. No formal stone tools such as scrapers or backed segments were recovered.

Ceramics

Shape

The densest concentration of ceramics was found in the area centered on squares 13–19E, 0–18N. Interestingly, in the northwestern part of the site many of the potsherds were highly corroded. Ceramics from the same depth in all the other units were well preserved and not corroded. Because the age and soil matrix were the same, one possibility is that this part of the site was used for some special activity such as boiling seawater for salt in the manner described during the historic period by Proyart in Chapter 7 (1814: 574; Vansina 2010: 13). This would have had a corrosive effect on the pottery.

Of the 274 decorated and rim sherds examined, 101 were excluded from the analysis because they were too small for vessel shapes to be accurately determined. The remaining 173 sherds, comprising 63 vessels belonging to four vessel types, included (1) necked jars, (2) collared jars, (3) round-shouldered bowls, and (4) collared or barrel-shaped bowls. The two collared shapes are CBG wares associated with the Phase 2 occupation. The remaining necked jars and round-shouldered bowls belong to Phase 1 Herringbone wares that date between the last century BC and the second century AD. For the site as a whole, jars were far more numerous than were bowls, especially during the Phase 1 occupation. Figure 6.4 illustrates a handle decorated with an incised herringbone motif from one of the few decorated Phase 1 bowls recovered. Table 6.1 summarizes the distribution of vessel forms by rim diameter and shape.

Most of the sixteen vessels complete enough for rim diameters to be measured were necked jars belonging to the Phase 1 occupation. Generally, the collared jars of the Phase 2 occupation had larger rim diameters than did Phase 1 vessels; they were also more standardized in size with an average diameter of 22 centimeters.

Table 6.1. BP 113 shapes and rim types

	Total no. vessels	No. measured for rim diameter	Rim diameter range (cm)	Rim diameter mean (cm)	Beveled rim	Flat rim	Round rim
Necked jar	37 (59%)	12	14–24	18	35		
Round-shouldered bowl	1 (2%)						
Collared jar	23 (36%)	3	22	22		3	1
Barrel-shaped bowl	2 (3%)	1	20	20		1	1

Figure 6.4. Example of a decorated handle from a Phase 1 Early Iron Age Herringbone vessel.

Nearly two-thirds of the vessels (*n* = 41) from Phase 1 had preserved rims. One of the most distinctive characteristics of these jars is the thickening and beveling treatment of the rim (Figure 6.5). Finds of beveled rim jars at eight additional sites during the reconnaissance indicate this was not an idiosyncratic characteristic of the Phase 1 Herringbone wares from BP 113. Beveled rims were not found, however, on the jars recovered at Tandou-Youmbi, Meningue, or Kayes, which bracket the BP 113 horizon on its earlier and later ends.

It is unclear why so few bowls were recovered from the Phase 1 Herringbone occupation at BP 113, particularly when these were so common at earlier CLSA sites and at later Phase 2 and Phase 3 EIA sites. Because bowls are usually the most elaborately decorated pottery encountered in the EIA, one possibility is that food was served in wooden bowls rather than ceramic containers.

The collared jars and barrel-shaped beakers and bowls belonging to Phase 2 at BP 113 are very different in shape, decoration, and tempering characteristics. Many also had decorated lugs applied to their exteriors. The stratigraphy clearly places the CBG wares later than the Phase 1 occupation. The single AD 400 to 600 radiocarbon date for this phase is supported by another from the nearby site of Lac Ndembo discussed later.

Temper

Table 6.2 presents the distribution of temper types and grain size by vessel shape. All of the Phase 2 vessels have distinctive talc temper. This additive may have served a variety of functional and perhaps stylistic purposes. Talc is well known to reduce thermal expansion in ceramics, and its use

Figure 6.5. Examples of the beveled rims that characterize the Phase 1 Early Iron Age Herringbone wares at BP 113. The lower example appears to have been decorated using a knotted string roulette rolled across the wet clay.

in cooking vessels might have been an important consideration for Phase 2 potters. The talc also resulted in a very slippery surface that could have helped prevent food from sticking (Rice 1987: 150). The find of one CLSA vessel with talc temper at Lamba suggests this material may outcrop locally, but its source is presently unknown. No other vessels containing talc were recovered during the reconnaissance or excavations.

Most of the Phase 2 vessels also had mica in the clay, which gave them a glistening appearance. Mica was also present in a few of the round-shouldered bowls in Phase 1 levels. Because bowls were used for serving food, as well as cooking, it is possible the glittering mica was added for decorative purposes.

Firing and Surface Finish

The reddish-brown exterior of the ceramics from both EIA phases indicates they were fired in a more oxidizing atmosphere than were the gray CLSA wares discussed in the last chapter. Fresh breaks on the ceramics also indicate that most were fired red throughout, rather than having a contrasting, sandwich-like dark interior and red exterior indicative of lower firing temperatures. Experimental refiring of a sample of Phase 1 ceramics from BP 113 indicated these vessels were

Table 6.2. Temper type and size by shape

	Scoria	Quartzite	Anthill	Talc	Mica	Grain size	
						Coarse	Fine
Necked jar	35	37	7		4	2	35
Round-shouldered bowl		1			1		1
Collared jar	16	23	15	24	18		24
Barrel-shaped bowl	1	1	1	1	1		1
Total	62	71	23	25	24	2	81

Figure 6.6. Phase 2 Carinated Broadly Grooved (CBG) ware from BP 113.

indeed fired at temperatures of between 700°C and 800°C, approximately 100°C higher than the temperatures determined for a sample of CLSA ceramics (Hargus 1997).

Table 6.3 summarizes the decoration techniques by vessel shape found at BP 113. Phase 1 vessels were decorated using a variety of tools and techniques that included incising (27 percent), comb-stamping (14 percent), and cord-wrapped sticks or string roulettes (1 percent). All the Period 2 ceramics were decorated with deep grooving. In two cases, circular punctates were also used to decorate the round lugs applied to the sides of barrel-shaped pots (Figure 6.6).

Vessel Typology

The main typological subdivisions of the BP 113 ceramics are presented in Figure 6.7.

These include the following:

Class 1 jars decorated with obliquely hatched lines on the neck.
Class 2 jars and a bowl decorated with single or multiple bands of incised or comb-stamped herringbone in the neck.

Table 6.3. Decoration technique by shape

	Incising (I)	Comb-stamping (CS)	Roulette (R)	I + CS	I + R	Grooving	Grooving & Punctates
Necked jar	17	14	1	1	4		
Round-shouldered bowl					1		
Collared jar						23	
Barrel-shaped bowl						1	1
Total	17 (27%)	14 (22%)	1 (2%)	1 (2%)	5 (7%)	24 (38%)	1 (2%)

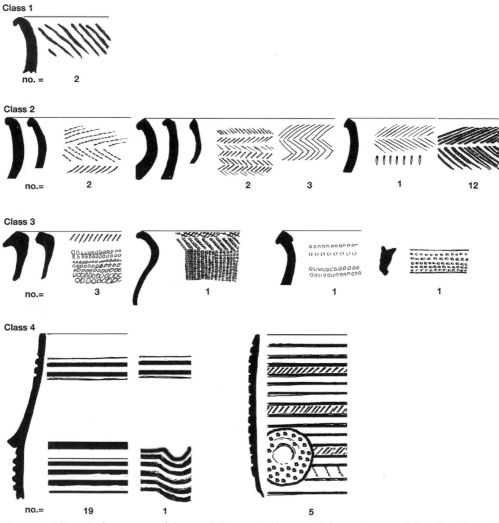

Figure 6.7. Numerical summary of the vessel shapes, rim forms, and decoration motifs found on the Early Iron Age Phase 1 vessels (classes 1–3) and Phase 2 (Class 4) ceramics at BP 113.

Table 6.4. Motif layout by shape

	Class 1	Class 2	Class 3	Class 4
Necked Jar	2	30	5	
Round-shouldered bowl		1	1	
Carinated jar				23
Barrel-shaped bowl				2
Total	2 (3%)	31 (48%)	6 (9%)	25 (40%)

Class 3 jars decorated with horizontal string impressions or roulette (Figure 6.5, bottom). Class 4 carinated jars and barrel-shaped bowls or jars decorated with bands of deep horizontal grooving. All class 4 vessels belong to Phase 2 of the EIA occupation. Jars in this class commonly have a sharp carination at the neck-shoulder junction, sometimes with semicircular festoons or other geometric motifs below. Bowls often have decorated lugs.

Table 6.4 summarizes these classes by vessel shape, whereas Figure 6.7 records the number of vessels recorded for each shape and class.

Summary

The densest concentration of cultural materials was found in two localities: the units 20 meters west of the datum point, just before the hilltop begins its descent to the Louandjili stream, and the area near the gully on the eastern side of the site 70 and 80 meters east of the datum. In the western locality a dense scatter of heavily corroded and fragile potsherds suggests that an activity such as boiling salt water to obtain salt may have taken place in this area. Pits belonging to Phase 1 of the EIA were concentrated to the southeast of the datum. Some pits had dark, organic fill whereas others had lighter fill and contained the remains of nearly whole pots. Pits 1 and 4 also contained Phase 1 pottery along with fragments of iron, iron slag, and smithing tuyère fragments that suggest metalworking took place in these locales.

The Phase 2 occupation was concentrated near the head of the gulley where the densest scatter of these ceramics was found. No pits contained Phase 2 ceramics, and the spatially restricted scatter of these materials suggest the occupation was of fairly short duration. Desmond Clark recovered examples of nearly identical CBG ware at Dundo airfield in northeast Angola in the 1960s (Clark 1968: 201, nos. 1–4, 7) associated with a single radiocarbon date between the eighth and eleventh centuries. The ceramics Clark illustrates, however, include a variety of styles, including some that were decorated with false-relief chevron motifs similar to EIA traditions in the Democratic Republic of Congo discussed in Chapter 8. Dates for CBG ware should be treated with caution until more become available.

Finally, the large mango trees (*Mangifera indica*) growing on the eastern edge of the site are probably associated with the nineteenth-century occupation.[2] The upper 20 centimeters of the deposit near these trees contained historic Loango ceramics along with sponge decorated earthenware, glass beads, and other objects of European origin.

Kayes

The Kayes site lies at the foot of a high coastal terrace that overlooks the mangrove forest at the mouth of the Kouilou River approximately 3 kilometers east of the ocean. Two erosion gullies mark the eastern and western sides of the site. No ceramics or other cultural materials were observed on the surface, but potsherds eroding from the gullies indicated the presence of a buried site.

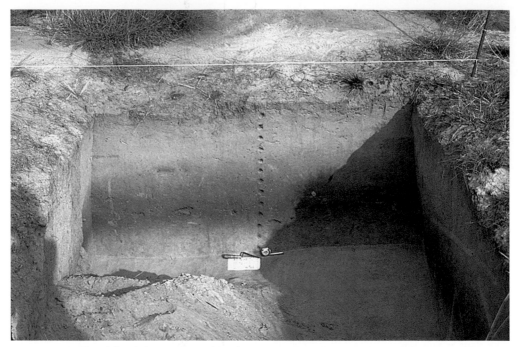

Figure 6.8. Profile of the dark, organic midden layer exposed in units 9–10N, 0 at Kayes. The yellow sand above and below the midden was sterile and contained no artifacts.

Two small cement markers were placed on a N-S magnetic line 20 meters apart to mark the 0, 0 and 20N, 0 points of the site datum. Figure 2.4 shows the 0, 0 marker, with the top of the 80-m terrace in the background. Around these markers, eleven excavation units were laid out, with each 1-by-1-meter unit labeled by its distance in meters from the marker at 0,0. Units that produced recognizable strata of organic-rich midden soils or other artifact concentrations were enlarged into 1.5-by-1.5- or 2-by-2-meter units. Just below the 30S, 0 unit, the terrace drops off steeply onto a flat surface that drains into the swamp approximately 300 meters to the south.

In the 20S unit, a light gray layer of humus from the surface down to 15 centimeters below the surface was observed. This layer was also found higher on the slope in the units at 10N, 0, but was missing from the downhill unit at 30–30S, possibly because it had been eroded away. In all the units, a sterile layer of light yellow sand 40 to 70 centimeters thick separated the humic layer from the buried cultural layers. Units closer to the hill had more sterile soil overlying the cultural deposits than those farther south. Table 5.2 summarizes the horizontal and vertical distribution of the materials recovered. The table includes only those levels that produced cultural materials. In all units, the EIA occupation horizon was overlain by sterile sand that varied in depth from 30 to 50 centimeters depending on the distance from the base of the hill.

In the units at 9–10N, 0–1E, a sealed midden deposit was exposed between 70 and 90 centimeters below the surface. This midden had a very dark, almost greasy, organic fill derived from refuse that had been deposited on the original land surface when the site was occupied (Figures 6.8 and 6.9). The midden contrasts with the pit fields used for rubbish disposal at the CLSA sites of Tchissanga, Lamba, and Mvindou and at BP 113. The 2-sigma calibrated dates for the midden range between AD 349 and 682 (Table 4.1, dates 31 and 32). A broader but overlapping 2-sigma calibrated date of AD 130 to 531 was obtained for the cultural horizon in Unit 19S, 0.

Figure 6.9. Sylvain checking the depth of the midden deposit at Kayes. The excavated hole and light sandy stain visible in the center of the square were produced by later rodent burrowing.

Iron and Lithics

Table 5.2 summarizes the distribution of lithic and iron materials recovered from the excavations. Two iron bangle fragments 1 centimeter in diameter were found in units at 10N, 0 and 30S, 0. A fragment of iron wire 10 centimeters in length and a subrectangular iron rod fragment 2 centimeters long were also recovered in different units along with several iron fragments of indeterminate shape. Iron slag and tuyère fragments from several other locations suggest that iron smithing may have taken place on the site. Evidence for smelting in the form of massive slag heaps or furnace remains was absent, however. No copper items were found.

Of the 181 quartzite flakes and fragments recovered at Kayes, 74 percent came from a pre–Iron Age horizon in Unit 0, 10W near the edge of the western gully; no chert materials were recovered (Table 5.2). A calibrated 2-sigma radiocarbon date of 724 to 180 BC (Table 4.1, date 30) was obtained for the LSA horizon. The remaining quartzite fragments were associated with the EIA occupation and indicate that occasional use of informal stone tools continued into the Iron Age. A single grinding stone was found in Unit 30S, 0, while a stone bead came from Unit 10N, 0. A polished stone axe similar in style and raw material to the one recovered at Tandou-Youmbi was also found on the surface near the eastern gully. The axe must have lain on the surface for a considerable time because its upper surface was highly corroded whereas the underside still retained most of its polish. These two polished stone axes are the only ones ever found along the Loango coast. Both came from EIA sites, not the CLSA contexts where they are more common elsewhere. Polished stone axes are also reported from Iron Age contexts in Gabon where one was discovered embedded in the shaft of an iron smelting furnace dated to 30 ± 80 BC. Its inclusion in the furnace could have been accidental, however (Clist 1986, 1989; Oslisly and Peyrot 1988; Eggert 1995: 302). Polished stone axes are also reported in association with CLSA Ngovo and EIA Kay Ladio ceramics dated to the last centuries BC and first centuries AD in the Democratic Republic of Congo and Angola (de Maret 1986; Clist and Lanfranchi 1992: 248; Eggert 1995: 302).

117

Several fragments of hardened tree resin or copal were recovered from Unit 30S, 0. Because copal was found in the natural soil at many locations during the survey, it is not certain whether it was intentionally collected by the prehistoric inhabitants of Kayes. Copal was used during the historic period, however, and in the eighteenth century, Proyart (1814: 576) remarked that

> [i]n the evening they light torches, which are made of an odoriferous gum, which distils plentifully from one of the forest trees, and which petrifies in rollers. Instead of putting their wick in the torch, they put the torch into the wick, by investing the rollers with flax and bits of dry wood. These torches throw up a light smoke, which spreads an agreeable odour to a great distance.[3]

Ceramics

Only 265 potsherds were recovered from the excavations at Kayes, which had to be cut short when I came down with appendicitis. No complete or nearly complete vessels were recovered. This made the determination of vessel shape difficult for the collection as a whole. To supplement the excavated material, an additional 257 sherds collected from the side of the erosion gully at the western edge of the site were included in the analysis. Of the 161 total decorated potsherds, 68, representing 53 vessels, were sufficiently large for vessel shape to be determined.

Shape

Five vessel shapes were identified: (1) necked jars, (2) globular jars, (3) round-shouldered bowls, (4) carinated bowls, and (5) hemispherical bowls. Table 6.5 summarizes the number of vessels of each shape, along with their diameters and rim types. The diameters of the necked jars showed the greatest variation, but no vessels were larger than 24 centimeters in diameter, indicating that they were all of fairly small capacity. This suggests that cooking and serving was for small groups of people rather than for large, extended families.

Of the vessels with preserved rims, unthickened beveled rims made up 52 percent of the collection. The beveled rims and the predominance of comb-stamped herringbone decoration in the vessel neck represent continuities with the earlier ceramic assemblage from BP 113. The higher frequency of bowls at Kayes (19 percent of the vessels), however, forms a significant contrast.

Temper, Firing, and Surface Finish

The major inclusions in the Kayes pottery were quartzite and scoria, both of which occurred in equal proportions for all vessel shapes (Table 6.6). These are followed by inclusions of fired clay derived from burning termitaria or anthills. One sherd contained grog or fragments of fired pottery as a temper. The grain size of all the inclusions was fine.

Similar to BP 113, the light red color of the potsherds indicates they were fired in an oxidizing environment at a reasonably high temperature that was experimentally determined to be between 700°C and 800°C. Such temperatures are consistent with those obtained with prolonged firing in an open bonfire (Barbour and Wandiba 1989; Hargus 1997).

Decoration

Traces of burnishing were found on the interior and exterior surfaces of all the decorated sherds; however, most, especially those collected from the surface, were severely corroded due to weathering. Such extreme weathering was not noted at the sites of Madingo-Kayes, Meningue, or Tandou-Youmbi, and it is possible that, being close to the sea, the corrosive effects of the salt air played a part in weathering the ceramics that had been exposed on the surface for a long time.

Very few potsherds were decorated below the rim/shoulder junction. Both incised and impressed decorations were found on the Kayes pottery, with comb-stamping and rouletted motifs the most common; only two vessels were decorated by incision alone. Tabulation of decoration technique by vessel shape found some potentially significant differences between jar forms, but sample sizes are small (Table 6.7). Necked jars, for instance, were more often decorated using

Table 6.5. Vessel size and rim form by shape

	Total no.	Rim diameter range (n)	Mean rim diameter (cm)	Flat rim	Beveled rim	Round rim
Necked jar	24 (45%)	14–24 (4)	19	3	12	
Globular jar	19 (36%)	18–21 (4)	20	9	9	1
Round-shouldered bowl	6 (11%)	12–22 (3)	17	5	1	2
Carinated bowl	3 (6%)	14 (1)	14		1	
Hemispherical bowl	1 (2%)					1
Total	53			17 (39%)	23 (52%)	4 (9%)

Table 6.6. Temper types

	Scoria	Quartzite	Anthill	Grog	Grain size	Coarse	Fine
Necked jar	24	24	9		3		21
Globular jar	15	19	5	1	2		17
Round-shouldered bowl	6	6	4				6
Carinated bowl	3	3	3				6
Hemispherical bowl	1	1	1				1

Table 6.7. Decoration technique

Vessel shape	Comb-stamping (CS)	Roulette (R)	Incision (I)	CS + I	R + I
Necked jar	8	14	–	–	2
Globular jar	12	5	–	–	2
Round-shouldered jar	–	5	1	–	–
Carinated bowl	2	–	1	–	–
Hemispherical bowl	–	–	–	1	–
Total	22 (42%)	24 (45%)	2 (4%)	1 (2%)	4 (7%)

knotted string roulettes rolled across their surface to produce herringbone motifs. Globular jars with less-well-defined shoulders were more often decorated with comb-stamped herringbone.

Vessel Classes

The most common decoration motif, whether comb-stamped or rouletted, was a herringbone band applied in single or multiple rows from the neck down to the shoulder. The vessel classes identified, based on combinations of vessel shape and design motif, are summarized in Figure 6.10 and Table 6.8. Figure 6.10 presents a quantitative summary of the vessel classes by shape, layout, and motif. Most of the collection consisted of necked or globular jars; unlike BP 113, several bowl shapes were also identified.

> Class 1: Jars and bowls in this class are decorated with single or multiple bands of herringbone running from the rim down to the shoulder (Figures 6.11a, c, d and 6.12a, b, c). One variant of this class is the round-shouldered bowl decorated with comb-stamping and incision shown in Figure 6.12d. This class made up more than 80 percent of the collection. Overall, multiple comb-stamped herringbone panels appeared on twenty vessels: eight

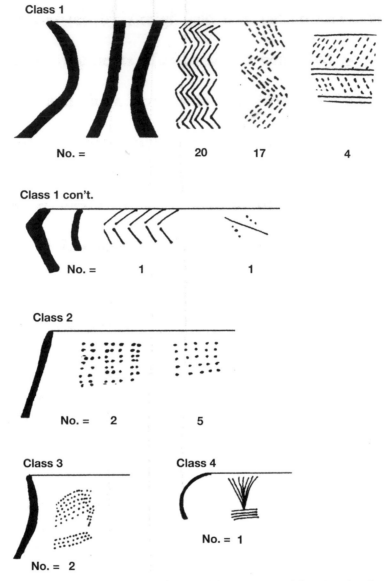

Figure 6.10. Numerical summary of the vessel shapes and decoration motifs found on the Phase 1 Early Iron Age ceramics at Kayes.

necked jars (Figure 6.11c, d), ten globular jars, and two carinated bowls (Figure 6.12a, b). In one case, oblique comb-stamping also occurred along the top of the lip (Figure 6.11a).

Class 2: This class is made up of necked jars with horizontal bands of comb-stamping or roulette in the neck (Figure 6.11f, g). In several cases, jars in this category also had beveled rims similar to those from the Phase 1 occupation at BP 113.

Class 3: Two necked jars decorated with a curvilinear roulette in the neck belong to this class (Figure 6.11b). In the illustrated example, a tool with seven studs was rolled across the body to create a looping curvilinear trace that could only have been made by rolling a roulette across the surface.

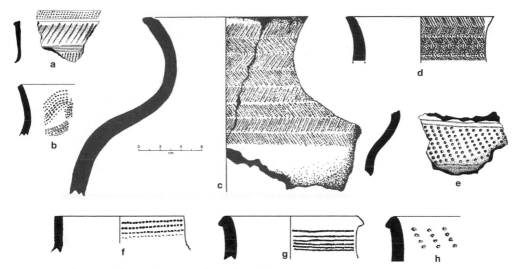

Figure 6.11. Phase 1 Early Iron Age necked jars from Kayes.

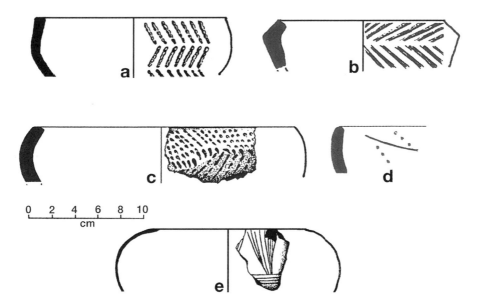

Figure 6.12. Phase 1 Early Iron Age bowls from Kayes.

Class 4: The only Class 4 vessel in the collection was a hemispherical bowl decorated with incised pendant triangles that rested on a horizontal incised band around the shoulder (Figure 6.12e).

The small ceramic assemblage from Kayes exhibits a high degree of standardization. Of the vessels with preserved rims, 52 percent had beveled lips, whereas 81 percent were decorated with single or multiple bands of herringbone, most created by impressed comb-stamping or roulette. Beveled rims and herringbone motifs are also characteristic of the Phase 1 EIA Herringbone occupation at BP 113, which is slightly older. The main difference between the two sites is the higher

Table 6.8. Vessel classes by shape

	Class 1	Class 2	Class 3	Class 4
Necked jar	22		2	
Globular jar	12	7		
Round shouldered bowl	5			
Carinated bowl	3			
Hemispherical bowl	1			1
Total	43 (81%)	7 (13%)	2 (4%)	1 (2%)

frequency of multiple herringbone bands and the greater incidence of jars with non-thickened, flat rims at Kayes. There was also a higher frequency of bowls in the Kayes collection.

Kayes Summary

The earliest occupation of the site is an LSA horizon that predates the main EIA occupation by 400 to 500 years. The EIA occupation produced calibrated radiocarbon dates clustering between AD 300 and 600. Although the Iron Age occupation at Kayes is later than that at BP 113, there is continuity in the frequency of jars with beveled lips decorated with comb-stamped or rouletted herringbone designs. These designs were also common at Tandou-Youmbi, which is the earliest dated expression of Phase 1 on the coast. The discovery of polished stone axes or hoes at both sites indicates these tools were part of the EIA toolkit. Quartzite flakes also consistently occur in the Iron Age levels at Kayes and BP 113, indicating that simple stone tools continued to be used well into the Iron Age. Both sites also contained iron tools and ornaments along with fragments of smithing tuyères that suggest that iron was worked on-site by local blacksmiths. No pits with organic-rich refuse were encountered at Kayes, though an organic-rich midden was exposed in Unit 9–10N, 0–1E.

Early Iron Age Phase 3: Madingo-Kayes and Lac Ndembo

Madingo-Kayes

The excavations at Madingo-Kayes carried out in 1987 and 1988 (Denbow 1990: 154) inadvertently combined materials from two separate cultural components: (1) Herringbone wares such as those found at BP 113 and Kayes (e.g., Figure 6.13, classes 1, 6a, 9a) and (2) new materials, now termed Spaced Curvilinear (SC) ware, that are stylistically different (e.g., Figure 6.13, classes 5; 6b, c; 7b, c; 8, 9b–f; 10). SC ware was recovered from excavations at Madingo-Kayes, Lac Ndembo, and surface collections at twenty-two other sites (Table 6.9). Distinguishing characteristics of SC ware include everted-neck vessels decorated with spaced horizontal bands of oblique incision and comb-stamping. In many cases, the borders of the comb-stamped bands are incised with wavy lines (Figure 4.6b, c); in some cases, the spaces between the bands are also either empty or filled with curvilinear or interwoven motifs in a variety of guilloche, triangular, and undulating forms. Two new accelerator mass spectrometer (AMS) radiocarbon dates from the site of Lac Ndembo correct the original second- to sixth-century dates from Madingo-Kayes that were thought to pertain to SC ware (Table 4.1, dates 25 and 26) and re-date this phase of the EIA to between the seventh and tenth centuries AD – rather than to the second or third century AD as had been proposed by Denbow in 1990 (Table 4.1, dates 39, 38).

The new dating for SC wares helps to explain an anomaly in dating between the SC wares in the Republic of Congo and similar materials dated between the seventh and ninth centuries AD at

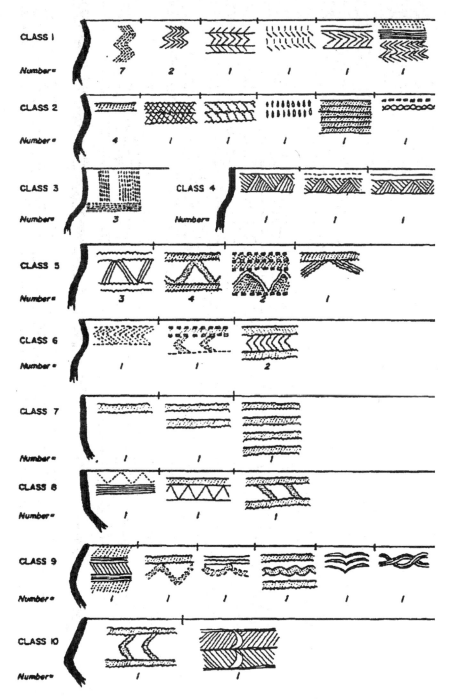

Figure 6.13. Numerical summary of vessel classes, shapes, and motifs identified at Madingo-Kayes.

Divuyu in Northwestern Botswana (Denbow 1990: 159; 2011). As is discussed in Chapter 8, both sites have vessels decorated with alternating bands of comb-stamping and incision, often separated by blank or empty bands. They also have jars and bowls decorated with horizontal comb-stamped bands bounded by wavy line incision, as well as with curvilinear motifs that relate these ceramics to the Naviundu Complex that dates as early as the fifth century AD in the southern Democratic Republic of Congo (Anciaux de Faveaux and de Maret 1984; Huffman 1989, 2007). The revised dating for SC

Table 6.9. Tabulation of the cultural components identified during the archaeological reconnaissance

	No. of cultural components
Pre–Ceramic Later Stone Age c. 1400–600 BC	10
Ceramic Later Stone Age, Phase 1 ca. 1000–500 BC	3
Ceramic Later Stone Age, Phase 2 ca. 400–200 BC	21
Early Iron Age Herringbone wares ca. 150 BC– AD 500	27
Early Iron Age Carinated Broadly Grooved wares ca. AD 300–600	30
Early Iron Age Spaced Curvilinear wares ca. AD 650–800	24
Indeterminate Early Iron Age	52
Later Iron Age ca. AD 1100–1500	23
Later Iron Age ca. AD 1500–1900	98
Indeterminate Later Iron Age	9
Total components	297

ware in Loango fits well with the proposition that these materials represent geographical facies of a widespread Naviundu Complex that had spread west to Loango and south as far as the lands border-ing the Zambezi River in Zambia and west to the Tsodilo Hills in northwestern Botswana at the end of the first millennium AD. These relationships are discussed further in Chapter 8.

Lac Ndembo

The site of Lac Ndembo (UTM coordinates: 0794807; 9518166) is situated approximately 12 kilometers east of the coast near the headwaters of the Louandjili stream that flows past Lamba and BP 113. The site lies on the eastern shore of Lake Ndembo in a shallow valley overlooked by rolling hills once covered with grassland but now planted in eucalyptus (Figure 4.2 and Figure 6.14). No artifacts were observed on the surface, but shovel tests placed across the area revealed ceramics at a depth of 40 centimeters below the surface. Decorated sherds (Figure 6.15) indicated the site belonged to the SC ware group first identified at Madingo-Kayes (Denbow 1990).

A central datum point (0, 0) was created by encasing a metal rod within a small cement marker 15 centimeters high. A second marker (see Figure 9.1) was placed 20 meters north of the first, creating a north-south datum line. Figure 6.16 provides the locations of the excavation units in areas A and B, which were labeled in meters north, south, east, and west of the datum point. A line of units extending east of the north-south line encountered a concentration of SC ceramics in the region marked "Area A" on the plan map. Twenty-five contiguous squares placed in this area revealed an occupation horizon with potsherds, small flecks of charcoal, and small fragments of burned anthill at 40 centimeters below the surface (Figures 6.17 and 6.18). Two 2-sigma calibrated AMS dates place the SC horizon in Area A between AD 659 and 943.

The consistent association of small particles of burned anthill with the occupation horizon was at first puzzling, especially because a similar association was also noted at Meningue. Investigation of cooking practices at neighboring households, however, revealed that because large stones to support cooking pots are absent on the Loango coast, people use three small, mushroom-shaped anthills – an object ubiquitous on the savanna – to support their cooking pots. In the fire, the ant-hills become oxidized and brittle, crumbling into small, red-fired pieces that accumulate around cooking areas and, eventually, become incorporated in the soil to become a distinctive horizon marker. The three-stone cooking technique has great symbolic meaning across Bantu-speaking Africa (Willoughby 1928: 285). In Loango, Dennett (1968:73; 75) found them carved on walking sticks and clothing where they symbolized stability or well-being. As a Vili proverb puts it, "a pot on three stones [makuku matatu or three lumps of ant hill] does not upset."

Figure 6.14. View over the excavations at Lac Ndembo showing the locations of Area A, which contained Phase 3 Early Iron Age wares, and Area B, where Phase 2 ceramics were uncovered. The lake can be seen behind the site with new eucalyptus plantations in the far distance. A brush fire had burned off the grass while the excavation was underway.

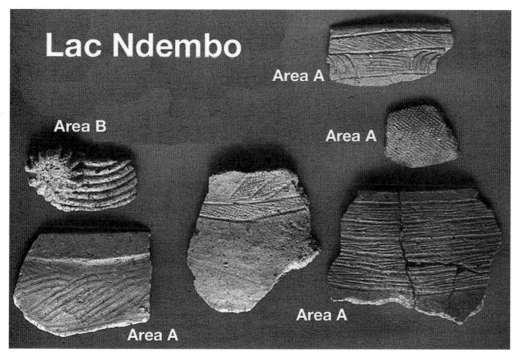

Figure 6.15. Examples of Spaced Curvilinear (SC) wares from Lac Ndembo. One lugged Carinated Broadly Grooved (CBG) sherd from Area B at the site is in the top left.

A second set of three contiguous 1-by-1-m units was excavated in the area marked "B" on the site map to investigate a horizon containing CBG ceramics. A 2-sigma calibrated AMS date situates these wares at Lac Ndembo between AD 418 and 597, which is nearly identical to the date obtained for CBG wares at BP 113. The occupation horizons in areas A and B were both very thin, with no artifacts occurring above or below a narrow 5-cm occupation horizon between 40 and 50 centimeters below the surface. No middens, pits, or other features were encountered.

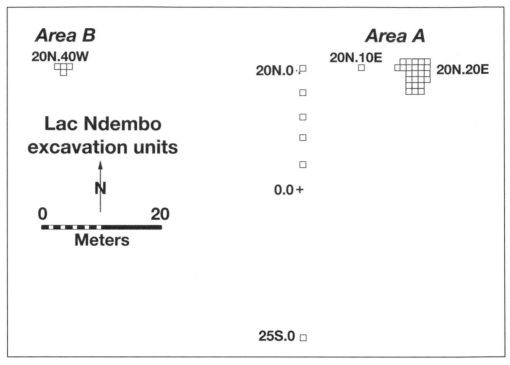

Figure 6.16. Layout of excavated units in areas A and B at Lac Ndembo.

Figure 6.17. View of the excavation at Area A, Lac Ndembo. Eucalyptus plantations can be seen on the hillside in the background.

Iron and Lithics

Table A.4 summarizes the spatial and stratigraphic distribution of the artifacts from Lac Ndembo. Two small fragments of iron slag were recovered from Area A while two iron fragments, one a small ring suitable for a finger or toe, came from Area B. Only two quartzite flakes and four

Figure 6.18. Gislain measuring the depth below surface of the narrow Phase 3 Early Iron Age horizon at 40 to 50 centimeters below the surface in Area A at Lac Ndembo.

rounded quartzite cobbles were recovered, along with thirteen fragments of burned limestone and seven small pebbles. Burned limestone was also recovered at BP 113, but the use to which this material was put is unknown.

Ceramics

At Lac Ndembo, 1,482 potsherds were recovered; most were undiagnostic body sherds that were eliminated from the analysis along with the decorated fragments that were too small for vessel shape to be determined. The remaining 168 sherds, representing 76 vessels, were used in the analysis. The Lac Ndembo vessels show considerable variation in decoration motif. Although this could be suggestive of a long occupation, the narrow stratigraphic horizon in Area A and the radiocarbon dates both belie this interpretation and indicate the site was occupied for a relatively short time. The reasons for the high ceramic variability are unclear.

Shape

Table 6.10 presents a summary of the vessel shapes and their average size and lip forms. Six vessel shapes were recorded from both areas of the site: (1) EIA Phase 3 necked jars ($n = 27$), (2) EIA Phase 3 globular jars ($n = 19$), (3) EIA Phase 2 sharply carinated jars ($n = 7$), (4) Phase 2 and Phase 3 round-shouldered bowls ($n = 20$), (5) Phase 3 slighted carinated bowls ($n = 8$), and (6) Phase 2 barrel-shaped bowls. Figures 6.19 and 6.20 illustrate the jar and bowl shapes as well as the decoration motifs identified for the Phase 3 EIA materials from Area A; Figure 6.21 illustrates the Phase 2 EIA vessel forms and motifs for Area B.

The fifty-nine vessels with preserved lips showed considerable standardization, with more than 80 percent of the vessels from both phases having flat lips, though the Phase 3 carinated bowls showed greater variability in lip form. Average rim diameter, an estimate of vessel size, also shows little variation though the shallow Phase 2 serving bowls were slightly smaller than the jars. The small size of the cooking and serving vessels from both phases suggests that food was prepared and

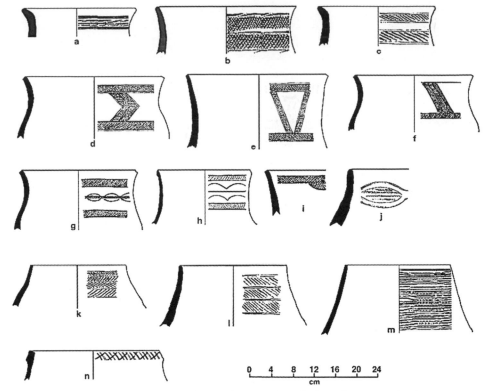

Figure 6.19. Phase 3 Early Iron Age Spaced Curvilinear (SC) necked jars from Lac Ndembo.

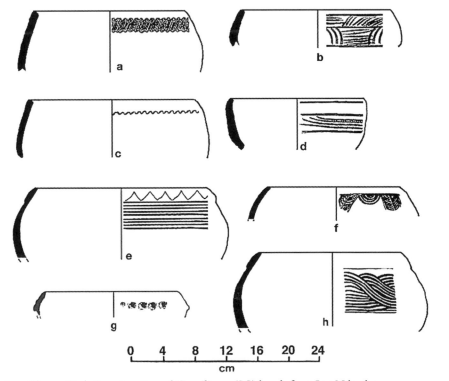

Figure 6.20. Phase 3 Early Iron Age Spaced Curvilinear (SC) bowls from Lac Ndembo.

Table 6.10. Vessel size and rim type by shape at Lac Ndembo

	No. of vessels	No. measured for diameter	Rim diameter range (cm)	Average rim diameter (cm)	Round lip	Flat lip	Flat, thickened lip
Necked jar	23	7	16–25	21		12	
Globular jar	19	9	16–24	20		16	2
Carinated jar	7	2	18	18		3	
Round-shouldered bowl	20	6	16–22	19	1	9	4
Slightly carinated bowl	8	2	16–20	18	4	7	
Barrel-shaped bowl	1						
Total	78	26			5 (9%)	47 (81%)	6 (10%)

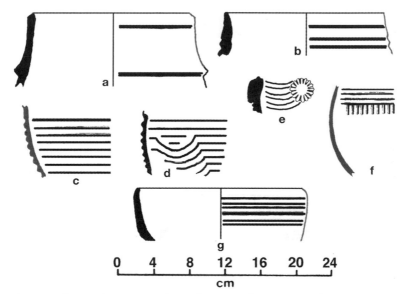

Figure 6.21. Phase 2 Early Iron Age Carinated Broadly Grooved (CBG) ware from Area B, Lac Ndembo.

served to small groups of people. The large number of bowls from Area A contrasts strongly with the EIA Phase 1 remains from BP 113, and Kayes, where relatively few bowls were recovered.

Temper, Firing, and Surface Finish

The most common inclusions in the clay of the Area A vessels were crushed quartzite, mica, and burned anthill (Table 6.11). A few ceramics also contained charcoal and talc. There is a correlation between vessels with elaborate decoration and those with mica in the paste. As was suggested for BP 113, mica may have been added to improve the aesthetic quality of serving bowls. Alternatively, it could point to different clay sources for the more elaborate ceramics. As was the case at BP 113, talc was found only in the CBG wares of the Phase 2 occupation.

The majority of sherds were fired red throughout, indicating high firing temperatures. Most also have firing clouds on the surface suggesting they were fired in an open bonfire. Experimental analyses found the firing temperatures ranged between 700°C and 800°C (Hargus 1997), which are identical to those determined for BP 113 and Kayes, and higher than those for the earlier CLSA ceramics.

Table 6.11. Temper by vessel shape at Lac Ndembo

	Scoria	Quartzite	Anthill	Talc	Mica	Grain size	
						Coarse	Fine
Necked jar	18	21	7		19	6	17
Globular jar	15	19	10		8	7	11
Carinated jar	7	7		7	5		7
Round-shouldered bowl	16	20	11		8	4	16
Slightly carinated bowl	5	8	4		4	3	5
Barrel-shaped bowl	1	1	1	1	1		1
Total	62 (28%)	76 (34%)	33 (15%)	8 (4%)	45 (20%)	20	57

Table 6.12. Decoration technique by shape at Lac Ndembo

	Incising	Grooving	Comb-stamping & incision	Wiping
Necked jar			23	
Globular jar	2		17	
Carinated jar		7		
Round-shouldered bowl	4		9	5
Slightly carinated bowl	3		6	1
Barrel-shaped bowl		1		
Total	9 (12%)	8 (10%)	55 (70%)	6 (8%)

Evidence for burnishing was found on all vessels. The decoration techniques at Lac Ndembo included incision, grooving, comb-stamping, and wiping or brushing (Table 6.12). Comb-stamping, which was used on 70 percent of the Lac Ndembo ceramics, was always found in combination with incision. Incision alone was used on only 12 percent of the vessels. Wiping with straw, grass, or a similar flexible tool was used to decorate several globular and necked jars. As at BP 113, wide grooving was confined to the Phase 2 CBG wares.

Vessel Classes

Seven ceramic classes were identified by combinations of decoration technique, motif, and shape. These are enumerated in Figure 6.22.

Class 1: These vessels include necked jars and round or slightly carinated bowls decorated with incised bands of hatching or herringbone. On bowls, the bands are sometimes "interrupted" to divide the decoration into quarters or halves around the vessel perimeter (Figure 6.20b).

Class 2: Vessels in this class are composed of necked or globular jars decorated with cross-hatched bands on the rim or neck (Figure 6.19b, n).

Class 3: This class includes globular jars and round shouldered or slightly carinated bowls with single or multiple bands of horizontal lines in the neck, sometimes with triangles extending above the band margin (Figure 6.19e). On some bowls, the boundary lines at the top and bottom of the band are made purposely wavy (Figures 6.19a, c).

Class 4: Jars, and occasional round-shouldered bowls, have open spaces between bands as a decoration motif. The spaces may either be left undecorated or contain a variety of spaced geometric or curvilinear designs that include chevrons, triangles, and ovals (Figures 6.19d–j). Some vessels from Madingo-Kayes also exhibited such motifs (Figure 6.23).

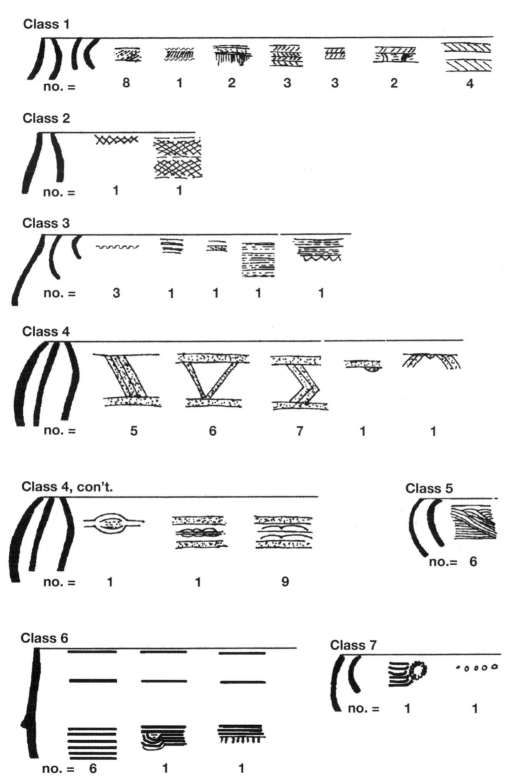

Figure 6.22. Numerical summary of the Phase 3 Early Iron Age (EIA) ceramic classes and motifs from Area A at Lac Ndembo. Classes 6 and 7 belong to Phase 2 of the EIA and were only found in Area B.

Figure 6.23. A Phase 3 Spaced Curvilinear jar from Madingo-Kayes illustrating a chevron motif in the space created between upper and lower comb-stamped bands.

Class 5: Round-shouldered bowls in this category are decorated with a distinctive ropelike pattern (Figure 6.20h).

Class 6: In this class are EIA Phase 2 carinated jars decorated with broad grooving in the neck, usually with another band of broad horizontal or curvilinear grooving below the carination (Figures 6.21a–d) These vessels are identical to the Phase 2 CBG wares from BP 113.

Class 7: CBG bowls that sometimes have lugs near the rim are included in this class.

Lac Ndembo Summary

The excavations at Lac Ndembo exposed two spatially separated areas of occupation, A and B, that contained stylistically different ceramic assemblages belonging to phases 2 and 3 of the EIA. Area A contained a narrow horizon between 40 and 45 centimeters below the surface. The ceramics recovered belong to the SC ware grouping also found at Madingo-Kayes (Denbow 1990). The most common vessels were necked jars decorated with geometric chevrons and other patterns that filled the open space between upper and lower hatched bands (Figure 6.22, Class 4); twisted rope-patterned bowls (Class 6) were also common.

Area B, approximately 50 meters west of Area A produced decorated ceramics identical to the Phase 2 ceramics from BP 113. In addition to their carinated shapes, broad line grooving, and applied lugs, they also used talc as temper. Calibrated dates for this material from both BP 113 and Lac Ndembo fall between the third and sixth centuries AD.

The elaborately decorated SC wares have no earlier precedents on the Loango coast. The intertwined motifs and other elements point to an origin in the Naviundu Complex to the southeast in the Democratic Republic of Congo. As is discussed in Chapter 8, similar decoration layouts, motifs, and decoration techniques link these wares to those found far to the south along the Okavango River in northwestern Botswana, the Caprivi Strip of Namibia, and southwestern Zambia (Huffman 1989, 2007; Seidel, Kose, and Mohlig 2007; Denbow 2011).

An Unexpected Digression from Research

The excavations at Kayes had to be cut short due to an unforeseen circumstance: I came down with appendicitis. When it happened, I remembered a conversation I had had many years earlier when sitting in a bar next to a wizened old colonial who, after a few whiskeys, pontificated that "[a]nyone wanting to do field work in Africa should have their appendix out as a matter of course before leaving home for the continent." I thought this was bizarre advice at the time: the idea that one would have an operation to ward off something that might not even happen. I never imagined it could happen to me.

We had been working for a couple of weeks at Kayes when one afternoon I came back to our camp at Tchissanga early, telling my wife Josie that I just "didn't feel right." The symptoms of generalized pain in my intestines and nausea that I described to her were not the classical ones of appendicitis – a pain in the lower right side. Going out to the beach where reception for the portable radio was better, my worried wife marched up and down next to the crashing waves for more than half an hour before she could catch a signal and contact our friend Dr. François Camus in Pointe Noire. When she described the symptoms to François, he was concerned enough that he told her he was setting out after dark for our camp – a difficult journey even in daylight over very bad roads.

After examining me by lantern light, he pulled Josie aside and said, "I think it's appendicitis. He has a fever, and I don't think he should travel back to town by road. There are too many potholes that could cause the appendix to rupture. I'm going to call Conoco for an emergency helicopter."

About an hour later the helicopter, its bright lights shining down through the sea fog, landed in a swirl of sand on a cleared stretch of beach next to our camp. Its appearance terrified the neighboring villagers on the hilltop overlooking our camp. Klaus and a couple of other Conoco workers put me on a stretcher and loaded me sidewise into the chopper for the ride back. It was my first and only ride in a helicopter, and I remember thinking as it clawed its way upward with the wind and sand rushing in through the open doors that I wished I could see out and watch the coastline as we traveled along. My wife traveled back by road with François.

Arriving in Pointe Noire, I was rushed through the town to its only hospital. Built in the 1930s and named after Adolphe Sicé, director of the Pasteur Institute in Brazzaville from 1927 to 1932, the hospital looked its age with its crumbling cement covered with a coat of blistering and faded yellow paint. Conoco (and perhaps other expatriate companies as well) had a permanent reservation for one "private" room on the second floor in case any of its personnel needed emergency care. Even so, the room had no blankets, sheets, or pillows – those had to be provided by the patient. The cracked and dingy tile floor was permanently gritty from decades of sand, and the toilet, although it flushed, had no seat – just the cold porcelain as I bent over it to vomit. Past my room, at the end of a dimly lit corridor, the building had collapsed into the waiting arms of the jungle. When the cleaners walked down the hall with their brooms, they simply swept the dust out the end of the building and onto a spoil heap of dirt, broken metal hospital beds, and other trash through which the jungle trees were now pushing their tangled roots.

After a blood test a French army surgeon who had been temporarily seconded to the hospital came in with the bad news. "We can confirm that your white blood count is high, and you have all the symptoms of appendicitis. You need to make a decision whether to have it out here or wait for a medevac plane to take you to Europe."

"So it needs to come out?" my wife asked with some trepidation.

"Yes," he replied. "It is a simple operation now, but if it bursts there could be serious complications. There is no medevac plane here in the Congo; it must come from Switzerland. That means it would be twenty-four hours before you could be on your way. And then it is another eight hours in the air back to Europe. Maybe things will be OK for that long, but if the appendix bursts … well, that would be bad."

"It looks as though I really have no choice," I said. "I'll have to have it out here."

"OK. But the next complication is that since you are not a citizen of the Congo you have no right to medical care. And as you are not directly working for one of the foreign companies here, you will have to buy all your own medicines and operating supplies from the pharmacy. They should have everything in stock."

He then wrote out a list of everything that would be needed: sterile cotton and bandages, disposable syringes, rubbing alcohol, ether, and so on. He gave it to my wife, who, along with Dr. Camus, took it down the street and handed it in at the Croix du Sud pharmacy. When she returned to the pharmacy a few hours later, they handed her the supplies in an old wooden beer crate. She brought them back to the hospital, gave them to the doctor, and then went to the market to purchase some sheets, a blanket, and a pillow. Luckily there were two iron-frame beds in the room, so she could arrange to stay there with me. The total cost for the operation, including later payment to the surgeon, came to approximately US$700.

The operation was to take place the following afternoon and the doctor, after seeing me the next morning, said, "You will have to walk down the stairs to the operating room. You are a big man, and we don't have anyone here who could carry you down the steps. We will give you the anesthetic after you are on the operating table."

As I walked through the door into the outer room of the operating theater that afternoon, I was surprised to see there was no furniture of any sort. The room was painted a dingy green, and the surgeon and anesthesiologist were crouched in the far corner washing their arms and hands with soapy water in a galvanized tub on the floor. The anesthesiologist, another French soldier, led me into the operating room and had me lie down on a scarred wooden bench that looked like it was as old as the building. It had a wood plank out to one side for my arm. After I lay down, he strapped my arm to the plank, and I looked up to see that the green paint was already blistering away from the wall due to the corrosive effects of the sea air. Placing a rubber mask over my face, the last thing I remember was his saying, "Count backwards from one hundred."

I woke up later back in my second-floor room. I have no idea how I got back there, but I was happy to see my wife waiting for me. The surgeon stopped by with a male nurse and assured her that everything had gone well. I had a drip of some sort in my arm, and the doctor said I should have an injection of an antibiotic, or painkiller, or something, every four hours through the night. The male Congolese nurse then rubbed my arm down with one of the cotton balls and alcohol that we had purchased and administered the first injection with one of the disposable needles. I was lucky to have those rather than the dull, reusable ones the hospital provided. When he finished, he carefully placed the used cotton ball in a metal tray on a corner of the bedside table and left. The next injection was scheduled for 11 PM.

After the nurse left, Josie immediately pitched the used cotton ball into the dustbin. We had lived long enough in rural Africa to know that he likely intended to economize on supplies by using it again.

When 11:30 PM came around, no one arrived for the next injection. Josie searched through the hospital and found him. She then learned that no one on the night shift had a watch so reminding them of the timing of my medication would be another duty for her – along with bringing my meals from a nearby hotel. When the nurse got to the room, we could see him searching the bedside table with a puzzled look on his face. My wife, ever the diplomat, said, "Are you looking for that piece of cotton? I'm really sorry; I thought you were finished with it so I threw it away. Just use another new one from the box. It's OK."

In those days, most African hospitals did not serve meals. Instead, relatives of the patient had to stay with them near the hospital in order to buy and prepare all the food for the patient. The bare-earth grounds surrounding the hospital were like a large visiting room with people chatting with one another as they cooked the meals for their ailing relatives over small wood fires lit under the overarching branches of large flamboyant trees. To meet people's needs, homemade kiosks selling small quantities of bread, butter, tinned meat, and cigarettes had sprung up in entrepreneurial fashion around the outside of the cement wall that enclosed the hospital grounds.

After the second day, the surgeon announced that I must now get up and start to walk around. "You will heal faster that way," he said. So that afternoon I took a short walk. By the next afternoon I could go as far as the outside wall where I passed along the line of kiosks, chatting with their vendors. As I did, I saw a curious sight: on the corner of almost every counter was a small pile of gray clay kaolin sticks about the size and thickness of a pencil; each cost 25 CFA.

"What are those for?" I asked.

"They are for pregnant women who come to the hospital to give birth. They eat them to make their babies stronger."

Later I would learn that this same white clay was also used in the past by iron smelters who painted it around the bellies of their smelting furnaces, which were shaped like women. Similar to the mothers in the hospital, they used it to ensure the iron "babies" growing in the furnace's womb would reach maturity and the furnace would give birth to its iron (Herbert 1993; Denbow 1999).

After three days in the hospital, we decided it might now be better to move into a hotel. It would be cleaner and meals would be easier. In a week I was well enough to catch a flight to London and then, after a few days rest, on home.

The following year old Bernard's son, also named Bernard, came to work one day feeling ill. He described for me the now familiar symptoms of appendicitis, and I took him to the same government hospital in Pointe Noire. I assured him that I would pay for whatever the government insurance did not. But one week passed and young Bernard was still in the hospital – and then another week went by. I then remembered that the French army surgeon who had operated on me had said that it was his last week and that he would not be replaced. Perhaps that was the reason for the longer recovery. When I asked Bernard why his son was taking so much longer to recover than I had, he pulled me aside and whispered the cause from his perspective on the world:

> "There are just too many jealous people here. It's the sorcerers," he said. "They are very strong. When the doctor would operate in one area, the appendix fled up his arm to another place. And when they operated there, they drove it down to a third. Because of the sorcerers, the doctors couldn't get it."

While young Bernard eventually recovered and returned home, that was the last time he worked for me. A few days later, Bernard the elder came to my camp with a white chicken: his way of saying thanks for having helped organize the operation for his teenage son. No doubt the white color was not an accident, but chosen for its cosmological symbolism (Jacobson-Widding 1979).

7

Later Iron Age Sites and the Historic Period

In ... crafts and arts, the Bakongo see a chronological order in which their own ancestors proceeded from one stage to another. Most overtly ... they honor relative chronology in cloth making. They distinguish the distant past – when their ancestors did not know how to weave and dressed in bark – from the past, when they already know how to weave and made pieces of cloth. (Volavka and Thomas 1998:144)

The Later Iron Age

A gap in the Loango archaeological sequence presently exists between approximately AD 900 and 1100. Only one site, Lac Tchitembo – a shell midden with no decorated ceramics – dates to this period (Table 4.1, date 35). The remaining Later Iron Age sites located during the reconnaissance (Table A.1) can be grouped into two broad categories based on vessel shape, decoration, and the presence or absence of European trade goods. The first consists of twenty-four surface sites with no European trade goods. The pottery from these sites includes jars that continue the tall, everted-neck vessel forms of the Early Iron Age (EIA) but are decorated with diamond or lozenge "woven" motifs that resemble those also found on raphia cloth and other materials (Figure 4.7). Toward the end of this period other vessels include hemispherical and "chamber-pot" shapes with undecorated, sharply everted rims and bands of incised or impressed crosshatching on the belly; the decorated band is often bordered on the top and bottom with an applied strip (Figure 7.1). Calibrated 2-sigma radiocarbon dates from Condé and Loubanzi date these materials to between AD 1100 and 1500.

The second category, which accounts for ninety-seven sites, includes sites with hemispherical or "chamber-pot" shaped indigenous pottery along with European earthenware, stoneware, glass bottles, tobacco pipes, and other items. With the exception of a fragment from Loubanzi described in a later section, the only copper found during the reconnaissance was associated with these Phase 2 Later Iron Age sites.

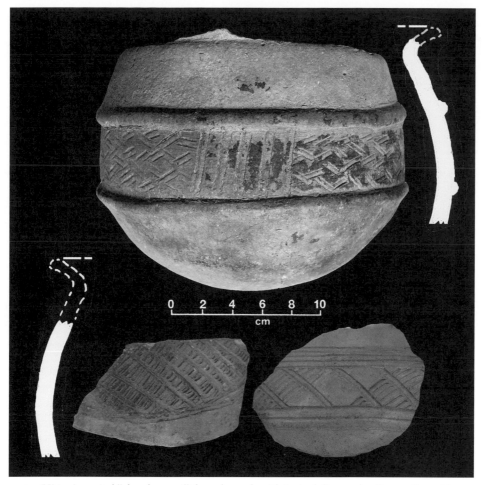

Figure 7.1. Historic period "chamber-pot" shaped vessels with incised diamond or "woven" motifs.

Phase 1 Later Iron Age: AD 1100–1500

Very few sites with definitive early second millennium ceramics were located during the reconnaissance. One explanation might be that, for unknown reasons, the area was depopulated following the Phase 3 Spaced Curvilinear (SC) ware occupation after AD 900. Alternatively, the population distribution could have shifted from one of dispersed, small settlements during the Early Iron Age to a more centralized pattern in which small villages coalesced into larger towns at the beginning of the second millennium, perhaps for defence. Because so few Phase 1 Late Iron Age (LIA) settlements were identified during the reconnaissance, test excavations could only be carried out at two, which were recognized by their distinctive, "woven pattern," ceramics. No European trade goods or ceramic wares were found at these locations.

Condé

The site of Condé is situated in the Konde province of the former Loango Kingdom on a terrace overlooking a stream feeding into Ntombo Marsh (Figure 4.2). No archaeological materials

Figure 7.2. View over the excavations at the site of Condé.

were visible on the surface and the site was discovered by systematic shovel tests that were placed across an unplowed savanna (Figure 7.2). Because little cultural material was recovered, only eight 1-by-1-meter test squares were excavated. All the artifacts were concentrated in the upper 30 centimeters of the deposit (Table 7.1). The 2-sigma calibrated date places the site between AD 1040 and 1281 (Table 4.1, date 39). No metal was found.

Only fourteen decorated potsherds and eleven chert and quartzite flakes were recovered. Although the pot shapes continue the everted-neck forms of the Early Iron Age, the decoration motifs are completely different and include the earliest dated examples of the diamond or woven motif – a design that would later become widespread on raphia cloth, ivory, wood carvings, and other materials of the historic period in Loango, northern Angola, and the Democratic Republic of Congo (Dennett 1968; Hagenbucher-Sacripanti 1973; Bassani & Monzino 1987: pl. 5, 6, 11, 12–15, 18–23; Clist 2012a).

Loubanzi

The Loubanzi site is located approximately 4 kilometers east of Tchissanga on a small rise that overlooks Ntombo Marsh to the north. From here, the marsh extends eastward along a tributary that leads past Condé to Mvindou (Figure 4.2). When the site was discovered, approximately half of it had already been plowed and planted in eucalyptus. Decorated ceramics, quartzite chips, and flat pieces of mica schist that might have served as grinding stones were collected from the plowed area. No goods of European manufacture were found. Because the pottery was different from that recovered at most of the other sites examined during the reconnaissance, the unplowed portion was signposted for conservation to protect it from further plowing, and a small excavation was undertaken (Figure 7.3). A single 2-sigma calibrated date placed the occupation between AD 1415 and 1633, with the highest probability falling toward the earlier end of this range (Table 4.1, date 40). The absence of European trade goods supports this dating. Given its date and location, it is possible that Loubanzi was an early ward or precinct on the outskirts of the larger

Table 7.1. Provenience of artifacts from the excavation at Condé

Unit	Depth (cm)	Later Iron Age rim	body	Undecorated rim	Undecorated sherds	Quartzite	Chert	Mica-schist	Sand-stone	Pebble
1	0–10				1					
1	10–20				18	1				
1	20–30				12	1				1
1	30–40				2					
2	0–10				3					
2	10–20	1		2	35					1
2	20–30				8					3
2, ext.	0–10				10					
2, ext.	10–20	1	3	2	184	2	4			
2, ext.	20–30		2	1	28		1		2	6
3	0–10				4					
3	10–20				2					
3	20–30	2			2					
3	30–40				1			2		
4	10–20				8					
4	20–30				3					
4	30–40				3					
5	0–10				1					
5	10–20	1	1		10					2
5	20–30			1	13					2
5	30–40		2		3					
6	0–10									
6	10–20				30					6
6	20–30	1		1	27					1
6	30–40				8					
7	10–20				6					
7	20–30				4					1
7	30–40				3					1
Total		6	8	7	429	4	5	2	2	24

Figure 7.3. View to the north over Ntombo Marsh from the Later Iron Age site of Loubanzi, which was signposted for preservation. The archaeological crew included students from the University of Texas in Austin and Marien Ngouabi University in Brazzaville. The cement marker erected as the excavation datum is under the sign to the right of the students.

settlement of Bouali (Bwali), the capital of the Loango kingdom described in the sixteenth and seventeenth centuries. No reconnaissance was possible on the hilltop behind Loubanzi because it was heavily overgrown with forest. The more open savanna across the tributary of Ntombo Marsh to the north was unsafe for reconnaissance because it was part of the firing range used by the Cuban military.

A small cement marker was constructed next to the conservation signboard to serve as the datum point for the test excavations (Figure 7.4). A line of six 1-by-1 meter squares was placed adjacent to the plowed area, with two additional units placed 10 meters east of this line at a distance of 10 and 20 meters north of the datum. Table 7.2 summarizes the results of the excavation. All the cultural materials were concentrated between 20 and 50 centimeters below the surface.

Ceramics

From the surface of the plowed area, twenty-one decorated potsherds were recovered, with another fourteen coming from the excavated units. None of the excavated ceramics was large enough to determine rim diameter, but four of the vessels from the surface collection had rims large enough for measurement. The vessels were all small and ranged from 14 to 18 centimeters in diameter. All the vessels were tempered with sandy grit, and all but one of the necked jars were decorated with the "diamond" or woven motif similar to that found at Condé. The decoration looks as though it was made by rolling a carved wooden roulette across the wet surface of the clay prior to firing the pot (Figure 4.7).

The other decorated sherds resembled the "chamber-pot" shapes found at later historic period sites, suggesting that a change in ceramic style was underway (Figure 7.1). These vessels have very sharply everted lips and are decorated around the belly rather than in the neck. The most common motifs consisted of a panel filled with hatching or cross-hatching. The single excavated

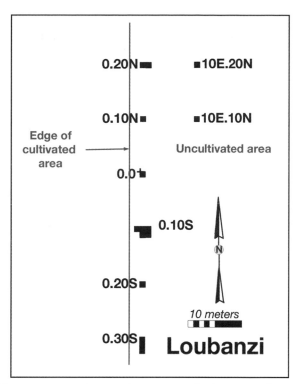

Figure 7.4. Layout of the excavation units at Loubanzi. 0, 0 marks the cement datum marker at the site.

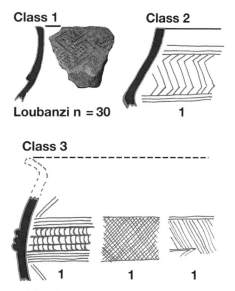

Figure 7.5. Numerical summary of the Phase 1 Later Iron Age ceramics from Condé and Loubanzi.

example of this style has the incised panel filled with stamping produced with the scalloped edge of a cockleshell (Figure 7.5, Class 3a). Shell-impressed vessels of this type were also noted occasionally at some historic sites during the surface reconnaissance (see Figure 4.8).

Clist (2012a) has recently grouped the LIA ceramics from the Democratic Republic of Congo into a new complex he refers to as the Mbafu Tradition, which dates between AD 1400 and

Table 7.2. Provenience of the artifacts recovered at Loubanzi

Unit	Depth (cm)	Decorated & rim sherds	Undecorated sherds	Iron	Slag	Copper	Quartzite	Chert	Ferricrete	Mica schist	Hematite	Sand stone	Human premolar	Oyster shell
0, 0	0–10													
0, 0	10–20		1											
0, 0	20–30													
0, 0	30–40													
0, 10N	0–20	1	8	1			1							
0, 10N	20–30		35											
0, 10N	30–40	2	25				1							
0, 10N	40–50		32				1		6		2	3		
0, 10N	50–60		23				2		3	0	2	0		
0, 10N	60–70		5	1							1	0		
0, 10N	70–80		8								1			
0, 20N	0–20	1	35	1			2							
0, 20N	20–30	1	26						1	0	1			
0, 20N	30–40		13						1	1	1			
0, 20N	40–50		2											
0, 20N	50–60													
0, 10S	0–10		6								1			
0, 10S	10–20		22						4					
0, 10S	20–30	1	31				1			3				
0, 10S	30–40		3											
0, 10S	40–50		2						1					
0, 11S	0–10		24						2		1			
0, 11S	10–20		32				4		7		5			
0, 11S	20–30		18						8		3			
0, 11S	30–40		9			1	1		1					
0, 20S	0–10		8											
0, 20S	10–20		9											
0, 20S	20–30		6											
0, 20S	30–40	1	27		1									
0, 20S	40–50	2	47				1		1		1			
0, 20S	50–60		4				0				1	0		
0, 20s	60–70		1											

142

Region / Depth													
0, 30S 0–10		8											
0, 30S 10–20		8							1				
0, 30S 20–30		19											
0, 30S 30–40	1	40		1		2				1	2		2
0, 30S 40–50										1			
0, 30S 50–60													
0, 31S 0–10		8											
0, 31S 10–20		36	1		1				1				
0, 31S 20–30		32							1				
0, 31S 30–40		23				2							
0, 31S 40–50		20							1				
0, 32S 0–10		6											
0, 32S 10–20		12											
0, 32S 20–30	1	23				1							
0, 32S 30–40	1	37		1		3			1		1		
0, 32S 40–50		22				1			2				
1W, 10S 0–20		60											
1W, 10S 20–30		25											
1W, 10S 30–40						4							
1E, 11S 0–10		23						3	2				
1E, 11S 10–20		23						3		3	1		1
1E, 11S 20–30		25											
1E, 11S 30–40		4				1							
0–1E, 10–11S 40–50		41		2		2		25	1		2		2
1E, 20N 0–20		37						2	1	4			
1E, 20N 20–30	1	18				2		4		5			
1E, 20N 30–40		28				1		1					
1E, 20N 40–50													
1E, 20N 50–60													
10E, 10N 0–20		7				1		1					
10E, 10N 20–30		39				1		2					
10E, 10N 30–40	1	20						6	1	2		1	1
10E, 20N 0–10		8				1		2					
10E, 20N 10–20		34						7	3		1		
10E, 20N 20–30		16						5	2	2			
10E, 20N 30–40		9				2	1	1	1	1			
Total	14	1173	1	7	1	38	1	97	23	38	10	1	2

143

1800. Although the earlier ceramics from Condé and Loubanzi share some of the same design elements or "cultural aesthetic" found on these wares, the pot shapes and placement are different – perhaps because the excavated Loango examples are older. As mentioned earlier, the necked pot shape of these Phase 1 LIA wares has a greater resemblance to the EIA wares of the first millennium AD than to the sharply everted rim "chamber-pot" shape of the European contact period.

The post-AD 1500 ceramics from Loango do share many of the Mbafu Tradition design motifs and shapes, especially the diamond or lozenge motifs of Clist's Mode 1 and the bordered bands of alternating triangles of his modes 2 and 5 (Clist 2012a: 190–195). But there are sufficient differences in detail to suggest that the Loango materials represent a separate regional facies of this tradition. For instance, the borders that outline the decorative panels on Loango ceramics are usually fashioned from applied strips of clay (Figure 7.1 top), rather than being incised or stamped as they commonly are on Mbafu wares. Given the association of the Mbafu wares with Kongo-speaking peoples, the appearance of these ceramics on the Loango coast indicates they moved there at the beginning of the second millennium AD, perhaps following a period of depopulation or population restructuring at the end of the first millennium AD.

Lithics, Fauna, and Metal

Lithics
Table 7.2 summarizes the stratigraphic distribution of cultural materials from Loubanzi. Thirty-eight flakes and chunks of quartzite were recovered, along with a single chert flake; no unmodified quartzite cobbles were found. In addition, ninety-seven fragments of ferricrete and thirty-eight pieces of hematite were recovered. These had clearly been collected and brought to the site, but their purpose is unknown. They were not found on the EIA sites, and they do not appear to be ores suitable for smelting. Twenty-three fragments of mica-schist were also found, some of them flattened on one or both sides from use as grinding stones. The relatively large number of grinding stones recovered is unusual when compared to the EIA sites where they are less common.

Fauna
A single human molar and two oyster shells were recovered in the excavation. Although no evidence for shell middens was found at Loubanzi, small shell middens were frequently encountered at historic period sites during the reconnaissance (Figure 4.10). The absence of shells at EIA sites could mean that the oysters, cockles, and other shellfish that abound on the coast today were not utilized by EIA peoples. However, the extensive shell middens at Lac Tchitembo indicate this was not the case (Table 4.1, date 35). More likely, the highly acidic soils and high rainfall of the Congo worked against shell and bone preservation apart from the deep shell middens at Lac Tchitembo, which were sufficiently large to have changed the soil pH enough to preserve the shells. All of the sites with small LIA shell middens also had goods of European origin.

Metal
The five fragments of iron recovered were too corroded for their function to be determined. A twisted piece of flat copper sheet approximately 8 by 2 centimeters in size was also found at the base of the unit at 0.11S between 30 and 40 centimeters below the surface. This and the copper fragment from the nineteenth-century occupation at BP 113 were the only two excavated copper artifacts found during the Congo project.

Knowledge of copper smelting in sub-equatorial Africa is at least as old as iron smelting (Herbert 1984), so there is no technical reason it should not have been present at Loango from an early date. Loango is only 250 kilometers as the crow flies from the Niari-Djoué region near Mindouli and Boko Songho in the Democratic Republic of Congo where some of the richest copper deposits in Central Africa are located (Herbert 1984; Volavka and Thomas 1998). Nonetheless, no early copper was found during the reconnaissance, which suggests that the rugged terrain of the

Mayombe Mountains may have worked against a trade in copper until European contact stimulated demand for it. It is also possible that the Kingdom of Kongo to the south controlled the copper trade before Europeans upset the balance of power. In any case, by the beginning of the seventeenth century, copper and other metals were present in some quantity at Loango, at least in elite households, as Van den Broecke (La Fleur 2000: 95; 100–101) reports:

> [The king] has tremendous income, with houses full of elephant's tusks, some of them full of copper, and many of them with *lebongos* [raphia cloth], which are common currency here and are made from grass and are woven by the natives. ... During my stay, more than 50,000 lbs. [of ivory] were traded each year. ... There is also much beautiful red copper, most of which comes from the kingdom of the Isiques [Tio] (who are at war with Loango) in the form of large copper arm-rings weighing between 1½ and 14 lb., [which are] smuggled out of the [Tio] country. Learned also that there lie silver, tin, and copper mines inland which are not worked.

Dapper (1686: 328) describes how the copper was procured from these distant mines and brought to Loango. He makes it clear that it was blacksmiths from the coast, not smelters in the interior, who organized its production and transport (author's translation):

> [T]hey seek [copper] in very distant mines such as at Sondi, which is on the road to Pombo before [one reaches] the country of the Abyssinians. In the month of September a group of blacksmiths leave for Sondi and, arriving at the mountains where the copper mines are, they work them with their slaves. There they smelt and purify the copper. ... The blacksmiths return in May bringing the copper along with a few elephant teeth.[1]

Currently, the earliest evidence for copper mining in the interior of the Congo also dates to the second millennium AD at sites such as Misenga in the Democratic Republic of Congo and Kitsounga in the Republic of Congo. Although rich copper mines occur in these areas, the dates for copper working are inexplicably much later than those presently available for iron working (Lanfranchi and Manima-Moubouha 1984; Dupré and Pinçon 1997; Clist 2012b: 183, 199). It is likely that this anomaly will be resolved as more research is undertaken there.

Since iron ores do not outcrop on the Loango coast, the iron recovered in the excavations must have been obtained farther inland, perhaps through barter with smiths on the western slopes of the Mayombe or by expeditions sent there to produce it in a manner similar to that described above for copper. Nonetheless, even in the early sixteenth century it was still so scarce that "even a nail from a ship is taken in exchange for a whole elephant's tooth. This must be either because no iron is found here, or the working of it is unknown" (La Fleur 2000: 57).

Phase 2 Later Iron Age: The Historic Period (AD 1500–1900)

Although the archaeological excavations occasionally found nineteenth-century historic materials in their upper levels, no extensive excavations were carried out at historic component sites. Nonetheless, much can be gleaned from the surface reconnaissance and from historical documents pertaining to this period. The indigenous ceramics recovered from these sites were decorated with the diamond and other designs characteristic of the Mbafu Complex. In many cases these decorations appear to replicate the woven motifs used in raphia cloth manufacture. The indigenous ceramics occur in association with a variety of European porcelain and earthenware (Figure 7.6), the most recent with maker's marks that date between ca. 1860 and 1929 (Table A.1, notes). Earlier materials have no maker's marks, especially the salt-glazed Westerwald stonewares, soft-paste cream wares, and string-lipped gin or brandy bottles.

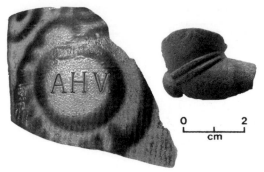

Figure 7.6. (Left) Nineteenth-century blue-and-gray stoneware stamped AHV for "Africaansche Handels-Vennootschap," a Dutch trading concern that operated on the Loango coast under this name between 1856 and 1880. (Right) Indigenous clay smoking pipe.

Bwali or Bouali, the Capital of Loango

Van den Broecke visited the Loango coast three times at the beginning of the seventeenth century and described its capital as lying close to the shore and surrounded by a wall. His description bears some resemblance to the somewhat fanciful etching published by Olfert Dapper in 1668 (Figure 7.7, taken from Prévost 1748:239).
Dapper never traveled to Africa, however, and it is possible that his illustration was guided by Van den Broecke's earlier description:

> The king keeps his residence less than a mile inland in a town named Bansa de Loango, which lies on a very high hill and is an extremely pleasant location. The king's court covers almost half of the city and is surrounded by palm-wine trees. Inside the *pagger* [fence] stand three or four large houses and another 250 small ones, in which live the king's wives, who are said to total more than 1,500 in number. (La Fleur 2000: 94)

Andrew Battell, a long-term resident of Loango in the same period, is probably more accurate in placing the number of king's wives at 150 rather than 1,500. His description of the capital also indicates it had a royal compound separated from the rest of the town, a royal court where war and other matters of national import were deliberated, and a great market where palm-cloth, "elephant's teeth," red dyewood, and several varieties of grain were sold. However, he makes no mention of a surrounding wall:

> The town of Mani Longo is three miles from the waterside, and standeth on a great plain. This town is full of palm and plantain-trees and very fresh, and their homes are built under the trees. The streets are wide and long and always clean swept. The King hath built his houses on the west side, and before his door he hath a plain, where he sitteth, when he has any feastings or matters of wars to treat of. From this plain there goeth a great wide street; some musket-shot from the place; and there is a great market every day. (Ravenstein 1901: 43)

A sixteenth-century visitor to San Salvador in northeastern Angola describes a much greater European impact on the Kongo capital than is evident at Loango. The city, for instance, had several enclosure walls (Lopes et al. 1881: 66–67):

> The city [San Salvador/Mbanza] is placed in a corner or angle of that summit, towards the south-east, and was enclosed with walls by King Dom Affonso, the first Christian, who gave

146

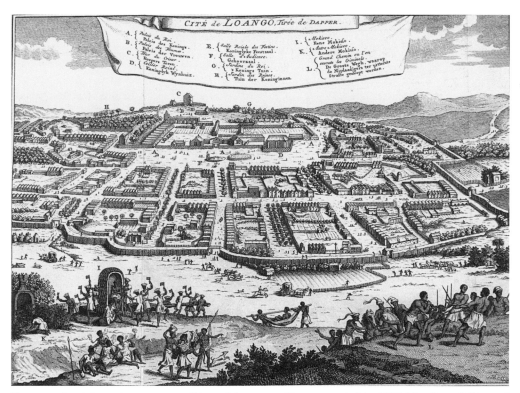

Figure 7.7. An eighteenth-century rendition of the town of Loango copied by J.V. Schley from O. Dapper's original etching published in 1686. The two "mokisso" (*nkissi*) Labeled K and I resemble European religious shrines rather than the *nkissi* figurines of the Congo.

the Portuguese their own separate part shut off with a wall, and enclosed his palace in the same way, as well as the other royal houses. A large space was left between these two enclosures, in which stands the principal church, with its square in front, the gates of the houses of the nobles and of the Portuguese being built so as to face the said church, and where the square commences live certain great nobles of the Court. ... Beyond these walls, in which the royal residences and the city of the Portuguese are enclosed, there are several buildings belonging to nobles, every one taking the most agreeable to him near the court. So that it is impossible to determine the size of this City, the whole country beyond the two boundaries of the walls being covered with houses and palaces, each noble having his houses and lands enclosed like a town. ... The walls are of great thickness; the gates are not shut at night, nor even are sentinels posted.

The small number of sites that could be assigned to the sixteenth to eighteenth centuries by the archaeological survey suggests that Loango populations were more centralized than they were in the first millennium AD. It is not yet possible to determine, however, whether this change in settlement pattern coincided with the exigencies of European contact and the disruptions of the slave trade or whether it had occurred earlier as a result of tensions or conflict within the wider Kongo kingdom. Certainly Loango was already an independent entity at the time of European contact (Martin 1972). Although there is no conclusive evidence that a perimeter wall surrounded the capital of Loango in the seventeenth century, centralization of population into large towns and the construction of defensive perimeter walls would both point to a need for defense and perhaps competition between competing local polities.

Turning to the capital itself, Proyart expresses surprise that there were few material distinctions between the inhabitants of the Loango capital, its architecture, and the conditions found in smaller surrounding villages:

> [They are] properly speaking, only great villages; they differ from them solely in containing a greater number of inhabitants. Grass grows in them, as in the villages; the streets are merely narrow path-ways. A great town is really a labyrinth; whence a stranger could never get out if he had not the precaution to take a guide with him. The citizens have nothing which distinguishes them from villagers; they are neither better clothed nor better lodged. The female citizens of the capital go to work in the fields like the peasant girls of the smallest hamlet. ... The King of Loango's palace is composed only of five or six huts, rather larger than those we have been speaking of. ... A house of this kind has nothing disagreeable in its appearance; it is a sort of large basket turned upside down. The rich and knowing ones sometimes have their dwellings worked with a deal of art, and lined with mats of different colours, which are the ordinary tapestry of the country. (Proyart 1814: 561)

It would be a mistake, however, to conclude that there were no social distinctions or other material ramifications brought about by the new wealth derived through trade with Europeans. But in Africa, in contrast with European practice, wealth was usually not hoarded for long periods in vaults or treasuries or even conspicuously displayed. Such behaviors could easily lead to jealousy and its counterpoint – witchcraft (Denbow 1999). Moreover, as Ekholm (1972: 100) remarks, Kongo kings "did not control land or any other means of production – instead they had control over goods" – prestige objects which were not needed for actual material support of life, but were definitely needed for social and political position. Africans used the material goods they acquired to create and reinforce power by circulating it (Sahlins 1965) much like contemporary politicians redistribute funds from their "campaign chests" in order to tilt the balance of political power in their favor. As Joseph Miller (1988: 49) explains,

> The quest for imports, once begun, tended to gain uncontrollable momentum in the rate of importing and, while not destroying local production, created a political dependence on foreign trade. These material goods, in turn, were used to establish debt and status – allowing a wealthy man to increase productivity through organizing and controlling people. What ambitious men struggled to achieve was not direct supervision over others, and still less stocks of the physical products of their labor beyond immediate needs, since both people and their fabrications were all too perishable, but rather a general claim to unspecified future labor and its product at whatever moment need for them might arise. ... Control over the "means of production" in its highest human form brought deference rather than storehouses filled with spoiling fish or rotting grain.

But trade with Europeans also brought eventual political collapse as the Kongo kingdom, based in the interior, was challenged by elites on the coast in a better position to conduct trade directly with Europeans (Vansina 1966). Loango's coastal position enabled it to profit as a middleman.

The exchange of prestige goods such as beads and cloth for needed foodstuffs by Europeans on the coast, however, also disrupted in a subtle way traditional systems of power and authority based on the control over the circulation of prestige goods by the elite. In normal circumstances, one could never exchange food for prestige items directly because these goods functioned in two separate spheres. This prevented peasants from entering directly into the prestige sphere controlled by the elite. By exchanging luxury goods directly for food, Europeans undercut the traditional system of circulation through which prestige goods passed from king to lesser nobles as a form of patronage. Now even ordinary farmers had "the opportunity of acquiring what otherwise had to come down from their chiefs" (Ekholm 1972: 114). Thus, the Atlantic slave trade was not only a direct threat to African communities through the loss of valuable labor and political support; it also fundamentally undermined the system of prestige goods circulation that the elite used to regulate access to power and status.

Indigenous Money: Salt and Weaving

Iron and copper, cowry shells from northern Angola, salt, and raphia cloth were all important stores of wealth that functioned as money on the Longo coast. In the case of salt, Proyart (1814: 574) found that it was made by "peasants of the villages near the sea, [who] are mostly salters. All their art consists in evaporating sea water over a great fire, which deposits the salt at the bottom of vessels employed for the purpose." So important was salt that the capital of the Kongo, M'banza Kongo or San Salvador, was reputed to have been established at the crossroads where the trade routes bringing copper from the north and salt from the sea intersected (Ekholm 1972: 107, 123–124). Indeed, the Bushong word for *price* in the Democratic Republic of Congo derives from the term for commercial salt cake (Vansina 2010:13).

Palm cloth served as an even more important form of money. Men in Loango produced a variety of raphia cloth types that included "velvets, satins, taffetas, damasks, sarsenets, and such like" (Purchas 1617:873; Vansina 1998). These were so valuable that seventeenth-century Portuguese administrators in Angola commissioned Loango weavers to produce palm cloth for use as currency to pay their soldiers (La Fleur 2000: 74–75). As Proyart (1814: 574) explains, "The best workmen make no more than the length of an ell [1.25 yd] of cloth in the space of eight days. Their little pieces, which we call *macoutes*, serve as the current money of the country." So valuable was cloth at the beginning of the seventeenth century, especially the imported variety, that Battell reported that a piece he used to wrap up his rifle was more valuable than the firearm itself: "Our author [Battell] inhabited a little Reed house, after the Loango maner, and had hanging by the wals, in a Cloth case, his Peece, wherewith he used to shoot Fowles for the King, which, *more for love of the Cloth then for the peece, was stoln*" (Purchas 1617: 875, emphasis added). Of course, raphia cloth also had more mundane uses, as Van den Broecke (La Fleur 2000: 97) explains:

> They [women] are attentive in their dress, which are just *labongos* made of grass and are about a square ell in size, which they wear on their right side and which just covers their nakedness, front and back. They have their hair cut with a razor and smear their entire bodies with red paint made from stone-ground *taccola*. These women always go with a mat under their arms on which to sit when they go somewhere for a chat. Many have good numbers of beads, which they know how to make themselves from shells, and which are held in great esteem.

> The men wear on their heads caps of grass, very pretty and neatly stitched with a needle, some of which are decorated with feathers of different colours. Their clothes are also made of grass and bound like a skirt, which they tie around their middle with a quarter ell of cloth, but more often with bark from trees, so that their bodies are usually covered from their hips down and above that they are naked. On top of that, decorative skins from exotic animals, such as leopards, monkeys, civet cats, and others, hang in front of their bellies. Also many copper and silver arm-rings, and most of them have buffalo-tails over their shoulders, to shoo away flies off their naked upper bodies as needed.

Palm cloth was thus a central metaphor in Loango society, one that resonated throughout many areas of indigenous life (Nsondé 1995: 189–191), as Martin (1986: 6) explains:

> The newborn was laid on a piece of raphia cloth; young people at initiation wore raphia cloth skirts; the suitor of a young girl carried palm wine and cloth as presents for her

family; cloth was used to pay legal fees. The elders and the wealthy could manipulate power through controlling the circulation of raphia cloth and passing it on to their juniors and dependents who lacked cloth or the means to acquire it. At the same time, higher and lower chiefs in the administration of the kingdom celebrated their authority through the exchange of cloth on important political occasions. Thus, there was reciprocal cloth-giving at the installation of the rulers of Ngoyo and Loango. ... Those who could afford to do so hoarded baskets of cloth in their homes as savings for such extraordinary expenses and for times of crisis. It was reported of the Maloango in 1612, for example, that at his court there were "houses full of ivory, copper, and libongos." (Martin 1986: 3)

The woven diamond-shaped and crosshatched designs that were incised and stamped into the early ceramics at Condé, Loubanzi, and other sites were thus a reflection of the wider polysemic role played by raphia cloth in the cultural aesthetics of the coastal peoples of the Congo and Angola for more than a millennium.

Cloth and the Slave Trade

When Europeans first arrived on the Loango coast, they found that domestic slavery already existed, but it differed in fundamental ways from the commoditized slavery that came to dominate relations with Europeans over the next four centuries. Ekholm (1972: 92) provides a useful description of the social dimensions of pre-European domestic slavery in Kongo society:

What we are up against here is not *Slavery* in the usual meaning of the word: it can neither be compared with slavery in the antique world nor with that which developed in 16th and 17th century America. Here we are dealing with an individual who was transmitted from his own lineage to another, in exchange for prestige articles, thereby losing his lineage membership and becoming a *muana* [child], *a nonmember of low social age*. He was not classified as a slave – as something quite other than a free human being – and his situation did not differ in any decisive way from that of other *muana*. He could not be treated badly, and he was not the object of the kind of contempt which is continually present in real situations of oppression and subjugation. To be sure, *tata* [parent or father] had the power of life and death over his "slaves," as long as they remained with him, but this was the position in which even a "free" sister's son found himself vis-à-vis his uncle, who could sell him to Europeans just as well as he could a "slave."

By the mid-eighteenth century the trade in dyewood and ivory mentioned for the Loango Coast by Lopes, Battell, Van den Broecke, and others had largely given way to slaves, as Proyart (1814: 586; 584) observes:

[Trade in] ivory, monkeys, parrots, and some other merchandize ... forms an object of so little importance that they reckon nothing of it. ... The principal trade of these people is that in slaves, whom they sell to the ... French, the English, and the Dutch, who transport them to their American Colonies. ... They are taken in war by those who sell them. In the interior of the territory there are hostile people irreconcilable to those of whom we are speaking. ... It is by way of reprisals that they themselves wage open war on them, and they pretend that they treat them humanely, contenting themselves with selling them to the Europeans at the same time when they have a right to deprive them of life. This war, though continual, does not however trouble the tranquillity of the kingdom, because it is carried on far beyond the frontiers by certain individuals, and, properly speaking, it is less a war than a chase; but one in which the hunter is often liable to become the prey of the game he follows. Those who have made captives sell them to merchants of the country, or bring them to the coasts, but they are not allowed themselves to sell them to the Europeans; they are obliged to address themselves to brokers, nominated by the minister of commerce, who treat with the captains of ships. These slaves are estimated according to their age, sex, and strength; they pay for them in European goods.

All trade took place under the watchful eye of the M-souka or Mafouque (Mafuka), a "minister of commerce" appointed by the MaLoango to oversee transactions with foreigners. According to Proyart, the trade in human beings was confined to the "rich and mighty ones of the country"; ordinary people had "no need but that of food and clothing in the grossest and simplest manner" (Proyart 1814: 587). A complex pricing system evolved as European commodities were bundled into "virtual" money termed *pieces*:

> At Loango they reckon by pieces, and every sort of goods is entered in a line of the account with the stuffs to form the piece; thus, when they say a slave costs thirty pieces, it does not mean he costs thirty pieces of stuffs, but thirty times the ideal value which they think fit to fix on, and call a piece. ... This difference in the manner of reckoning is nothing at bottom, and the price of slaves is nearly the same in all the kingdoms bordering on Loango. (Proyart 1814: 585)

Proyart gives the example of a twenty-two-year-old slave named Makviota who was purchased for a bundle of goods worth thirty pieces. More than half the value of the bundle, 16.5 pieces, was composed of 95 yd of cloth; the remaining commodities included "2 guns, 5 lbs. of gunpowder, 6 lbs. of musket shot, 2 swords, 24 sheath knives, 2 lbs. of iron bar, 5 dutch pots, and 10 strings of beads." A musket, an item once thought to be essential to the conduct of the slave trade in Africa, was worth only one piece or the same as nine yards of imported cloth, enough to make three or four waist skirts.

Although European traders focused on the commoditized value of their goods, and attempted to extract the maximum profit from each exchange, the symbolic value of these items in indigenous terms was more complex. At the time of European contact, Africans already had a long familiarity with pottery manufacture, metalworking, and the production of alcohol in the form of palm wine and sorghum beer. In many cases, the cloth woven by Loango men from raffia palm fronds was seen, even by Europeans, as comparable in quality to the finest imported varieties (Nsondé 1995: 189–190; Vansina 1998).

So what incentives from the African side would create a demand for European goods so great it could only be satisfied through the exchange of human lives? Two stand out. First, African economic systems revolved around the circulation of debt and obligation, rather than the accumulation or hoarding of material goods for their own sake (Sahlins 1965, J. Miller 1988; Nsondé 1995: 190–191). As Ekholm remarks (1972: 106), "Those red, white and blue glass beads corresponded to a certain type of shell [money], *nzimbu* (*Olivancillaria*), Kongo's prestige article above all others." Second, it was widely believed that the vast quantities of goods made available by Europeans could only have been produced and acquired through witchcraft and sorcery. They were therefore invested with supernatural agency, as Schrag (1990: 51) explains:

> Nineteenth century BaMboma believed that foreign-manufactured goods had a magical quality. According to one account of this belief, foreigners did not weave the cloth that they brought to Mboma's port. This was the work of the *simbi* spirits who lived beneath the oceans that the trade vessels crossed on their way to the African coasts. The foreigners, who had found the hole leading to the aquatic *simbi* factory, simply sailed to the *simbi* hole and rang a bell whenever they needed cloth. ... As payment to the *bisimbi*, the captains threw into the hole the bodies of BaMboma and other Africans who had been sold to them through witchcraft.

The Archaeology and Ethnography of Central Africa

Central Africans thus interpolated meaning not only into the European goods themselves but also into the remarkable *quantities* of items that European ships brought to their shores and the astonishing number of human lives demanded in exchange for them. European bowls, basins, and bottles thus had spiritual as well as functional valence, and it was the former attributes that caused them to be heaped over graves as an accompaniment for the dead as they journeyed to the land of their ancestors (Thompson and Cornet 1981). The Vili justified their trade in slaves by arguing that selling their captives to Europeans was more humane than simply killing them, which was within their traditional right. Although he was a religious figure, Proyart (1814: 563) also justified the slave trade to himself in a way that was likely soothing to the conscience of European and African alike – a rationalization that demonized the victim while praising the perpetrator:

> They who give to the negroes of Loango, Kakongo, and other neighbouring states, the characters and manners of the slaves whom we draw from among them for our colonies, are the most grossly mistaken of all; since they judge of a nation by its most deadly enemies, and by the most desperate of its subjects. If they do sell us some slaves of the country, they are those whom their crimes have rendered unworthy of being citizens. But most of those whom we buy are taken in war from other savage nations, and who sympathize so little with the people in question, that they have never had either peace or truce with them. Those slaves in general have many bad qualities without any mixture of good ones; they must be made into good men before anything can be done towards making them Christians. … [T]he despair of slavery seems to close their heart against virtue.

The raphia cloth monetary system that underwrote the slave trade continued in diminished form in Loango up to the end of the nineteenth century when "French coinage [was] gradually taking its place" (Dennett 1968: 49). Older reckonings of value were yet submerged, however, and one of the terms still in use for slaves at that time was "children of the cloth" (Dennett 1968: 49). But it was now cloth imported from outside Africa, not the locally made *libongo* (Nsondé 1995: 189–191). And a good deal of this cloth was "sacrificed" to accompany the burials of the elite. In one famous case such large quantities of cloth were wrapped around a king in Cabinda that wheels had to be borrowed from a European ship's cannon so that the cloth-wrapped body, more than 9 meters in length, could be transported to its final resting place (Degrandpré 1801: plate between pages 152 and 153). But even when imported cloth was used as burial wrappings, it was reworked into the traditional diamond patterns. Dennett describes a nineteenth-century elite burial in which red cloth was chosen to cover the coffin, but white strips were then nailed over it to produce the traditional diamond shapes. His (Dennett 1898:230) following description parallels in many respects Degrandpré's (1801: 146–153) account of a century earlier:

> His body is smoked and watched by his wives in the back room [of the funeral house], while in the front half of the shimbec the prince's wealth, in the shape of ewers, basins, figure ornaments, pots, pipes, glassware, etc., is on view. One of his wives will generally be found walking about in front of the shimbec, throwing her arms about and crying. This may last for a year or more before the body is buried. The coffin is a case, perhaps 15 feet long, 4 feet broad, 6 feet high, covered over with red save-list. White braid is nailed by means of brass-headed chair-nails in diamond shaped designs, all over the red cloth. The coffin (into which the dried body, wrapped in cloth is placed) is then put on the funeral car. Stuffed tigers [leopards?], an umbrella, and other ornaments are placed upon the top of the coffin. The whole is then drawn to the burial ground by hundreds of assembled guests, who sing and dance by the way. The grave is ready; and the coffin is lowered into it. Then one or two of his wives (10 years ago) jumped in, or (as is the case to this day, a little north of Loango) two small boys are placed in the grave beside the coffin; and all are buried.

The choice of red and white colors reflects time-honored symbolic associations between color, the ancestral world, and other liminal states of initiation and rites of passage (see Jacobson-Widding 1979; Denbow 1999). Such symbolism also underlay the demand for red dyewood along the coast remarked upon by Van den Broeke and others. In Central Africa wood rather than rock-ochre was only the material available to produce the red pigment used for ritual purposes such as female initiation well into the colonial period. Dennet and others often remarked on the "paint houses" where the Loango girls were secluded during their initiation into womanhood (Dennett 1968).

The End of the Slave Trade and Colonial Rule

Both Burton and Dennett were witness to the social consequences of four centuries of Loango involvement in the slave trade. But, instead of condemning the trade, they mocked the transformations they saw in indigenous culture while minimizing their own society's complicity in it. In doing so, they failed to recognize that the values of their own societies had also been warped through four centuries of complicity in the slave trade. Although their nations profited from it materially, their values and beliefs had also become debased as its brutality and inhumanity were disguised in an ideology of justification and colonial superiority. That arrogance is evident in Burton's vilification of the Vili as "land sharks … a tribe of bumboat men, speaking a few words of English, French, and Portuguese, and, dealing in mats and pumpkins, parrots, and poultry, cages, and Fetish dolls called 'idols'" (Burton 1876 vol. 2: 4–5). Dennett (1887: 44), no admirer of the Catholic faith, further diminished Vili religious beliefs, commenting that they had become "neither a Christian or a heathen, or whatever he was before, but a priest-ridden fearer of the evil spirit, and would-be reverer of the Virgin Mary, or *Nzambi* [God]. … Roman idolatry was in days gone by a dangerous method to Christianize. … Thus Christianity worked hand in hand with *Nkissism* [his generalized term for indigenous spiritual beliefs]." For both observers, hybridity was visible only in the "other," not themselves.

And African cultural values were about to be reworked yet again as colonial conquest and occupation left the Vili with even less control over their political and economic affairs than they had had before. During the nineteenth century, the rigid social stratification of the Vili also changed as Europe and the New World shifted from economies based upon slave labor to more industrialized forms of production. The ambitious aristocracy of Loango was now in decline as the opportunities for prosperity offered by the slave trade declined. Indeed, so impoverished did the coast become that Dennett was told that MaLoango Prati, who died at the end of the eighteenth century, had to wait almost a century to be buried. It took that long before a new king could accumulate the wealth needed to complete the expensive coronation process (Dennett 1968: 6).

With economic and political collapse, the end of the slave trade, and with them the need for centralized, fortified communities, commoners once again dispersed from Bwali (Bouali/Buali) to settle in small villages scattered across the surrounding hinterland where the archaeological reconnaissance found their remains. In the 1920s, however, populations began to shift once again toward the new city of Pointe Noire as people responded to the new economic opportunities provided by the construction of the rail line and port. Apart from a few villages and fishing camps, the hinterland was once again deserted, leaving behind only a few lonely tombstones and scattered fragments of broken earthenware and glass bottles to mark their presence.

A Less-Well-Known, but Lasting, Consequence of the Slave Trade

A daily reminder of the Atlantic slave trade had an impact on our archaeological work in the Congo: the inadvertent introduction by slaving vessels of a species of sand tick known locally as

Figure 7.8. Henri, one of the archaeology students from Marien Ngouabi University, removing a chique from Josie's foot. Many painful mornings were spent removing these pests, which were transplanted to the shores of Africa in the ballast of slave ships from the New World.

a chique (*Tunga penetrans*). When one walks on these infested beaches they burrow into the feet, especially under the toenails, where they rapidly grow into a painful, pea-sized creature that must be carefully dug out before blood poisoning or gangrene can set in (Figure 7.8). The creature arrived on the Congo shores in the sand ballast of slave ships as they returned to Africa lightly loaded from Central and South America. The chiques were deposited on the beach when the ballast was dumped in preparation for taking on a new cargo of slaves bound for the New World. The tick and its associated disease, *tungiasis*, has now made its way southward from the slave coasts of Central and West Africa to the Cape of Good Hope. It is now continuing northward up the East African coast.

We first noticed them when a few weeks into the project we all had sore feet that caused us to hobble around. Looking closely, we found red sores that were usually concentrated around our toenails. The Congolese crew members, who were also suffering, explained that although chiques were a common problem in their villages, they had never seen so many of them in one place. They knew that in winter the chiques tended to live in the wet sand along the shore, and they suggested that we may have inadvertently spread them throughout our camp when Conoco workers laid down a layer of beach sand to cover the mud around our buildings. The intention was to use the sand to prevent hookworm, which tends to infest muddier ground. The chiques cost us many painful visits to the doctor in Pointe Noire, who cut them out with a razor blade. My wife, Josie, had over a hundred chiques removed in this way at one go, which led to blood poisoning. If she didn't respond to medication, François told her she would have to be evacuated. We were all relieved when, after a short rest in Pointe Noire, she was able to return to camp. Later we learned that the local Congolese had a somewhat less painful and less dangerous approach. They looked for the chique's airhole, enlarged it with the sharpened point of a palm frond, and then levered them out whole. We then burned them in alcohol. Over the following weeks a daily rite evolved in camp as we took turns removing chiques from each other's feet. This made for many glum mornings in our camp. Our mood was not improved when we learned that Congolese children play a tag-like game in which the person who is "it" is called a "chiquer,", the Congolese equivalent of someone with "cooties." At the end of the field season, we were still removing chiques from our feet two weeks later in France. And we burned them again to prevent spreading them to a new location.

8

Opening Pandora's Box: From Loango to the Okavango

Archaeological surveys have a limited distribution in Angola and excavations *sensu stricto* are few. ... The Neolithic and Iron Ages, everywhere old, have received little attention from archaeologists and at the moment it is very difficult, with such fragmentary data, to integrate Angola into larger syntheses pertaining to the early settlement of this part of Africa. (Clist and Lanfranchi 1992: 261, author's translation)

Introduction

From a homeland in west-central Cameroon 3,000 to 4,000 years ago, peoples speaking Bantu languages spread across most of Central, eastern, and southern Africa. By AD 300 they had covered a region roughly the size of North America, differentiating in the process into what are today 400 to 600 separate languages. The first stages of this expansion likely followed river courses southward through the equatorial forest, but little is yet known in detail about the prehistory of this process (Eggert 1984, 1987, 1992; Wotzka 1995; Mercader et al. 2000). Other routes followed the Atlantic coastline as early fishermen and farmers brought new technologies and languages south from Gabon to the Loango coast during the last millennium BC (Denbow 1986, 1990, 2011, 2012; Eggert 1994/1995, 1995; Vansina 1995; Clist 2005, 2012b; Neumann et al. 2012). Over the ensuing centuries this expansion continued southward to reach the northern fringes of the Kalahari and Namib deserts by the middle of the first millennium AD (Denbow and Wilmsen 1986; Clist and Lanfranchi 1992; Vansina 2004; Kose and Richter 2007; Kose 2009; Campbell, Robbins, and Taylor 2010; Denbow 2008, 2010; Wilmsen and Denbow 2010; Wilmsen 2011).

Archaeological investigations into the prehistory of the area from Gabon and Loango in the north to the Cunene-Cubango-Zambezi watershed in the south are thus few and far between, with many gaps in coverage. Compounding the sparse archaeological coverage, the high rainfall and acidic soils of West-Central Africa have often worked against the preservation of plant and animal remains. As a result, archaeological interpretations of the development and expansion of Iron Age peoples across Angola resemble working with the proverbial "black box"– we know something about what went into the box in the north and what came out in the south, but we have little direct knowledge of the internal transformations that took place within it as the prehistoric societies that once existed there evolved into the foraging, pastro-foraging, agricultural, and agro-pastoral economies known in more recent times.

These transformations were as complex and varied as the environments of Angola, which range from mixed topical forest and savanna in the North to the dry deserts of the Kalahari and Namib in the South. Miombo woodlands cover the central highlands whereas more open grasslands interspersed with Mopane (*Colophospermum Mopani*) and Baikea (African teak) forest dominate the south and southeast (Cruz de Carvalho, Vieira da Silva, and Morais 1973). The first Bantu-speaking farmers and fishermen to cross the Congo River in the last millennium BC entered a cultural mosaic as diverse as the new environments they encountered. Today the region is home to speakers of languages that belong to three separate language families: Niger-Congo (Bantu subgroup), Khoe-Kwadi, and Northern San or Ju-≠Hõa (Vansina 1995, 2004; Ehret 2008; Güldemann 2008). As Ceramic Late Stone Age (CLAS) and Early Iron Age (EIA) peoples moved south across the Congo River they interacted with and absorbed a varied population of indigenous foragers, in the process incorporating new ideas, values, and practices. Hence, as Vansina (2004: 33) remarks, "[i]t is absolutely wrong to think of all the resulting societies as consisting of a single invariant forager input and a single input of Bantu agriculturalists."

Languages

Some insight into the cultural and economic developments that took place inside the "black box" can be developed through an examination of contemporary languages and the history of technological and social change they preserve. For instance, historical linguistics can suggest hypotheses regarding the sequence of adoption of specific plants and animals by a language group and, in some cases, can posit possible origins and routes of movement for the new or borrowed terms associated with these practices. But specific dates – and the geographical areas and social means through which new productive technologies and terminologies were transferred – are more difficult to determine from linguistic data alone. Identified and dated faunal remains, carbonized seeds, plant phytoliths, and other data from archaeological sites can provide minimum dates for some linguistic reconstructions, helping to ground them in time and place (Vansina 2004; de Luna 2012). Stylistic and technical analyses of excavated ceramics can also contribute to the reconstruction of past social geographies and networks of regional interaction (Huffman 1989, 2007; Wilmsen et al. 2009).

Other than by sheer coincidence, which is unlikely in most instances, there are two principal reasons why languages could come to share a common word for a particular item or practice. The first is because they inherited it from a common ancestor or "protolanguage." The second is because the term was acquired at a later date through borrowing. Sometimes earlier word forms can be linguistically reconstructed using phonological rules and semantic comparisons. Such terms are called "starred terms" by linguists because they are written with an initial asterisk (e.g., *-búmb- a common term meaning "to make pottery" found in both the Eastern and Western branches of Bantu). Generally, the more geographically widespread a term is, the older it is – particularly if it occurs in languages belonging to distinct branches or sub-branches of an ancestral "protolanguage" (Bostoen 2007a: 175–176).

Tracing the spread of borrowed terms is more complicated because languages that share a common ancestry could both borrow the same word from a more distant or even unrelated language. For instance, when maize and manioc were introduced to West-Central Africa from the Americas in the sixteenth century, new terms for these crops spread inland as Bantu-speaking farmers adopted them and then passed both the plants and the new terminology for them on to their neighbors. When the crops reached southwestern Zambia, the borrowed terms cut across a much older linguistic division between Eastern and Western Bantu languages, blurring the earlier distinction between them (Bostoen 2007b: 26).

Bantu Languages

Present evidence indicates that proto-Bantu diverged from a wider group of Bantoid languages in westernmost Cameroon around 4,000 years ago. One model, termed the "Early Split Model," suggests that soon afterward these languages differentiated into Eastern and Western subgroups with one branch, Eastern Bantu, expanding north of the tropical forest to arrive in the Great Lakes area of East Africa in the last millennium BC. The second branch, Western Bantu, expanded at about the same time directly southward toward the lower Ogooué area of Gabon (Vansina 1995: 186). More-recent linguistic research suggests a revision, termed the "Late Split Model," in which the Eastern branch separated from the Western branch at a later date in a "secondary nucleus" south of the equator near the Atlantic Ocean in West-Central Africa (Heine, Hoff, and Vossen 1977; Vansina 1984; Kahlheber et al. 2009; de Filippo et al. 2012). Over time, the Western meta-group (sometimes referred to as Narrow West Bantu) diverged into the Coastal (D), Inner-Congo Basin (C) and Southwest (E) groupings shown in Figure 8.1 (Vansina 1995: 184–185; Bostoen 2007a: 185). The hypothesis of a late rather than an early split between Eastern and Western branches of Bantu also finds support in some recent genetic data; however, "subsequent contact between Bantu languages and populations has strongly affected the signal of the initial migration" (de Filippo et al. 2012:7; see also Bostoen 2007a, 2007b; Alves et al. 2011: 13).

In the 1960s the linguist Malcolm Guthrie (1967/1971) subdivided the modern Bantu languages into different geographic zones to which he assigned the letters A–S; individual languages within these regions were given unit numbers (e.g., R10, R20, etc.). The Western Bantu languages found in the region from Loango in the north to northwestern Botswana in the south belong to Guthrie's zones H, R, and K. The Vili of Loango and the Kongo and Chokwe of northern and northwestern Angola, for instance, all speak languages of the Coastal subgroup of Western Bantu and belong to Guthrie's zone H10. The Ambundu who live south of the Kongo in the northern parts of the central highlands of Angola also speak a Coastal language belonging to Guthrie's zone H20. The neighboring Chokwe to the southeast and the Ovimbundu on the southern edge of the highlands, however, speak languages belonging to the Southwest Bantu subgroup in Guthrie's zones K10 and R10 (Bostoen 2006/2007: 189). On the dry Kalahari sands between the central highlands and the Okavango Delta, other Southwest Bantu languages are spoken. These include the languages of the Herero (R30) and Ovambo (R20) of southwestern Angola, northern Namibia, and northwestern Botswana, the Yei (R41) in the Okavango Delta, and the Mbukushu (K43) who live between the Delta and the Zambezi Valley. As a result of long-term interaction with the Khoe-Kwadi and Ju-≠Hõa language families, the latter two groups have adopted many clicks in their languages (Güldemann 2008; Ehret 2008; Bostoen and Sands 2012).

"Khoisan" Languages

In a series of recent papers, Güldemann (2008, forthcoming), Güldemann and Elderkin (2010) and Ehret (2008) have proposed a dramatic revision of the so-called Khoisan language family, arguing that its two major branches – Khoi and San – did not emerge together from a proto-Khoisan ancestor in southern Africa. Instead, they hypothesize that the proto-Khoe-Kwadi languages had a long history of separate development in East Africa prior to their arrival in southern Africa approximately 2,500 years ago. As Güldemann (forthcoming: 16, 20–21) summarizes it,

> This argues against the common assumptions that (a) Khoe-Kwadi is an old lineage in southern Africa and that (b) all its speakers were originally foragers. I propose instead that the Proto-Khoe-Kwadi population colonized southern Africa relatively recently as a pastoralist group and was thus responsible for the first introduction of food production into this region. That is, not all populations lumped together under "Khoisan" have entirely emerged

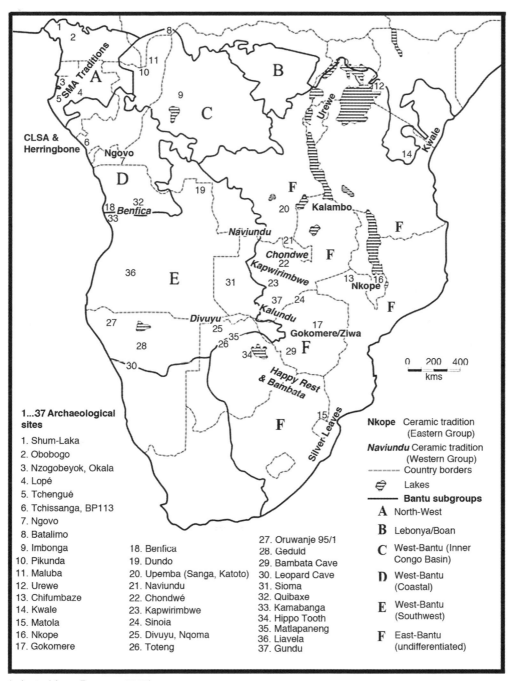

(adapted from Bostoen 2007)

Figure 8.1. Map of archaeological sites and ceramic traditions in central and southern Africa and their geographic relationship to the linguistic subdivisions of Western Bantu (adapted from Bostoen 2007a: 180).

in southern Africa and represent "pristine" hunter-gatherers. ... [A]t the earliest historical stage, the original population initiating the above change is assumed to have (a) possessed a non-Khoisan genetic profile, (b) subsisted on small-stock pastoralism, and (c) spoken an early chronolect of Khoe-Kwadi. All these population characteristics are compatible with or

159

even specifically suggest an ultimate origin of Khoe-Kwadi in eastern Africa. … it is very probable that Khoe-Kwadi had a wider geographical distribution in the past and other such groups existed at least in Zimbabwe and the eastern parts of Botswana and South Africa where they gave way to incoming Bantu.

The hypothesis of separate origins for the Khoe-Kwadi, Ju-≠Hõa and Tuu (Southern San) finds support not only in linguistic analyses (Figure 8.2), but also in archaeological and genetic studies (Vossen, Keuthamnn, and Köhler 1986; Sadr 1997; Ehret 1998, 2008; A. Smith, 2005, 2006; Henn et al. 2008; Coelho et al. 2009; Schlebusch et al. 2012). Henn et al. (2008: 10696; but see Mitchell 2011), for instance, conclude that a "direct haplotype sharing between Sandawe/Kxoe and !Kung/Hadza/Datog leads us to argue for a migration between Tanzania and … northern Namibia and southern Angola."

Taken together, these data argue that prior to the arrival of Bantu-speaking populations from the north, proto-Khoe-Kwadi speaking herder-foragers occupied the dryer wooded grasslands of southern Angola, northern Namibia, and Botswana. Along the river systems of the Cubango-Okavango-Boteti, they relied on fish and other riverine resources to supplement their diet (Denbow 1986, 2008; Denbow and Campbell 1986; Turner 1987a, 1987b; Robbins et al. 2000a, 2000b; van Zyl et al. 2013). It was from these early herder-foragers that advancing EIA immigrants acquired sheep and possibly cattle (Vossen 1997; Robbins et al. 2005; Kose and Richter 2007; Robbins et al. 2008; A. Smith 2008; Kose 2009; Pleurdeau et al. 2012). Both the immigrant Khoe-Kwadi and Bantu populations settled among indigenous hunter-gatherers who spoke Ju-≠Hõa languages. The ceramics found on early Ceramic Later Stone Age (CLSA) herder-forager sites in southern Africa may represent (a) an independent in situ invention of pot-making on the part of herder-foragers in southern Africa (Sadr 2008); (b) an origin in the "Pastoral Neolithic" of East Africa, with ceramics being part of the cultural knowledge that accompanied the migration of proto-Khoe-Kwadi peoples to Southern Africa (A. Smith 2005); or (c) ceramics acquired through trade with Bantu agriculturalists north of the Cunene-Okavango-Chobe rivers, such as those at Benfica in Angola (Huffman 1994, 2005; Denbow 2008).

Pygmy Languages?

Whether there was another autochthonous language family in the northern regions of Angola and Loango when the first Bantu-speaking agriculturalists arrived is more contentious. Although hunting-and-gathering populations may have evolved as a genetic and cultural isolate in the forests of Central Africa during the late Pleistocene and early Holocene, issues of chronometric dating, the relationship between shifting forest boundaries and archaeological horizons, and the fluid and complex history of contemporary identities, make the assignment of past cultural identities problematic (Denbow 1990; Mercader et al. 2000; Mitchell 2010; Jarvis et al. 2012). No languages apart from those belonging to the Bantu, Khoe-Kwadi and Ju-≠Hõa families remain that could attest to the earlier existence of a now-lost language family spoken by isolated foraging populations in the tropical forest. If there was such a family, all traces of it have disappeared (Blench 1999; Klieman 2003) apart for some possible subsistence vocabulary used by the Aka and Baka pygmies of the northern and eastern Congo Basin (Bahuchet 1992, 1993a, 1993b).

Although some genetic analyses suggest the former existence of a "pygmy" isolate (Jarvis et al. 2012), in the current state of research one may question how contemporary self-identification as a member of a pygmy community is related to deeper historical reconstructions across such a vast region and over so many thousands of years. As for the southwestern fringes of the tropical forest in the Congo and northern Angola, the only cultural signals for the existence of a distinct late Pleistocene/early Holocene hunter-gatherer adaptation are the scattered finds of Tshitolean lithic assemblages in northern Angola that are distinct from Wilton materials further south (Clark

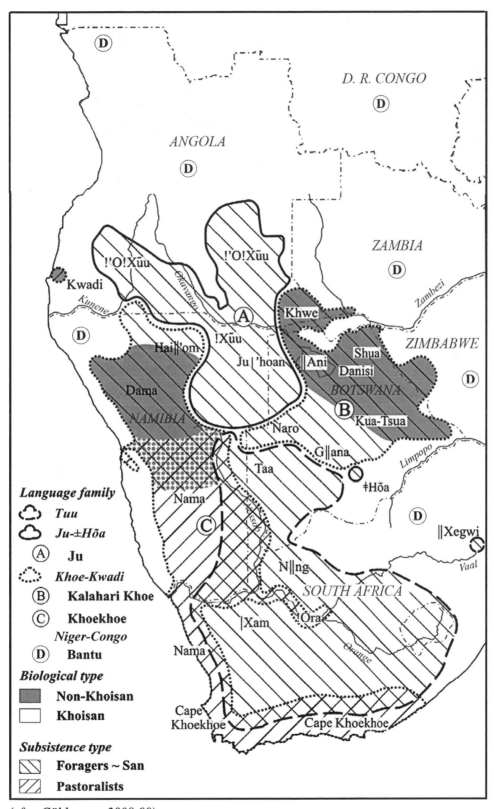

(after Güldemann 2008:99)

Figure 8.2. Linguistic map of central and southern Africa showing the general distribution of Bantu, Khoe, Ju-≠Hõa, and Tuu languages (adapted from Güldemann 2008: 99).

1966; Rudner 1976; Ervedosa 1980: 150). Differences in lithic technology, however, cannot be used as direct proxies for language or cultural groupings. And some differences in toolkit would be expected in any case given the environmental differences between northern and southern Angola. Whether such differences constitute sufficient evidence for the existence of a long-standing genetic and cultural isolate, glossed by an all-encompassing term such as *pygmy*, may therefore be problematic.

Food Production

Domesticated Crops

Linguistic reconstructions indicate that the proto-Benue-Congo ancestors of proto-Bantu speakers were familiar with oil palm (*E. guineensis*) and cola nut (*Cola* sp.) trees. Archaeological evidence for the intensive exploitation of the oil palm, along with the oil-rich *Carnarium schweinfurthii* or bush candle tree, is also widespread from Ghana to Cameroon and at CLSA sites in Gabon and Loango (Denbow 1990; de Maret 1994/1995; Sowunmi 1999; Bostoen 2005). According to Phillipson and Bahuchet (1994/1995), proto-Bantu farmers also cultivated several varieties of yam of the *Dioscoraceae* genus (*-bàdá, *-kódó), as well as two species of ground bean: *-kúndé or cowpea (*Vigna unguiculata*) and *-júgú or Bambara groundnut (*Vigna subterranean*). A more recent reconstruction to proto-Bantu is the term *-cángu for pearl millet or *Pennisetum glaucum* (Bostoen 2006/2007: 189–190). Today this term is confined to Southwest Bantu speakers, although some Coastal and Inner Congo Basin languages now apply it to maize. Almost all Eastern Bantu languages use a different term, *-bèdé, which appears to have been introduced as a loan word from a Nilo-Saharan source (Ehret 1974, 1998; Phillipson and Bahuchet 1994/1995; Kahlheber et al. 2009). Archaeological corroboration for the early presence of domesticated pearl millet in the Western Bantu branch comes from carbonized pearl millet seeds recovered from coastal sites in the Cameroon dated to the late first millennium BC (Eggert et al. 2006), where it could be associated with "the beginning of the break-up and spread of 'Narrow West Bantu'" (Neumann et al. 2012: 57–58).

Although there is no direct archaeological confirmation of farming at CLSA sites in Loango or the Democratic Republic of Congo, on linguistic grounds it is likely they cultivated pearl millet and perhaps bananas (Vansina 1995, 2004; Mbida et al. 2001; Bostoen 2006/2007: 202–203; Neumann 2006; Kahlheber et al. 2009: 259–260; Neumann and Hildebrand 2009; Neumann et al. 2012). Deep pits containing large quantities of carbonized oil palm nuts along with grinding stones and polished stone axes possibly used to harvest and process oil palms and domestic grains have also been recovered from the Loango coast and from Ngovo Group sites in the Democratic Republic of Congo (de Maret 1986). Vansina suggests such sites, which he associates with the "proto-Njila," may represent a group ancestral to the Coastal and Southwestern subgroups of Narrow West Bantu. He postulates that proto-Njila first emerged from Narrow West Bantu in Northeastern Angola "after its speakers had acquired pottery and horticulture, but before metals reached them, for the metallurgical vocabulary is not proto-Njila" (Vansina 2004: 42). Small quantities of iron appear on the Loango coast and adjacent Democratic Republic of Congo after 300 BC and by AD 100 iron working was solidly present at Herringbone settlements such as BP 113.

To the south in the Tsodilo Hills of northwestern Botswana (Figure 8.3), excavations at the seventh- to ninth-century AD site of Divuyu uncovered large quantities of carbonized mongongo nuts (*Schinziophyton rautanenii*) that hint at the importance of wild plant foods in the diet (Denbow 2011). Remains of these nuts, along with carbonized grains of sorghum (*Sorghum bicolor*), were also recovered from the nearby site of Nqoma in a level dated between the eleventh and twelfth centuries AD (cal AD 1020 ± 60, Beta-13260; Wilmsen and Denbow 2010).[1] Direct

Figure 8.3. View of the "female" hill at Tsodilo in northwestern Botswana showing the locations of the Early Iron Age sites of Divuyu and Nqoma.

evidence for millet cultivation was not recovered at either Divuyu or Nqoma. Stable carbon isotope analyses of three human skeletons from Nqoma and one from Divuyu, however, indicate a diet dominated by the consumption of cultivated rather than wild plants (Mosothwane 2011: 122).

Carbonized remains of domesticated sorghum, pearl millet, a cucurbit seed, and wild *Grewia* seeds were also recovered using flotation methods at the EIA site of Matlapaneng near Maun on the southern edge of the Okavango Delta (Denbow and Wilmsen, field notes).[2] The two hut floors from which grain was recovered are dated between the tenth and twelfth centuries AD (cal AD 930 ± 110, Beta-10563, and AD 1100 ± 50, Beta-10562, respectively). The Matlapaneng ceramics link it partly with Nqoma, but also with Dambwa wares of the broader Kalundu Tradition in the Victoria Falls region of southwestern Zambia (Vogel 1971a, 1971b, 1973, 1975; Wilmsen et al. 2009; Wilmsen and Denbow 2010).

Domesticated Animals

Goats

Proto-Benue-Congo speakers had a term for domesticated goat, *-búli,* that is ubiquitous in both the Eastern and Western branches of Bantu (Ehret 2002: 278; Bostoen 2005). The tropical forests of Loango and northern Angola harbor the tsetse fly (*Glossina* sp.), which today limits livestock to small herds of goats that, along with sheep, are more resistant to trypanosomiasis than cattle (Connor 1994; Gifford-Gonzalez 2000; Badenhorst 2002). Although the linguistic evidence thus suggests that goats may have been kept by the CLSA and EIA inhabitants of the Loango and Congo coasts, there is as yet no archaeological confirmation of this. The widespread use of the *-búli* term in the Western and Eastern branches of Bantu languages, however, suggests that Narrow West Bantu speakers may have been able to traverse the forest with small numbers of these animals, retaining their proto-Bantu term for them. Alternatively, they may have reacquired them at a later stage through contact with Eastern Bantu speakers, either retaining the earlier *-buli term or reacquiring it as a loan word.

For the Khoe and Ju≠Hoa in southern Angola, the linguistic evidence (Ehret 2008: 18) suggests that goats were acquired from Bantu sources in three sequential adoptions at dates later in time than their acquisition of sheep or cattle. These terms include the following: (a) the term *khobo-de*, which was introduced into Kwadi from the Southwest Bantu *-kombo*; b) the Bantu root *mpene*, which was introduced into Khoe languages as a borrowing from nearby Southwest Bantu languages such as Yei (*impènê*) in the Okavango Delta; and (c) the term *m-buli* that was acquired at a later stage through interaction with another Southeast Bantu language.

Sheep

A proto-Khoe term for sheep, *gu,* that is widespread amongst the Southwest Bantu languages indicates a complex history of interaction between Bantu and Khoe/Kwadi speakers in Angola, Namibia, and northwestern Botswana (Ehret 2008: 15). Most Ju-≠Hõa dialects also use the term (Ehret 2008: 17), and it is widespread as a loan word in some of the languages of southwestern Zambia and most of the Southeast Bantu languages spoken east of the Kalahari in Eastern Botswana and South Africa. Dates for sheep bones from Leopard's Cave in Namibia, Toteng on the banks of Lake Ngami in Northwestern Botswana, and Bambata Cave in Southwestern Zimbabwe (Figure 8.1) place these animals in LSA or CLSA contexts during the last three centuries BC. This is several centuries before the arrival of EIA settlements in the region (Walker 1983; Bousman 1998; Robbins et al. 2005; Blench 2006; Pleurdeau et al. 2012). The linguistic and environmental data suggest that proto-Southwest Bantu speakers did not initially possess sheep in northern Angola, but acquired them later though contact with proto-Khoe-Kwadi pastroforagers living on the dry grasslands of southern Angola, northern Botswana, or Namibia (Ehret 2008; Güldemann 2008; A. Smith 2008).

Currently, the earliest archaeological dates for sheep and goats in EIA contexts in Northern Botswana come from Divuyu and the lower levels of Nqoma (Denbow and Wilmsen 1986, Wilmsen and Denbow 2010; Denbow 2011; Wilmsen 2011). Although it is often difficult to separate the bones of sheep from goats archaeologically (Badenhorst 2006: 47), this has been possible at these two sites. Of the 1,550 faunal remains identified to species level at Divuyu, 479, or 31 percent, came from sheep (*Ovis aries*). These make up 25 percent of the minimum number of individuals (MNI) identified at the site. Goats (*Capra hircus*) were represented by just fifteen bones, or less than 3 percent of the MNI (Turner 1987a; Denbow 2011). Undifferentiated sheep/goat (*Ovis/Capra*) remains accounted for another eighty-one bones, or 15 percent of the MNI. Cattle bones accounted for less than 2 percent of the MNI. At Nqoma, it is more difficult to separate the faunal remains into earlier Divuyu and later Nqoma components because of the longer chronology and more complex stratigraphy. But of the 1,721 MNI identified, sheep account for 123 or 7 percent; undifferentiated sheep/goat remains account for 42 individuals, or 2 percent of the MNI, whereas goats make up just 0.2 percent of the MNI (Turner 1987a; Wilmsen 2011: 106). Cattle, on the other hand, were more common and composed 19 percent of the MNI. At Matlapaneng, cattle were even more prevalent and accounted for 31 percent of the 121 MNI identified whereas sheep accounted for 4 percent, goats 2 percent, and undifferentiated sheep/goats 17 percent (Turner 1987b).

Cattle

Tsetse fly infestation of the forested regions of west-coastal Africa would have prevented cattle from diffusing southward through the tropical forest with Narrow West Bantu peoples, and even today almost no cattle are raised in the northern provinces of Angola, the Democratic Republic of Congo, and Loango. As with sheep, cattle would have had to be reacquired at a later stage farther south in Angola. Because of differences in the way cattle are used, Vansina (2004: 83) proposes a two-stage incorporation of cattle into the EIA economies of central and southern Angola:

> from a line running to Caconda and eastward, people such as the northern Ovimbundu and the Ambundu did not drink milk or milk their cattle, which they keep only for their beef. Indeed the northern limit of milking is also the limit to which agropastoral systems prevail. Beyond this line, cattle, however much prized, remained unimportant compared to farming. The existence of this border then makes it clear that there were two different sorts of acquisition concerning cattle, in which Divuyu and Camabanga [Kamabanga] represent the earlier one but not the transition to true pastoralism.

Radiocarbon dates for cattle remains at CLSA herder-forager sites in northern Botswana are almost as early as those for sheep at Toteng, and at Lotshitshi near Matlapaneng (Denbow and Wilmsen 1986; Robbins et al. 2005). However, these domesticates make up only a very small percentage of the faunal remains. Unlike the linguistic terminology for sheep, no unique proto-Khoe-Kwadi or proto-Khoe terms for cattle have survived. Instead, all Khoe and Ju-≠Hõa speakers use words such as *gomo, *gumi,* or *be* that can all be reconstructed to the Eastern Bantu root *-ngombe.* Ehret (2008: 20–22) suggests that the transfer of cattle from Eastern Bantu to Khoe and Ju-≠Hõa speakers took place in different parts of the Kalahari at different times and through two different intermediary languages. The terms for cattle in Southwest Bantu languages also derive from the *-ngombe* root. In an interesting turn about, however, the terms for cattle and sheep in the Southeastern Bantu languages of Eastern Botswana and South Africa (such as the Tswana terms *kgomo* and *nku)* were adopted from Khoe – suggesting that they possessed few or no cattle or sheep before their arrival in southern Africa, when they acquired them from Khoe sources.

While cattle make up only 2 percent of the MNI at Divuyu, there was an abrupt change to a more cattle-oriented economy at Nqoma after AD 900 when they make up 19 percent of the MNI. Cattle also outnumber sheep and goats at the coeval site of Matlapaneng on the southern edge of the Okavango Delta where they make up 31 percent of the MNI (Denbow 1986; Denbow and Campbell 1986; Turner 1987a, 1987b; Wilmsen 2011). The ceramics from these two sites, discussed in the following section, indicates this economic change correlates with an influx of new peoples from two areas in western Zambia (Wilmsen et al. 2009; Wilmsen and Denbow 2010). At Tsodilo, these immigrants absorbed or displaced the earlier Divuyu population that possibly spoke a Western Bantu language.

Although the archaeological evidence for herding is presently meager in Angola, domestic cattle are also present along the coast at Kitala and Kamabanga south of Luanda in the ninth century AD, a date coterminous with Nqoma and Matlapaneng. Clist and Lanfranchi also suggest these cattle could represent "the first traces of contact and mutual influence between eastern and western bantu" (1992: 261–263, author's translation).

The archaeological evidence thus suggests that intensive cattle herding and probably the Eastern Bantu term *-ngombe* for them only became common in northwestern Botswana at the end of the first millennium AD. The timing of this economic shift, and the ceramics associated with it, suggest it was related to the appearance of more intensive cattle-keeping economies in southwestern Zambia at the end of the first millennium AD (Vogel 1971a, 1971b, 1975; Huffman 1989; de Luna 2012: 238–243). Eastern Bantu languages may have been introduced at the same time. Some of these herders expanded west to the margins of the Okavango – perhaps in search of new grazing lands or in response to the expansion of LIA, Kalomo Tradition, agro-pastoralists into the Victoria Falls region at the beginning of the second millennium. The valuable specularite deposits of the Tsodilo Hills would have formed another attraction (Robbins, Murphy, and Campbell 1998).

In summary, the linguistic evidence suggests that goats may have been important early domesticates among Narrow Western Bantu communities prior to their breakup into Coastal and

Southwestern Bantu subgroupings in the last centuries BC or first centuries AD. Late last millennium BC dates for carbonized pearl millet from coastal Cameroon indicate that farming was also practiced by early Western Bantu speakers along the coast (Eggert et al. 2006; Neumann et al 2012). In northern Angola, linguistic evidence (Ehret 2002: 198) tentatively suggests that sheep may have been reacquired from Bantu sources living farther east, but there is as yet no archaeological evidence in this region to confirm this hypothesis. Farther south, sheep were certainly adopted at a later stage by Southwest Bantu peoples from proto-Khoe-Kwadi sources. While the location of such transfers is presently unknown, sherds of Bambata-like pottery similar to that recovered at some CLSA sites in Botswana are dated to the second century AD at Benfica (Ervedosa 1980; Huffman 2005).

Combining agriculture with small-stock pastoralism could have fueled the spread of proto-Southwest Bantu agro-pastoralists across the dry plains of southern Angola and northwestern Botswana. Cultivation of pearl millet along with small stock would also have helped Early Iron Age agro-pastoralists cope with the loss of significant resources such as the oil palm, fish, and shellfish as they moved southward. Although the economy at Divuyu was dominated by sheep-herding, supplemented to an important extent by hunted game, fish, and mongongo nuts, nearby sites such as Xaro and Qogana in the northern Okavango Delta with similar ceramics had economies based on the exploitation of riverine resources and wild game, with no domesticated animals (Turner 1987b; van Zyl et al. 2013). No evidence of lithic technology was found at either Okavango site, and it is uncertain whether they represent early ceramic-using Khoe adaptations to the Delta similar to those of present-day Bugakhoe and Dxericu or were instead the remains of Bantu-speaking peoples who had developed a specialized riverine adaptation such as is found among contemporary Yei peoples (Tlou 1985; Denbow and Thebe 2006). Stable carbon isotope analyses of two human skeletons from Xaro confirm a diet of fish and wild plant foods, with little evidence for the consumption of domesticated plants (Mosothwane 2011: 122–123).

Cattle appear in large numbers only after AD 900 at Nqoma and Matlapaneng along with new ceramic assemblages that align them with the makers of EIA Kalundu and Sioma wares in western and southwestern Zambia (Vogel 1971a, 1971b, 1973, 1975; Wilmsen et al. 2009). The earliest dates for cattle in Angola fall into the same time frame as Matlapaneng and Nqoma.

Pottery and Iron Working

Recent linguistic reconstructions indicate the existence of two very old words for pot-making in Eastern and Western Bantu languages: (a) a *-mà- term that is found in some of the Group A Northwestern Bantu languages of the Cameroon and a few Southwestern Bantu languages of Group E in southern Angola (Figure 8.1) and (b) a *-búmb- term that is much more widespread in most Eastern (Group F) and many Western Bantu languages, but not in the Northwest Bantu group (Bostoen 2007a: 193–194).

Bostoen has proposed a two-phase spread of pot making to explain this distribution in the western half of sub-equatorial Africa. First, an early strata of Western Bantu-speakers brought the *-mà term south along the coast to Angola, where it was retained by a few Southwest Bantu speakers. This was followed by a second stratum using the *-búmb- term that spread westward to replace *-mà in all but a few languages (Bostoen 2007a: 194). What is not known is when the change in pot-making terminology took place or whether it was also accompanied by a change in potting styles such as is evident between Divuyu and Nqoma in the Tsodilo Hills.

Early Iron Age Ceramic Traditions

The wide geographic split in the distribution of the *-mà- term argues that it is very old and was likely present along the Loango coast prior to the diversification of Narrow West Bantu into its

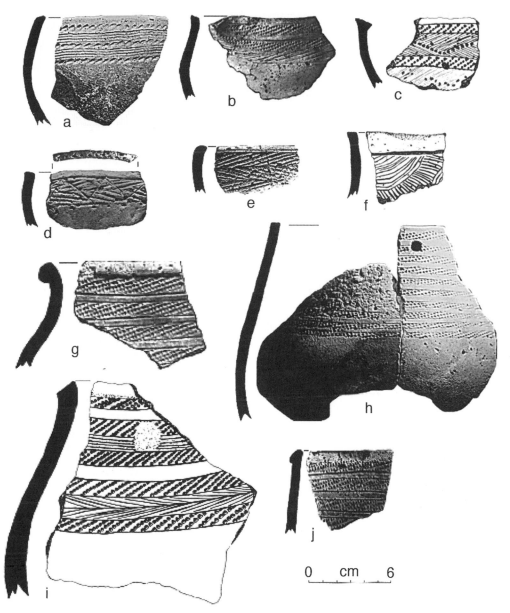

Figure 8.4. Examples of Early Iron Age Divuyu Tradition ceramics, part of the Naviundu complex, from the Tsodilo hills.

Coastal and Southwest branches. Although the archaeological data are meager, this could suggest that the *-mà-* term was used by the earliest Iron Age communities in southwestern Angola. On present evidence, this would be the Divuyu Tradition (Figure 8.4) dated between the sixth and ninth centuries AD (Denbow 1990, 2011; Denbow and Wilmsen 1986; Kose and Richter 2007; Kose 2009). This tradition, in turn, is related to the Spaced Curvilinear (SC) wares of Loango and the early ceramics from Naviundu in the Lubumbashi area of the Democratic Republic of Congo (Huffman 1989, 2007: 335; Denbow 1990).

Dates for the expansion of the Naviundu complex place peoples making SC wares on the Loango coast in the seventh to the ninth centuries AD (Table 4.1, dates 37 and 38). The dates for Divuyu are slightly earlier, with most falling in the sixth to eighth centuries (Kose 2009; Denbow

167

2011). The calibrated dates for Gundu, which Huffman also attributes to Naviundu, are slightly later and fall in the ninth to the eleventh century range (Huffman 1989: 60).

Huffman (1989, 2007: 335) contrasts the Naviundu complex with the Kalundu Tradition of southwestern Zambia, which is widely associated with the early expansion of Eastern Bantu languages (Phillipson 1977, 2005). In a ceramic comparison of Naviundu (including Madingo-Kayes or SC wares) and Kalundu, Huffman argues they belong to two co-occurring complexes with separate origins during the EIA. The origin of Kalundu he associates with sites such as Benfica and Quibaxe in Northwestern Angola, which, he argues, "must have been made by Eastern Bantu speakers ... [who] left the proto-Bantu homeland in West Africa with an already developed Central Cattle Pattern ... Kalundu is quite distinct from the contemporaneous Naviundu style in Zaïre" (Huffman 1989: 114).

No cattle, goat, or sheep remains were found at Benfica, however, and the occupants of the lagoon site appear to have been focused on the exploitation of fish and shellfish, rather than herding; no faunal remains are reported from the inland site of Quibaxe (dos Santos and Ervedosa 1970; Ervedosa 1980; Valdeyron and Da Silva Domingos 2009). It is highly unlikely that an economy centered on pastoralism or cattle herding could have diffused southward through the tsetse infested forests to Central Angola. Cattle economies, and the Central Cattle Pattern (CCP) associated with them in southern Africa (Huffman 1986, 1993, 2007), must have developed at a later stage farther south.

Nevertheless, the suggestion that the ceramic assemblage at Benfica represents an early branch of proto-Eastern rather than Western Bantu speakers, although provocative, would not necessarily conflict with the Late Split linguistic model. It does, however, necessitate the early coexistence of two ceramic traditions in the same region at the same time: one derived from Herringbone, Kay Ladio, or Naviundu and associated with Narrow West Bantu (de Maret 1986; Gosselain 1988; Denbow 1990), and the other associated with the proto-Eastern Bantu Kalundu Tradition. At present there is no evidence for a Naviundu presence in central or northwestern Angola before the second half of the first millennium AD. Only the enigmatic Carinated Broadly Grooved (CBG) wares have been reported there (Clark 1968: 201). In the sixth through the eighth centuries, however, an expansion of the Naviundu complex left SC wares on the Loango coast, the Divuyu Tradition wares (Figure 8.4) in northwestern Botswana and the Caprivi Strip, and Gundu settlements in southwestern Zambia (Figure 8.2). Some of the ceramics illustrated by Clark from Dundo and dated to the ninth century AD (Clark 1968: 194) bear similarities to Naviundu rather than to CBG wares and could provide additional evidence for a westward expansion of the Naviundu complex into northeastern Angola. The driving force behind this expansion is unknown, but at Divuyu it is associated with a mixed agro-pastoral, fishing, and foraging economy based on small-stock sheepherding.

Around AD 900, new agro-pastoral settlements appear on the western and southern margins of the Okavango Delta at Nqoma and Matlapaneng. The ceramics from these sites are not related to those from Divuyu or to the wider Naviundu Complex. Instead, they have their origins in two separate traditions of the Iron Age in western Zambia. At Nqoma, the ceramic assemblage is characterized by collared, bag-shaped jars with tall, thickened rims decorated with comb-stamping or, later, incised hatching and cross-hatching (Figure 8.5, g–i). None of these charcoal-tempered vessels has decoration on the neck or shoulder. The bowl forms are generally small, carinated, and very elaborately decorated with red slip and a variety of pendant triangles or hatched or crosshatched bands executed with incision or comb-stamping (Wilmsen and Denbow 2010; Wilmsen 2011). False relief chevron or ladder stamping sometimes borders the decoration.

The Nqoma assemblage is most closely related to the ceramics reported by Vogel (1973) from the Sioma Mission site along the Zambezi River approximately 300 kilometers northwest of Victoria Falls (Figure 8.1). Although the jar forms at Sioma are different from those at Nqoma, many of the bowl forms and decorative motifs are the same. Based on a detailed ceramic

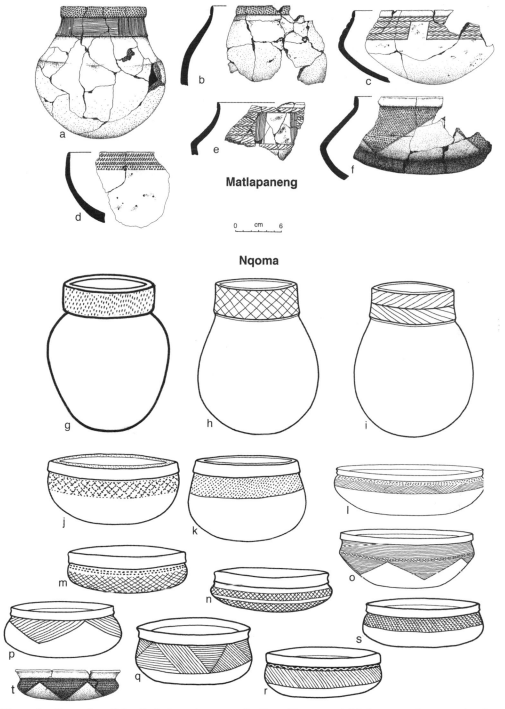

Figure 8.5. Examples of the Early Iron Age ceramics from Nqoma and Matlapaneng that are related to ceramics from Sioma and Dambwa, part of the Chifumbaze complex found in southwestern Zambia.

comparison with other sites in Zambia, Huffman (1989: 87–91) suggests that Sioma best fits as an early phase of the Later Iron Age Kalomo Tradition, rather than as a separate facies or a phase of the EIA Kalundu Tradition. Its appearance at Nqoma around AD 900 correlates with the appearance of a more cattle-based, agro-pastoral economy. A greater emphasis on cattle herding is also

169

found in southwestern Zambia at that time (de Luna 2012), as well as at Matlapaneng near Maun on the southern edge of the Okavango Delta.

The ceramics from Matlapaneng include a few of the same vessel styles as Nqoma (Figure 8.5f), suggesting there was some interaction between the two sites. But most of the jar and bowl forms are related to the Dambwa phase of the Kalundu Tradition in the Victoria Falls region, rather than to Sioma (Vogel 1971b, 1975; Huffman 1989). The charcoal-tempered jars from Matlapaneng have thickened rims decorated by comb-stamping or incised hatching, along with bands of neck decoration that often include horizontal bands, sometimes with vertical interruptions (Figure 8.5a). Such jars are also common in Dambwa. Slightly carinated bowls decorated with multiple bands of incised or combstamped hatching interrupted with blank vertical spaces or panels are also common at Dambwa sites and at Matlapaneng (Figures 8.5c, e).

In addition to stylistic similarities, the paste of some of the vessels from Nqoma and Matlapaneng has mineral inclusions that indicate they were imported from the wider Victoria Falls region (Wilmsen et al. 2009). Given the Kalundu (Dambwa) and early Kalomo (Sioma) affiliations of the ceramics from Matlapaneng and Nqoma, respectively, it is possible that Eastern Bantu languages, and new potting traditions associated with the term *-búmb-, were introduced to the Okavango region at the end of the 1st millennium AD, replacing an earlier Western Bantu presence at Divuyu associated with the early Western term *-mà for potmaking. The Eastern Bantu term for cattle, *ngombe, may also have been introduced at the same time.

Metalworking

Although iron fragments, jewelry, and tools were consistently recovered with the Herringbone and SC wares in the Loango sites, none has been reported at Benfica or the more inland sites with similar pottery. The earliest dates for metallurgy presently available for northern Angola are a tenth century AD date for iron from Ricoco II (Lunda Norte) and an eighth-century date from Liavela (Clist and Lanfranchi 1992: 261). Both sites are on the northern edge of the central highlands. Dates for metallurgy will undoubtedly be pushed back as more research is conducted.

Iron is associated with Divuyu ceramics dated as early as the fifth century AD along the Kavango River in the Caprivi Strip of Namibia (Kose and Richter 2007; Kose 2009). At Divuyu itself, more than 200 iron and copper artifacts were recovered. These include barbed arrowheads with long tangs (Figure 8.6) that suggest they could have been coated with poison in a fashion similar to those used by contemporary Khoe and Ju-≠Hõa hunters in the northern Kalahari. The heavy-duty iron chisels, picks, and axes recovered at both Divuyu and Nqoma might have been used as mining tools in the specularite mines at Tsodilo. More than 1,000 tons of rock are estimated to have been removed from these mines, which are dated between AD 700 and 1100 (D. Miller 1996; Robbins et al. 1998; Denbow 2011). In historic times sparkling specularite powder was widely traded as a valued cosmetic powder that was mixed with fat and sprinkled on the skin or hair to create an effect much like modern hair glitter (Campbell 1835: 112; Livingstone 1858: 108).

There are no iron or copper ores at Tsodilo, however, and there is no direct evidence that iron or copper smelting ever took place there. All the materials were obtained through trade with smelters living elsewhere, most likely in exchange for specularite. Most of the copper and iron at Divuyu was made into jewelry that included a variety of helix bangles to adorn the arms and legs, metal clips that were probably attached to clothing or hair, delicate chains to be draped over the body or clothing, and beads. At Nqoma, the metal assemblage is even richer, with more than 2,700 beads, chains, helixes, clips and other artifacts recovered (D. Miller 1996; Wilmsen 2011; Wilmsen and Denbow, in preparation). One of the four copper specimens from Nqoma that was examined chemically by Duncan Miller was unusual because it had a phosphorous content of approximately 4.5 percent. This would have made it much harder to work, but it would also have

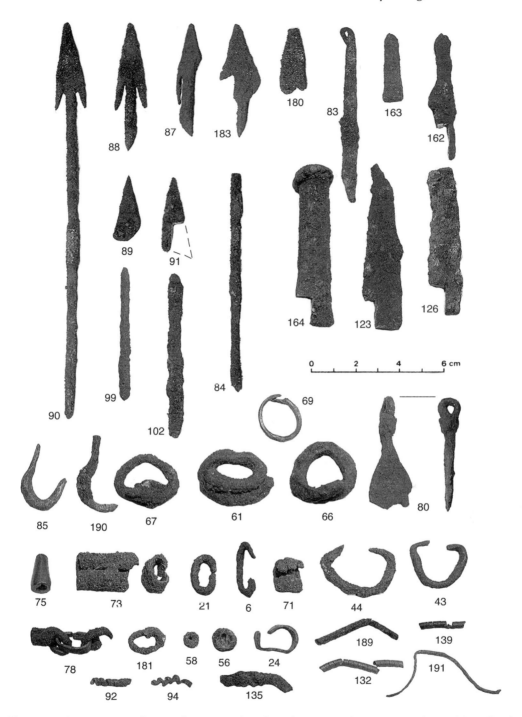

Figure 8.6. An assortment of iron and copper tools and jewelry recovered at Divuyu in the Tsodilo Hills of northwestern Botswana. Artifact numbers refer to samples discussed in D. Miller (1996).

made it particularly bright in color. D. Miller (1996: 89) argues that the variability in trace element inclusions found in the copper artifacts indicates they were derived from a diversity of ore sources in neighboring regions. The closest copper mines to Tsodilo are more than 200 kilometers distant in the Kwebe Hills south of Toteng; mines that might also have contained inclusions of phosphorous and nickel are even farther away in the Democratic Republic of Congo, Eastern Botswana, and South Africa.

It is likely that trade in specularite enabled the inhabitants of Divuyu and Nqoma to acquire the luxury copper and iron goods from such far distances. Indeed, the inhabitants of Nqoma were so rich that they were even able to acquire glass beads and marine shells from the Indian Ocean more than 1,500 kilometers to the east. These are the most distant East Coast trade goods ever recovered in the interior of Southern Africa and their presence at Tsodilo underscores the wealth of the Nqoma community. According to Duncan Miller (1996), at the beginning of the second millennium AD Nqoma was the richest site in all of Southern Africa in terms of the quantity and diversity of its iron and copper jewelry. All of the metal was imported and metallurgical analyses indicate that most of it was reworked many times into new forms. Two smithing tuyères from a burned structure at Nqoma prove that some of this reworking was carried out on-site by local smiths (D. Miller 1996; Wilmsen and Denbow 2010).

The Later Iron Age: AD 1100–1800

Nqoma came to an end around AD 1200 as powerful, cattle-based chiefdoms and kingdoms emerged in the Limpopo valley and eastern Botswana to take control of the inland trade routes in luxury goods. Now demand for ivory and gold, not specularite, fueled exports along trade routes to the Indian Ocean. Nqoma and Matlapaneng, with their complex record of shifting interactions between Western Bantu, Eastern Bantu, Khoe, and Ju-≠Hõa, waned in the centuries after AD 1200 as trade routes for luxury goods were reoriented to meet the demands of new political economies based on cattle, gold and ivory. Drying climates may also have had an adverse impact on farming and livestock production in some areas (Denbow 1986 1990; Denbow and Campbell 1986; Denbow and Wilmsen 1986; Denbow and Miller 2007; Denbow et al. 2008; Huffman 2008). Archaeological visibility in northwestern Botswana picks up again in the eighteenth century, however, as LIA ceramics related to those made by contemporary Kavango, Mbukushu, and Yei peoples appear along the northern waterways of the Kavango, Kwito and Okavango (Gibson, Larson, and McGurk 1981; Tlou 1985; Wilmsen and Denbow 2010; Wilmsen 2011; van Zyl et al. 2013).

On the Loango coast, there is presently a hiatus following the SC period and, with the exception of the shell middens at Lac Tchitembo, no sites have been found that date between approximately AD 900 and 1100. After this, as described in Chapter 7, LIA settlements with very distinctive ceramics decorated with "woven" or lozenge motifs appear. These motifs are widespread in Kongo ceramics, art, and raphia cloth (Hagenbucher-Sacripanti 1973; Bassani and Monzino 1987; Clist 2012a; Denbow 2012). Their appearance marks the arrival of peoples speaking Coastal Bantu languages associated with the emergence of the Loango and Kongo kingdoms in the early centuries of the second millennium.

Although copper was highly valued and widely traded throughout the Iron Age (Herbert 1984), it is only after approximately AD 1400 that there is any evidence for it in Loango. By the seventeenth and eighteenth centuries, however, the storehouses of the Loango elite were filled with copper goods, ivory, and raphia cloth – all indigenous stores of value that continued to finance social alliances and political aspirations well into the colonial era alongside the newly introduced European cloth, ceramics, beads, guns, and brandy (Martin 1986).

9

Summation

The reconnaissance and excavation results presented in this book provide an initial cultural chronology of expansion and transformation on the equatorial coast of Central Africa. Data from more than 200 surface locations and excavations at 15 archaeological sites are documented by 40 radiocarbon dates. These findings provide a preliminary glimpse into the expansion of Western Bantu peoples over the last 3,000 years. The detailed findings from Loango, which are unusual in their scale, could only have been realized through a program of cooperation that joined private corporate interests and academic concerns to provide tangible benefits to both sides (Simpson and Pitcher 1988).

The Ceramic Later Stone Age

Deep pits filled with organic-rich soil, the fragmented remains of ceramics, carbonized oil palm nuts, and occasional chert or quartzite flakes mark the earliest Ceramic Later Stone Age (CLSA) or Neolithic sites on the Loango coast. The shapes and design motifs found on these early vessels relate them to other material found along the coast between Gabon in the north and the Democratic Republic of Congo in the south. The first appearance of CLSA sites correlates with evidence for the appearance of a dryer, more open savanna-forest mosaic around 1000 BC. Whether the environmental changes recorded in pollen cores for the end of the second millennium BC were the result of forest clearing, perhaps by initial agriculturalists, or were instead the result of longer-term processes of climatic change, is a subject of current debate (Brncic et al. 2007; Ngomanda et al. 2009). The data suggest that an initial migration along the coast by land and water around 1000 BC may have introduced an early Northwest Bantu language south of the tropical forest. It is possible that this language was later submerged as Iron Age immigrants bringing Herringbone wares and perhaps Narrow West Bantu languages settled in Loango in the last centuries BC.

The Iron Age

Iron first appears on the Loango coast in the third or fourth century BC. No smelting furnaces or slag heaps were found on the coastal savanna, and iron production appears to have taken place at more inland locations on the forested slopes of the Mayombe Mountains that were closer to the sources of iron ore. From the third century AD, iron was in common use. Remains of barbed arrow points, bangles, and other materials were recovered from excavations at Madingo-Kayes, Gray Sand, BP113, Lac Ndembo, Kayes, and Loubanzi.

The new ceramic styles characterized by herringbone decoration that appear in the last two centuries BC dominate ceramic assemblages in the first half of the first millennium AD. Given its distinctness from the earlier Neolithic or CLSA material, it is likely these were introduced by population movements from the northeast or east of the Mayombe Mountains. Pearl millet could have been introduced at the same time from sources farther north where it was cultivated from at least 400 BC (Eggert et al. 2006; Neumann 2006; Kahlheber et al. 2009; Neumann et al. 2012). Whether banana cultivation was practiced at the same time is still uncertain (Mbida et al. 2001, 2004; Vansina 2003).

Toward the middle of the first millennium AD, another new ceramic tradition appears on the Loango coast. The distinctive ceramics, termed Carinated Broadly Grooved (CBG) ware, are characterized by carinated and deeply grooved decorations on pots and bowls. Only two excavated sites produced this material, but it is clearly related to ceramics first recovered at Dundo Airfield in northeastern Angola more than forty years ago (Clark 1968; Ervedosa 1980). Little is presently known about this tradition either in Angola or in the Congo, but present evidence suggests that its origins lie south of the Congo River in northeastern Angola.

In the seventh and eight centuries AD, another cultural intrusion brought Spaced Curvilinear (SC) ware into the region, most likely from the area south and east of the Congo River. These elaborately decorated wares have no earlier precedents on the Loango Coast and their intertwined motifs and other elements point to origins within the Naviundu complex first described in the Lubumbashi region of the Democratic Republic of Congo (Anciaux de Faveaux and de Maret 1984; Huffman 1989). Ceramic decoration layouts, motifs, and decoration techniques link these wares to those found far to the south along the Okavango River in northwestern Botswana and the Caprivi Strip of Namibia where they date between the seventh and ninth centuries AD and, slightly later, those from Gundu in Southwestern Zambia (Denbow and Wilmsen 1986; Huffman 1989, 2007; Denbow 1990, 2011; Kose and Richter 2007; Seidel et al. 2007; Kose 2009).

The archaeological project found almost no sites dating to the period between AD 900 and 1100 in Loango, suggesting that the region was either depopulated at that time or that the formerly dispersed settlement pattern of the Early Iron Age (EIA) coalesced into a few large communities that were not located by the reconnaissance because they lie within the populated areas between Diosso and Pointe Noire that were not covered by the survey.

In southwestern Angola, northwestern Botswana, and northern Namibia, linguistic evidence indicates that proto-Southwest Bantu peoples had shifted from agricultural to mixed agropastoral economies by the middle of the first millennium AD. They acquired domesticated sheep from proto-Khoe-Kwadi speakers who had settled the region almost 1,000 years earlier. Present evidence suggests they were also immigrants to the region – but from East Africa. Both groups settled among populations speaking unrelated languages belonging to the Northern San or Ju-≠Hôa family. The earliest Iron Age sites in this area, represented by Divuyu in the Tsodilo Hills, had domestic economies that were dominated by sheep, with few cattle or goats. The centuries between AD 900 and 1200 were a period of rapid cultural and economic change as cattle-keeping Eastern Bantu peoples moved westward from the Zambezi Valley to the Okavango region to settle at Nqoma and Matlapaneng. They may have been in search of new pastures while exploiting other rich resources such as the specularite mines at Tsodilo. They either displaced or assimilated earlier Khoe, Ju-≠Hôa Ju and Western Bantu speakers at sites such as Divuyu.

The Late Prehistoric and Historic Periods

Early in the second millennium ceramics with "woven" motifs appear on the Loango coast at sites such as Condé and Loubanzi that date between the twelfth and fifteenth centuries AD. The decoration motifs on these ceramics suggest that the social and economic values attached to cloth and its decoration in historic times had developed in the centuries before European contact. With the arrival of Europeans, coastal economies rapidly shifted from trade in commodities such as red dyewood and ivory to slaves – most obtained through raiding the savannas to the east and south of the Mayombe. Although slavery existed in Africa prior to the arrival of Europeans (Miers and Kopytoff 1979), the scale of the demand for human lives, along with the tremendous quantities of manufactured goods unloaded onto Africa's shores, led Africans to comprehend the Atlantic slave trade in terms of the ideological structure of indigenous religion and witchcraft. In African eyes, the imported goods were not simply commodities that replaced earlier indigenous products, but goods whose very mode of manufacture and exchange associated them with sorcery, the supernatural, and *Mputu* or the land of the dead – a term still sometimes conflated even in modern times with Portugal and "Europe" (MacGaffey 1983: 131; 1986: 5; Denbow 1999: 405).

In the case of imported textiles, the traditional values already embedded in raphia cloth were amplified and transformed as imported cloth – even more than guns or brandy – became the principal commodities in the bundle of goods or *pieces* exchanged for a human life (Proyart 1814: 585; Nsondé 1995). The symbolic relationship that developed between cloth and slavery was so strong that even as late as the end of the nineteenth century, the most common metaphor for slaves in Loango was "children of the cloth" (Dennett 1968: 49). Over the ensuing centuries, European cloth, ceramics, and metal rapidly replaced indigenous products in domestic contexts. The cloth has long since disappeared, a good deal of it wrapped around the dead in potlatch-like burial ceremonies that introduced the departed to the land of their ancestors or *Mputu*. What remains as mute testimony to the grisly trade in human life that took place on the now-deserted coastal plains of Loango are the shards of painted earthenware, Rhenish stoneware, and shattered fragments of wine and gin bottles which peek almost innocently from the tall grass.

To the south the trade in luxury goods to northwestern Botswana, which early-on had included iron and copper jewelry along with glass beads and marine shell from the Indian Ocean, ended around AD 1200 as powerful kingdoms centered in the Limpopo Valley cut off the long-distance trade routes across the Kalahari to the far interior. This, possibly combined with a drying climate, led to a diminished archaeological presence until early Kavango settlements reappear in the eighteenth century, settling the Okavango region "like a scattering of flies across a milk pail" according to some traditions (Denbow and Thebe 2006: 8).

The State of Cultural Heritage Management

The archaeological project ended in 1993 when the eucalyptus planting ended; civil war broke out shortly afterward. Sadly, ineffective protection of cultural resources, coupled with corporate greed and false Western assumptions about the supposed emptiness and circularity of the African past, hindered our ability to develop a more nuanced account of the cultural achievements and historical changes that took place in this poorly known part of the African continent. Although such activities had a devastating impact on the cultural heritage of the Loango coast, much was also learned as resources were marshaled to undertake a conservation and excavation program with the help of Conoco, Congolaise de Développement Forestier (CDF), and Shell. It is encouraging that in 2011 a team of archaeologists led by Dr. Ibrahima Thiaw of the Laboratoire d'Archéologie in Dakar, Senegal, was invited to conduct an archaeological survey around

Figure 9.1. View of the concrete datum marker for the excavations at Lac Ndembo. The photo, taken in 2012 by archaeologists from the Laboratoire d'Archéologie IFAN-UCAD, in Dakar, Senegal, indicates that the site had been protected since its discovery in 1990. (Photograph courtesy of Dr. Ibrahima Thiaw, Nexus Heritage/IFAN, Dakar.)

Madingo-Kayes in advance of a proposed industrial development. He found that some of the important sites designated for conservation such as BP 113 and Lac Ndembo had indeed been preserved and protected over the intervening years (Figure 9.1). Clearly, the Loango coast is no longer "off the map" in terms of conservation and heritage management.

One cannot be complacent, however. Although the sites of Divuyu and Nqoma have been afforded greater protection because the Tsodilo Hills have been declared a World Heritage Site, other sites have not been so fortunate, and there are immense gaps between the legal protection of sites at the international and national levels and the practical actions of local district and town councils that are often unaware of heritage issues – or powerless to do anything because the sites are on private property. Benfica has been destroyed by centuries of lime-works activities, for instance (Valdeyron and Da Silva Domingos 2009). Portions of the Matlapaneng site on the banks of the Thamalakane River near Maun were destroyed to build a house. Construction at safari camps continues to have an impact on Xaro and Qogana in the Okavango Delta, and valuable sites at Serondella in the Chobe Game Reserve and Nyungwe in Kasane in northern Botswana have been torn up by local development activities related to the tourist industry, which in this case is focused on wild game – not archaeology or cultural heritage.

Finally, deeply ingrained Western prejudices about the more recent African past as empty, circular, and uninformative remain all too common, despite changes in corporate mentality that have led in some cases to increased conservation measures being taken (see, for example, Lavachery et al. 2010). The cultural resources of the continent are increasingly threatened by the greater scale of new development carried out by multinational corporations from both Western and

Eastern nations, some with very different notions about their obligations and responsibilities toward the environment and cultural heritage. Legal protection for cultural heritage sites and the funding needed to conduct environmental and cultural impact assessments remain, with few exceptions, rudimentary for most of Africa. And in many countries, site protection measures, even if they are encoded in law, are in practice unenforceable due to a lack of interest, an absence of personnel trained in heritage management, and inadequate funding. As a result, the cultural resources and historical patrimony of the continent are under greater threat today than they were thirty years ago, despite a few bright spots where archaeologists, governments, and multinational corporations have found ways to cooperate to conserve important sites. Increased protection for heritage resources is vital because the information they contain provide important tools with which to scientifically fight the dark legacy of prejudice that continues to marginalize the continent and its past.

It Takes a Village …

"It takes a village to raise a child" is one of the most widespread proverbs in Africa. It means that everyone in the community has a responsibility to look after every child in the village with love and discipline. Parents cannot be everywhere to see what is happening, so everyone must be a parent. To do otherwise would be to shirk one's responsibility to the community. The end result is that children are socialized into the community as a whole, learning from those around them their responsibilities and obligations to one another as well as the social skills and cultural knowledge needed to comprehend their world and survive in it. In setting out to do archaeological projects in countries and environments with which I was not initially familiar, I was often a child in new worlds – with much to learn about their past, their peoples, and the historical trajectories that had unfolded to inform the present. Let me explain.

In our work in Loango we could not afford to stay in hotels in town, eat out in restaurants, and drive the hour and fifteen minutes each way over rough tracks to work at Tchissanga. Although this is often the procedure with fieldwork in the United States, I made the decision to live in the field close to the excavation. Tchissanga is in a fairly isolated location, however, so we had to construct a camp that included the local and international university students, the Congolese workers hired from Pointe Noire, those from villages in the more distant countryside, and ourselves. This meant that our camp on the beach became its own village as a water bowser, makeshift showers, pit latrines, storerooms, and tents were erected to house us all. Everything was done communally as we cooked, ate, and faced calamities such as the daily removal of chiques from our feet. In the process we all, Congolese and Americans alike, became both teachers and students – the roles shifting constantly as we dealt with the daily problems and pleasures of living together and getting to know one another. The Congolese taught us about the chiques, why we had become infested with them, and how to remove them from our feet. We learned through experience that younger eyes were better than old when searching for the tiny air hole through which the chiques breathed, and through which they could best be taken out. It was Albert who knew how to repair our machete by taking the stomach from a large fish caught by Bernard, stretching it like a wet sleeve over the wooden handle and then putting it in the sun for two or three days until it dried into a clear, plastic-like cover that pulled the handle tight again over the metal shaft. It was Casimir who led the attack with sling shots on the dangerous, 7-ft viper that had taken up residence around the rafter above our six-year-old daughter's bed, and Bernard who helped to diplomatically resolve an issue of a stolen pocketknife.

One cannot write of all the multicultural experiences, many small in themselves, that served to broaden our horizons and the cultural understandings that would expand our knowledge of place and past. In both Loango and the Kalahari we learned to eat, if not enjoy, meals of smoked porcupine or python with steamed manioc, or snacks of dried mopane worms (caterpillars) and sour milk. We came to appreciate in a practical way the processes through which the meat was procured by local hunters and smoked or dried for preservation in the absence of refrigeration. We learned the best types of firewood to provide heat and avoid smoke and saw how our food was prepared and cooked, divided into morsels, and served according to values grounded in gender, status, and age. My daughter learned how to select and soak the plant fibers needed to weave a basket, her hands guided by Albert's skill and knowledge. Such acts are simple but fundamental to the development of more textured understandings of different ways of life and the lenses through which people come to view their world and construct its meaning from the constellation of past and present objects and memories surrounding them. Through the daily interactions, dialogues, and cultural misunderstandings that took place in our camps in the Congo and the Kalahari, we absorbed the essence, as well as the lessons, of ethnoarchaeology as we excavated (See Denbow, Mosothwane, and Ndobochani 2008).

One of those lessons was how wry humor is a useful tool to cope with a precarious, fickle, and sometimes painful world over which we, as ordinary people, usually had little control. I am reminded, for example, of the strained laughter that accompanied my failed attempt to have a supply of Strongbow Cider available at lunch time at Divuyu. The site was a 3-kilometer, 180-meter vertical climb from our camp at the base of the hill: too far to return to camp each day for lunch. One day I had the idea that it would be great to carry a case of Strongbow up to the site and cache it under the rocks. With visions of a much improved lunch experience the workers, a polyglot crew drawn from several nearby Ju-≠Hõa, Herero, Tswana, and Mbukushu communities, took turns scrambling over the rocks up to the site bearing the heavy case on their heads. Once there, we put the cider under a rock overhang to keep it cool and out of sight of any passing hunters. The plan worked well for a few days until it unraveled one night when a passing hyena discovered the cache and proceeded to bite open each and every tin to drain it of its alcoholic contents. It evidently got drunk and fell into one of the excavation units for the next morning we could see where it had left its frantic claw marks around the edge of the unit as it tried to paw its way out. Once free, and perhaps to get even, it ate the dry leather strap from our theodolite case on its way back to the bush. Now, more than two decades later, the strap, still un-mended and held together with a small piece of wire, is a reminder of that day. Many good stories about that hyena were created in the evenings around the campfire as we ate our meals: stories about how hungry that hyena must have been to eat the dried out old leather strap; about whether it might come to visit us one night in our camp to eat our belts, shoes, or even us; and, no less important, about who might have been jealous enough to have sent the hyena to play its evil joke and consume our alcoholic stash. To all of us, through the process of working and living together, archaeology became far more than the sum of its dry, dusty bones and potsherds.

Appendix

Appendix

Table A.1. Sites located during the archaeological reconnaissance

Site No.	Site Name/location	Status	Pre-ceramic LSA 1400–650 BC	Ceramic LSA Phase 1: 1300–400 BC	Ceramic LSA Phase 2: 400–100 BC	EIA 1 Herringbone ware 150 BC–AD 500	EIA 2 CBG ware AD 300–600	EIA 3 SC ware AD 650–900	Indeterminate EIA	LIA Woven ware AD 1100–1500	LIA AD 1600–1900	Indeterminate LIA
1	Tchissanga	Planted		I		I	I				I	
2	Madingo– Kayes	Planted						I		I	I	
3	Tandou Youmbi	Planted						I				
4	Meningue	Planted				I	I				I	
5	Kayes	Conserved	I			I						
6	Gray Sand	Conserved	I				I				I	
7	BP 113	Conserved				I					I	
8	Lamba	Conserved		I		I						
9	Mvindou	Planted		I		I						
10	Fignou 4	Planted							I			
11	Fignou 1	Planted							I			
12	Liambou 5	Planted										
13	Liambou 3	Planted			I							
14	Liambou 2	Planted				I		I	I			
15	Liambou 4	Planted							I			
16	Fignou 2	Planted				I		I				
17	Champ de Tire 1	Planted			I							
18	Champ de tire2	Planted			I							
19	Ngounou 1	Planted					I					
20	Ndombo 3	Planted										
21	Ndombo 3	Planted										
22	Lac Tchitmebo	Unknown										
23		Planted										
24		Planted								I		
25		Planted										
26		Planted								I	I	
27		Planted									I	
28	Bellelo 1	Unknown									I	
29	Bellelo 2	Unknown								I	I	
30	Bellelo near sea	Unknown						I		I	I	
31	Lac Loandjili	Unknown									I	
32	Loubanzi	Unknown							I			
33	Lac Tchitembo 1	Unknown	I									
34	Lac Tchitembo 2	Unknown	I									
35	Noumbi area.	Unknown								I	I	
36	Valley East of Madingo Kayes	Planted	I								I	
37	Base of Hill	Planted									I	
38	Top of Hill	Planted									I	
39	Small hill n/river	Planted			I							
40	Kouilou Tributary	Planted										

European Trade goods									Non-ceramic artifacts						Notes
Transfer ware ca. AD 1750–1810	Sponge ware	Annular ware ca. AD 1795–1855	Maestrict AD 1863–1958	Delph ware	Westerwald Rhenish stone ware ca. AD 1650–1900	Stoneware	African clay pipe	European clay pipe	Glass	Slag	Iron	Copper	Lithics	Shell	
					I		I			I	I				Deep pits that remain. Do not replant.
										I	I				
															Human burial exposed by bulldozer. iron bracelet on left wrist.
							I			I					
					I	I				I			I		Stoneware "Luneville France" (post-1850)
											I				
										I					
												I			
												I			
													I	I	
					I		I						I		
					I										
							I								
		I		I	I		I	I							Rhennish blue & grey stoneware; black & blue annular ware; green, red and blue floral sponge ware; Toby jug; European pipe stem.
														I	
													I	I	Shell midden with stone tools.
													I	I	Shell midden with stone tools.
							I						I	I	7 African clay pipes
													I		
								I						I	
								I						I	European clay pipe with molded emblem.
													I		
													I		White sand pit with lithics eroding.

(continued)

Table A.1 *(continued)*

Site No.	Site Name/ location	Status	Pre-ceramic LSA 1400–650 BC	Ceramic LSA Phase 1: 1300–400 BC	Ceramic LSA Phase 2: 400–100 BC	EIA 1 Herringbone ware 150 BC–AD 500	EIA 2 CBG ware AD 300–600	EIA 3 SC ware AD 650–900	Indeterminate EIA	LIA Woven ware AD 1100–1500	AD 1600–1900	Indeterminate LIA
41		Planted			I						I	
42		Planted			I							
43		Planted			I							
44		Planted			I							
45		Planted					I			I	I	
46		Planted					I			I	I	
47		Planted					I					
48		Planted										
49		Planted								I		
50		Planted								I	I	
51	cutline in forest	Planted									I	
52	cutline in forest	Planted									I	
53	cutline in forest	Planted									I	
54	Lac Ndembo	Conserved					I					
55		Planted		I			I			I	I	
56	Madingo	Planted					I				I	
57	Djenno 1 lagoon	Planted										
58	Djenno 3	Planted							I			
59	Djenno 2	Planted										
60	Pointe Noire	Planted										
61	in road	Planted										
62	cayene cote	Planted							I			
63	power line road	Planted										
64	power line road	Planted			I							
65	Pointe Noire	Planted							I			
66	hill behind camp	Planted			I		I					
67	behind Filao village	Planted							I		I	
68		Planted							I			
69		Planted				I				I	I	
70	East side of slope	Planted									I	I
71		Planted				I					I	
72	low ridge coastal plain	Planted				I					I	
73		Planted							I		I	
74		Planted							I		I	
75		Planted							I		I	I
76	Below eucalptus trees	Planted							I	I	I	
77		Planted						I			I	
78		Planted						I			I	
79		Planted							I		I	
80		Planted							I		I	
81	15 m beach	Planted	I									
82		Planted						I			I	

European Trade goods									Non-ceramic artifacts						Notes
Transfer ware ca. AD 1750–1810	Sponge ware	Annular ware ca. AD 1795–1855	Maestrict AD 1863–1958	Delph ware	Westerwald Rhenish stone ware ca. AD 1650–1900	Stoneware	African clay pipe	European clay pipe	Glass	Slag	Iron	Copper	Lithics	Shell	
													I		
													I		
													I		
													I		
					I			I					I		
							I								Set of canine/dog teeth
					I		I								
															Late 19th century blue hexagon bead.
					I		I						I	I	
													I		
													I		
													I		Above 2nd lagoon.
													I		1st lagoon overlooking ocean.
													I		Sand pit at Beninois village.
													I		
															Graded area on edge of stream.
													I		
										I				I	
									I				I		
													I		
									I				I		
									I				I		
					I		I		I						Herringbone ware with bevelled rims
									I				I		
							I		I				I		
								I	I			I	I		
									I				I		
									I				I		
						I			I				I		Stoneware with "NDFOCKINK TERDAM (Likely "Wynand Fockink Amsterdam")
I	I		I	I									I		"Societe Ceramique Maestricht" (1863–1958); blue and red floral spongeware; black transfer ware.
													I		
							I		I	I			I		

(continued)

Table A.1 *(continued)*

Site No.	Site Name/ location	Status	Pre-ceramic LSA 1400–650 BC	Ceramic LSA Phase 1: 1300–400 BC	Ceramic LSA Phase 2: 400–100 BC	EIA 1 Herringbone ware 150 BC–AD 500	EIA 2 CBG ware AD 300–600	EIA 3 SC ware AD 650–900	Indeterminate EIA	LIA Woven ware AD 1100–1500	LIA AD 1600–1900	Indeterminate LIA
83		Planted			I	I	I	I				
84	Spaep Toran 213/ radio site	Unknown			I	I	I	I		I	I	
85		Planted			I	I	I					
86		Planted			I	I	I					
87	Old number 1b/14/6	Planted			I	I	I	I			I	
88		Planted									I	
89		Planted									I	
90	Below radio site #84	Planted							I		I	
91	Jackal site	Planted									I	
92	19th-cent factory	Planted			I	I	I	I			I	
93		Planted							I		I	
94		Planted								I		
95		Planted						I			I	
96		Planted				I	I		I			
97		Planted							I		I	
98		Planted										I
99	Hill	Planted									I	
100	Area 2 near tree	Planted						I			I	
101		Planted									I	
102		Planted									I	
103		Planted									I	I
104	Near old conde area	Planted							I		I	
105		Planted									I	
106		Planted							I		I	
107		Planted							I		I	
108		Planted									I	
109		Planted							I		I	
110		Planted					I					
111		Planted									I	
112		Planted									I	
113		Planted					I				I	
114	Edge forest behind conde' I	Planted					I				I	
115		Planted									I	

European Trade goods									Non-ceramic artifacts						Notes
Transfer ware ca. AD 1750–1810	Sponge ware	Annular ware ca. AD 1795–1855	Maestrict AD 1863–1958	Delph ware	Westerwald Rhenish stone ware ca. AD 1650–1900	Stoneware	African clay pipe	European clay pipe	Glass	Slag	Iron	Copper	Lithics	Shell	
													1		
												1	1		Modern copper wire.
													1		
							1	1							European clay pipe with molded "D."
					1		1		1				1		SC ware sherds.
				1			1		1						
					1	1			1						Stoneware incised "1/?an."
						1			1				1		EIA sherds on 1st beach ridge.
									1				1		
						1			1		1		1		Stream to North of site; overlooks ocean.
					1	1							1		Stoneware marked "No. 11"
					1		1				1				Square cut iron nail.
			1					1					1		Whiteware with lion and "-Stricht" (post-1887); pipe marked "Noel Pat. 176"
									1						
													1		
						1			1				1		Round blue glass bead.
									1						
									1						
						1	1					1	1		
													1	1	
							1	1				1	1		
	1		1						1				1	1	"Societe Ceramic Maastricht, Made in Holland" (1887+); pink and green floral spongeware; green and yellow painted floral ware. Green "onion" bottle
													1		
									1						Dark green bottle glass with "-MA &-" (post 1860).
						1									
			1			1			1				1	1	Stoneware with "P. Regouta C Maastricht" (1834–1970).
													1		
									1						

(continued)

Table A.1 *(continued)*

Site No.	Site Name/ location	Status	Pre-ceramic LSA 1400–650 BC	Ceramic LSA Phase 1: 1300–400 BC	Ceramic LSA Phase 2: 400–100 BC	EIA 1 Herringbone ware 150 BC–AD 500	EIA 2 CBG ware AD 300–600	EIA 3 SC ware AD 650–900	Indeterminate EIA	LIA Woven ware AD 1100–1500	Indeterminate LIA AD 1600–1900
116	Conde 1	Planted								1	
117		Planted									1
118	Low terrace over Ntombo Marsh	Planted					1				
119		Planted									1
120		Planted									1
121		Planted									1
122		Planted							1		1
123		Planted									1
124		Planted									1
125		Planted				1	1				1
126		Planted								1	1
127		Planted									
128		Planted								1	1
129		Planted							1		1
130		Planted									
131		Planted						1			
132		Planted									
133		Planted							1		1
134		Planted									1
135		Planted							1		1
136		Planted							1		1
137		Planted									1
138		Planted									1
139	"Scattered Historic"	Planted							1		1
140		Planted							1		
141		Planted			1						
142	marker 01 x 18/6	Planted					1				
143		Planted						1	1		
144		Planted							1		
145	Surface in beach sands	Planted	1								
146	100% cubano	Planted							1		1
147	Fignou 3	Planted					1				
148	D1	Planted							1		

European Trade goods									Non-ceramic artifacts						Notes
Transfer ware ca. AD 1750–1810	Sponge ware	Annular ware ca. AD 1795–1855	Maestrict AD 1863–1958	Delph ware	Westerwald Rhenish stone ware ca. AD 1650–1900	Stoneware	African clay pipe	European clay pipe	Glass	Slag	Iron	Copper	Lithics	Shell	
															Woven ware sherd.
	I		I			I			I		I				"Societe Ceramique Maestricht Made in Holland" (1887+); green, yellow, and red painted floral plate; blue, red spongeware, tin cans.
													I		
					I		I		I				I		
									I				I	I	
							I								Villeroy & Boch Wallerfangen painted floral pattern (1836–1931).
									I				I		
						I			I						Green glass bottle with "V615 5" on base (post-1870).
									I						
					I				I						
										I			I		
						I	I								
						I							I		Stoneware with "wynand – amst – " (wynand amsterdam).
															Bone fragments and goat? teeth
							I						I		Tin bowl; homemade clay pipe with lead mouthpiece.
					I	I			I						
									I				I		
					I										
						I									
I						I			I				I	I	"Warrented Imperial Cro --" transfer ware (1890+); blue, pink and green floral spongeware; Power Bishop and Stonier green transfer vase, registered 64921 (1887).
													I		
													I		
													I		
													I		
						I							I		

(continued)

Appendix

Table A.1 *(continued)*

Site No.	Site Name/ location	Status	Pre-ceramic LSA 1400–650 BC	Ceramic LSA Phase 1: 1300–400 BC	Ceramic LSA Phase 2: 400–100 BC	EIA 1 Herringbone ware 150 BC–AD 500	EIA 2 CBG ware AD 300–600	EIA 3 SC ware AD 650–900	Indeterminate EIA Woven ware AD 1100–1500	LIA AD 1600–1900	Indeterminate LIA
149	D2	Planted							I	I	I
150	D3	Planted									
151	D4	Planted									
152	D5	Planted							I		
153	Koubotchi site 6	Planted				I					
154	Machelo site 1	Planted							I		
155	Mangolo site 1	Planted							I	I	
156	Tchisseka	Planted							I		I
157	Tchiniambi 1	Planted		I							
158	Tchiniambi 2	Planted							I		
159	Tchiniambi 3	Planted									
160	Diosso	In village								I	
161	Weka 1	Unknown				I				I	
162	Weka 2	Unknown							I	I	
163	Weka 3	Unknown							I	I	
164	Weka 4	Unknown				I				I	
165	Loubanzi	partially Planted								I	
166	Lac Ndembo Manger house	partially planted							I		
167	Lac Ndembo	Conserved								I	
168		Unknown									
169	Lac Ndembo north	Planted							I		
170	Lac Ndembo south	Planted								I	
171	Fipang (Fignou 1)	Planted							I		
172		Planted									
173	Yanika	Conserved					I				
174	Fignou 4b	Conserved									I
175	Litouba	Conserved					I				
176	Ntombo	Conserved							I	I	
177	Hinda 1	Conserved			I		I			I	
178	Hinda 2	Conserved							I	I	
179	Makola 1	Planted							I		
180	Makola 2	Conserved					I				
181		Conserved						I			
182		Conserved					I				

188

Transfer ware ca. AD 1750–1810	Sponge ware	Annular ware ca. AD 1795–1855	Maestrict AD 1863–1958	Delph ware	Westerwald Rhenish stone ware ca. AD 1650–1900	Stoneware	African clay pipe	European clay pipe	Glass	Slag	Iron	Copper	Lithics	Shell	Notes
European Trade goods									Non-ceramic artifacts						
						1							1		
										1					
					1										
					1		1	1	1				1		Whiteware with maker's marks.
						1							1		
													1		
						1		1	1	1			1	1	European pipe marked "SD". Possibly Samuel Decon ca. 1729
										1					Herringbone ware.
										1	1				
					1								1		
					1				1				1		EIA ware with roulette design.
			1										1		White ware with "Societe Cer-" (post 1851); plate with blue pic-crust rim.
															Nearly complete pot; quartz and chert flakes.
															Fignou 4-type sherds.
				1									1		Quartzite; upper part of hill has historic shell middens.
										1					Unusual early ceramics, lots of iron slag
										1					2 occupations: CLSA and LIA woven ware.
															Probably 2 occupations
															Cuban firing range; no decorated sherds.
										1			3		Cuban army trenches dug through deposit.
															Alongside erosion gully.
													1		Materials eroding from gully overlooking small lake.

(continued)

Table A.1 *(continued)*

Site No.	Site Name/ location	Status	Pre-ceramic LSA 1400–650 BC	Ceramic LSA Phase 1: 1300–400 BC	Ceramic LSA Phase 2: 400–100 BC	EIA 1 Herringbone ware 150 BC–AD 500	EIA 2 CBG ware AD 300–600	EIA 3 SC ware AD 650–900	Indeterminate EIA	LIA Woven ware AD 1100–1500	AD 1600–1900	Indeterminate LIA
183	Boumenga	Planted										I
184		Conserved										I
185	Tchibindou 1	Conserved								I	I	
186	Tchibindou 2	Conserved									I	
187		Planted									I	
188	Kangou	Planted	I									
189	Kangou	Planted									I	
190	Kangou	Conserved				I						
191	lac Loufoumbi	Conserved				I						
192	lac Loufoumbi	Planted							I			
193	lac Loufoumbi	Conserved							I			
194	behind Lamba	Conserved						I				
195	behind Lamba (Casimir)	Conserved							I			
196	behind Lamba	Planted				I						
197	south of L. Loandjiri	Conserved				I						
198	south of L. Loandjiri	Conserved	I									
199	south of L. Loandjiri	Conserved				I	I					
200	south of L. Loandjiri	Conserved				I						
201	Lac Loandjiri	Conserved			I		I					
202	Lac Loandjiri	Conserved				I						I
203		Planted						I				
204	Diosso edge	Planted									I	
Total			10	3	21	26	29	24	52	24	97	9

Note: Many were occupied during more than one time period or cultural phase.

Transfer ware ca. AD 1750–1810	Sponge ware	Annular ware ca. AD 1795–1855	Maestrict AD 1863–1958	Delph ware	Westerwald Rhenish stone ware ca. AD 1650–1900	Stoneware	African clay pipe	European clay pipe	Glass	Slag	Iron	Copper	Lithics	Shell	Notes
									I						
			I						I	I					"Societe Ceramique Maestricht" (1883–86?). Also some earlier historic material with woven motifs
									I		I		I		Several pots eroding from gully; case gin bottle.
		I		I	I			I						I	Grey and blue Rhennish stoneware "#4"; 2 annular ware cups (1795–1855); floral spongeware; pie crust rim transferware. "AHV" blue and grey stoneware (Africaanche Handels Vennootschap 1856–1880).
															On west side of large ravine and in bulldozer cut.
										I					Herrinbgone ware eroding from east side of large ravine.
										I					Herringbone ware with beveled rims eroding from 3 adjacent gullys.
										I					Slag eroding from gulley.
															SC ware eroding from gulley.
													I		SC ware eroding from gully.
															Unknown ceramic type.
															Eroding from side of gully.
													I		Quartzite flakes in side of gully.
															Talc tempered CBG ware.
													I		Herringbone ware with beveled rims.
															CLSA material on south shore of lake.
					I				I	I					Herringbone ware eroding from gully along with iron bangles.
I	I	I					I								Transfer ware (1750–1810?); annular ware (19th c.); homemade clay pipe; red, green & yellow spongeware; medicine bottle with stopper.
2	5	3	7	5	23	24	23	9	40	20	13	3	86	16	

Appendix

Table A.2. Provenience of the excavated Ceramic Later Stone Age materials from Tchissanga

Unit	Depth (cm)	Decorated Sherds	Decorated Rims	Undecorated Rims	Undecorated Sherds	Stone Flakes	Micaceous grindstone	Iron
TCHISSANGA EAST								
1.5N, 125E	0–15	1	0	2	13	2		0
	15–30	11	2	3	61	5		0
	30–45	26	4	3	80	3	1	0
1.5N, 130E	0–15	0	2	0	42	4		0
	15–30	3	0	0	18	4		0
	30–35	5	1	1	89	0		0
	35–45	31	3	7	175	3	1	0
	45–55	1	0	0	3	0		0
1.5N, 135E	0–15	0	0	0	2	1		0
	15–30	2	0	0	6	5	1	0
	30–40	39	7	9	191	2		2
	40–55	3	0	1	19	2		0
0N, 140E	0–15	0	1	0	2	3		
	15–30	0	0	0	3	1		0
	30–45	12	3	1	39	7		1
	45–60	1	0	0	16	7		0
1.5N, 140E	0–10	0	0	0	4	0		0
	10–20	0	0	0	10	3		1
	20–30	0	0	0	10	0		0
	30–40	3	0	1	17	1		0
	40–52	9	3	1	40	9		0
	52–60	2	0	1	7	1		0
3N, 140E	0–30	2	0	0	11	2		0
	30–40	4	1	0	23	1		0
	40–50	8	0	3	34	1		0
	50–60	0	0	0	3	0		0
Total		163	27	33	918	67	3	4
TCHISSANGA WEST								
40N, 0E	0–15	1	0	4	6	0		0
	15–30	16	5	2	51	19		2
	30–40	7	5	7	40	106	1	0
	40–60	1	0	0	4	5		0
50N, 0E	0–10	1	1	0	6	8		2
	10–20	5	1	3	47	7		0
	20–30	15	1	4	42	7	1	0
53.5N, 3W	0–15	1	0	2	30	22		0
	15–30	7	5	4	52	67		0
55N, 0E	0–20	3	0	1	30	19		0
	20–30	10	0	3	30	54		0
55N, 1.5W	0–20	4	0	1	25	38	1	0
	20–30	18	3	0	90	48	1	0
55N, 3W	0–20	1	0	0	22	25		0
	20–30	24	12	5	151	46		0
56.5N, 0E	0–15	6	0	0	40	32		0
	15–30	12	13	4	126	185	1	0
	30–50	2	0	1	6	16		0
	50–60	0	0	0	10	19		0
56.5N, 1.5W	0–20	0	6	1	24	35		0
	20–30	11	2	4	104	125	1	0
	30–45	2	0	0	1	10		0
55N, 20E	0–15	0	1	0	6	8		0
	15–30	0	1	2	21	10		0

Unit	Depth (cm)	Decorated Sherds	Decorated Rims	Undecorated Rims	Undecorated Sherds	Stone Flakes	Micaceous grindstone	Iron
	30–45	11	8	3	83	22		3
	45–55	3	2	2	24	53		0
	55–70	0	0	0	1	19		0
56.5N, 20E	0–20	1	0	0	10	2		0
	20–35	1	1	1	0	4		0
	35–50	21	2	0	63	17		0
Total		184	69	54	1145	1028	6	7

TCHISSANGA BASE

Unit	Depth (cm)	Decorated Sherds	Decorated Rims	Undecorated Rims	Undecorated Sherds	Stone Flakes	Micaceous grindstone	Iron
T-BASE	0–25	5	2	1	30	21		0
	25–40	0	0	0	11	29		0
	40–50	2	0	3	16	57		0
	50–60	31	4	10	148	196	1	0
	60–75	5	0	4	32	27	1	0
T-BASE FEA.	0–15	0	0	1	6	8		0
	15–30	0	0	0	1	10		0
	30–40	2	0	1	17	39		0
	40–50	3	1	1	62	74		0
	50–60	3	0	3	56	65		2
	60–70	14	3	3	30	49		0
	70–80	1	0	0	17	9		0
	80–90	1	0	2	18	14	1	0
	90–100	0	0	0	2	10		0
	100–110	1	1	1	2	8		0
	110–120	0	0	1	0	3		0
	120–130	0	0	1	2	3		0
	130–140	0	0	0	0	6		0
	140–160	0	0	1	0	2		0
Total		68	11	33	450	630	3	2

TEST UNITS

Unit	Depth (cm)	Decorated Sherds	Decorated Rims	Undecorated Rims	Undecorated Sherds	Stone Flakes	Micaceous grindstone	Iron
1.5N, 100E	0–15	2	1	1	70	1		0
	15–25	5	0	1	56	0		0
	25–35	27	8	6	188	3		2
	35–50	10	0	2	38	8		0
1.5N, 40E	0–15	1	0	1	4	0		0
	15–25	0	0	0	1	1		0
	25–35	8	1	1	48	1		1
	35–45	0	0	0	5	0		0
1.5N, 80E	0–20	5	0	1	16	0		0
	20–30	12	0	1	45	0		1
	30–40	10	0	0	66	0		0
1.5N, 20W	0–15	0	2	0	19	1		8
	15–30	1	3	3	34	3		0
	30–40	20	2	6	187	0		0
	40–50	3	0	1	7	0		0
	50–60	2	0	0	16	2		0
	60–70	0	0	0	1	0		0
1.5N, 60W	0–15	0	0	0	21	0		
	15–25	2	3	3	40	2		
40N, 60E	0–15	6	0	1	26	3		0
	15–30	10	0	4	41	0		0
	30–45	5	1	1	19	1		0
60S, 120E	0–15	0	0	0	0	0		0
	15–30	0	0	0	3	0		0

(continued)

Appendix

Table A.2 *(continued)*

Unit	Depth (cm)	Decorated Sherds	Decorated Rims	Undecorated Rims	Undecorated Sherds	Stone Flakes	Micaceous grindstone	Iron
	30–40	18	4	6	147	1		0
	40–50	1	0	1	13	0		0
40S, 120E	0–20	0	0	0	4	0		0
	20–35	2	0	0	9	0		0
	35–45	0	0	0	3	0		0
20S, 120E	0–15	0	0	0	23	0		0
	15–30	0	0	1	14	1		0
	30–40	6	2	0	74	0		0
	40–50	0	0	0	0	0		0
1.5N, 157.5E	0–15	1	0	0	37	0		0
	15–30	0	0	0	7	0		0
	30–45	0	0	0	3	3		0
60N, 190E	0–15	12	3	0	76	2		0
	15–30	33	12	7	174	1		0
	30–45	1	1	0	4	0		0
20N, 190E	0–15	0	0	0	1	0		0
	15–30	6	0	0	36	0		0
	30–45	3	0	0	12	1		0
	45–55	0	0	0	0	0		0
40N, 190E	0–15	8	0	2	18	0		0
	15–30	6	2	2	25	0		0
	30–45	6	0	1	2	0		0
21.5N, 1.5W	0–20	1	0	0	2	1		0
	20–40	12	4	4	22	27		0
	40–50	0	0	0	5	4		0
Total		245	49	57	1662	67	0	12
GRAND TOTAL		660	156	177	4175	1,792	12	25

Table A.3. Provenience of excavated materials BP 113

Unit	Feature	Depth	Ceramics decorated	Ceramics undecorated	Phase 1	Phase 2	Congo Historic	European trade	Iron slag	Iron object	tuyere	Copper	Lithics chert	Lithics quartzite	Notes
No.1		0–10		1											
No.1		10–20													
No.1		20–30													
No.1		30–40													
No.1		40–50		6											micaceous sherd
No.1		50–60		3		1									
No.1		60–70													
No.1		70–80													
No.1		80–90													
No.1		90–100													
No.1		100–110													
No.2		0–10													
No.2		10–20													
No.2		20–30													
No.2		30–40		6										1	
No.2		40–50		2											
No.2		50–60													
No.2		60–70													
No.2		70–80													
No.2		80–100		8											
No.3		0–20													
No.3		20–30													
No.3		30–40		13											
No.3		40–50		13										1	
No.3		50–60	2	1	2										
No.4,ext 3		0–40		44											
No.4,ext 3		40–50		72											
No.4,ext 3		50–60	1	31	1										
No.4,ext 3	Pit 7	50–74		2											
No.4,ext 3	Pit 7	60+		7											
No.5,ext.4		0–40													
No.5,ext.4		40–50	2	15	2										
No.5,ext.4	Pit 7	50–60													
No.5,ext.4		50–55		3										1	Top of Feature 1

(continued)

Table A.3. *(continued)*

Unit	Feature	Depth	Ceramics decorated	Ceramics undecorated	Phase 1	Phase 2	Congo Historic	European trade	Iron slag	Iron object	tuyere	Copper	Lithics chert	Lithics quartzite	Notes
No.5,ext.4	Pit 7	55–103	1	21	1										
13.14e,18n		0–10													
13.14e,18n		10–20													
13.14e,18n		20–30													
13.14e,18n		30–40													
13.14e,18n		40–50													
13.14e,18n		50–60													
13.14e,18n		60–70	5	30	6										
13.14e,18n	Pit 4	80–90	2	40	2									1	
13.14e,19n		0–10													
13.14e,19n		10–20													
13.14e,19n		20–30													
13.14e,19n		30–40													
13.14e,19n		40–50													
13.14e,19n		50–60	2	14											
13.14e,19n		60–70	5	25	5										
13.14e,25n		0–10													
13.14e,25n		10–20													
13.14e,25n		20–30													
13.14e,25n		30–40													
13.14e,25n		40–50													
13.14e,25n		50–60	1	8	1										
13.14e,25n		60–70													
13.14e,25n		70–80													
14.15e,18n		0–10													
14.15e,18n		10–20													
14.15e,18n		20–30													
14.15e,18n		30–40													
14.15e,18n		40–50													
14.15e,18n		50–60	3	9											
14.15e,18n		60–70	8	74	8										ceramics corroded
14.15e,1s		0–10													
14.15e,1s		10–20													
14.15e,1s		20–30	2	8		2			1					1	
14.15e,1s		30–40		7						1				1	

15.16e, 19n	0–10						
15.16e, 19n	10–20						
15.16e, 19n	20–30						
15.16e, 19n	30–40						
15.16e, 19n	40–50						
15.16e, 19n	50–60	3	11	3			
15.16e, 19n	60–70	2	6	2	1		large sandstone frag.
15.16e, 19n	70–80						
15.16e, 17n	0–10						
15.16e, 17n	10–20						
15.16e, 17n	20–30						
15.16e, 17n	30–40						
15.16e, 17n	40–50	16	15	16			
15.16e, 17n	50–60	6	102	6	3		ceramics corroded
15.16e, 17n	60–70		58				1 bowl fragment; ceramics corroded; granite fragment
15.16e, 18n	0–10						
15.16e, 18n	10–20						
15.16e, 18n	20–30						
15.16e, 18n	30–40						
15.16e, 18n	40–50						
15.16e, 18n	50–60	1	35				
15.16e, 18n	60–70	8	23				
15.16e, 18n	70–80	1	3				
18–19e,0	0–10	0	0				
18–19e,0	20–30	0	0				
18–19e,0	30–40	0	0				
18–19,0	40–50	0	1				
19–20e,0	20–30	0	2				
19–20e,0	30–40	0	0				
19–20e,0	40–50	0	18			1	
19–20e,0	50–60	1	4				grinding stone
19–20e,0	60–70	0	0				
19–20e,0	Pit 8 70–108	3	33				2 large decorated rims

(continued)

Table A.3. *(continued)*

Unit	Feature	Depth	Ceramics		Phase		Congo	European	Iron	Iron		Copper	Lithics		Notes
			decorated	undecorated	1	2	Historic	trade	slag	object	tuyere		chert	quartzite	
19–20e,2s		0–20	0	0	0										
19–20e,2s		20–30	0	0	0										
19–20e,2s		30–40	0	6	0		3							1	
19–20e,2s		40–50	0	24	0										
19–20e,2s		50–60	0	3	0										
19–20e,2s	Pit 8	70–108	0	0	0										
24.25e,1s		0–10													
24.25e,1s		10–20													
24.25e,1s		20–30													
24.25e,1s		30–40	10	4		10									
24.25e,1s		40–50	1	15		1									
24.25e,1s		50–60		7											
24.25e,1s		60–70		1											
24.25e,1s		70–80	3	4	1	2									
24.25e,22s		0–10													
24.25e,22s		10–20													
24.25e,22s		20–30													
24.25e,22s		30–40		7											
24.25e,22s		40–50	3	39	5								1	2	
29.30e,18n		0–10													
29.30e,18n		10–20													
29.30e,18n		20–30													
29.30e,18n		30–40	1	6	1										
3-4w,40n		0–10													
3-4w,40n		10–20													
3-4w,40n		20–30	4	20	4										ceramics corroded
3-4w,40n		30–40	2	39	2										many frags.from single vessel
34.35e,19n		0–10													
34.35e,19n		10–20													
34.35e,19n		20–30													
34.35e,19n		30–40													
34.35e,19n		40–50		27						1					
4.5e,11s		0–10													
4.5e,11s		10–20													

Provenience	Depth					Remarks
4.5e,11s	20–30					
4.5e,11s	30–40					
4.5e,11s	40–50	1	1		1	
4.5e,11s	50–60	3				
4.5e,11n	0–10					
4.5e,11n	10–20					
4.5e,11n	20–30	2	2	2		
4.5e,11n	30–40	23	5	5		
4.5e,11n	40–50	10	1	1		
4.5w,10n	0–10					
4.5w,10n	10–20					
4.5w,10n	20–30					
4.5w,10n	30–40	2	2			
4.5w,40n	0–10					
4.5w,40n	10–20					
4.5w,40n	20–30	30	11	11		
4.5w,40n	30–40	1				
39–40e,0	0–10					
39–40e,0	1–20	2	2	2		1 oyster shell; sherds w/mica temper
39–40e,0	20–30	2				
39–40e,0	30–40	7				
39–4e,0	40–50	23	18	18	1	sherds w/mica temper
39–40e,0	50–60	1	1			
39–40e,0	60–70					
39–40e,1n	0–10					
39–40e,1n	10–20					
39–40e,1n	20–30					
39–40e,1n	30–40					
39–40e,1n	40–50	23	4	4	1	sherds w/mica temper
39–40e,1n	50–62	5				
48.49e,10s	0–10					
48.49e,10s	10–20	1	1			
48.49e,10s	20–30					
48.49e,10s	30–40				1	
48.49e,10s	40–50	5	5			
48.49e,10s	50–60	8	2	2		1 sandstone chunk

(continued)

Table A.3. *(continued)*

Unit	Feature	Depth	Ceramics decorated	Ceramics undecorated	Phase 1	Phase 2	Congo Historic	European trade	Iron slag	Iron object	tuyere	Copper	Lithics chert	Lithics quartzite	Notes
48.49e,10s		60–70	1	9	1										
48.49e,19n		0–10													
48.49e,19n		10–20													
48.49e,19n		20–30													
48.49e,19n		30–40	1	10		1								1	
48.49e,19n		40–50	5	26		5								2	
48.49e,19n		50–60	6	15	6										
48.49e,20n		0–10													
48.49e,20n		10–20													
48.49e,20n		20–30													
48.49e,20n		30–40													
48.49e,20n		40–50													
48.49e,20n		50–60		6											
48.49e,20n		60–70	2	3	2										
48.49e,20n	Pit 2	70–140													
48.49e,21n		0–10													
48.49e,21n		10–20													
48.49e,21n		20–30													
48.49e,21n		30–40		3											
48.49e,21n		40–50	4	14		4									
48.49e,21n		50–60	1	10	1								1	1	
48.49e,22n		0–10													
48.49e,22n		10–20													
48.49e,22n		20–30		2											
48.49e,22n		30–40													
48.49e,22n		40–50		1											
49.50e,31n		0–10													
49.50e,31n		10–20													
49.50e,31n		20–30													
49.50e,31n		30–40													
49.50e,31n		40–50													
49.50e,31n		50–60	1	6	1									1	
49.50e,31n		60–70		7						1					iron point
49.50e,10n		0–10													
49.50e,10n		10–20													

Unit	Depth (cm)						Notes
49.50e,10n	20–30						
49.50e,10n	30–40	1				1	
49.50e,10n	40–50	1	1		2		
49.50e,10n	50–60						
49.50e,10n	60–70	3	6	1			
49.50e,10n	70–80	1	6	1	2	1	
49.50e,10n	80–90		2				
49.50e,21n	0–10						
49.50e,21n	10–20						
49.50e,21n	20–30						
49.50e,21n	30–40						
49.50e,21n	40–50						
49.50e,21n	50–60	2	2		2		
49.50e,21n	60–70	1	2	1			
49.50e,10s	0–10						
49.50e,10s	10–20						
49.50e,10s	20–30						
49.50e,10s	30–40						
49.50e,10s	40–50	6	6				ceramics corroded
49.50e,10s	50–60	2	2				
49.50e,10s	50–70	3	3				
49.50e,10s	70–80	4	4				
49.50e,19n	90–170	6	7	6			vessels from same pot
Pit 6							
49.50e,20n	0–10						
49.50e,20n	10–20		1				
49.50e,20n	20–30						
49.50e,20n	30–40	1	4		1		
49.50e,20n	40–50	13	30		13		
49.50e,20n	50–60	7	29	7			
49.50e,20n	60–70	2	9	2			
49.50e,20n	70–80	1	1	1			
49.50e,20n	80–90		6				
49.50e,21n	0–10						
49.50e,21n	10–20						
49.50e,21n	20–30						
49.50e,21n	30–40						
49.50e,21n	40–50	6	11	4	6		
49.50e,21n	60–144	4	13	4		1	
Pit 5							
49.50e,40s	0–10					2	1 piece of granite

(continued)

Table A.3. *(continued)*

Unit	Feature	Depth	Ceramics		Phase	Phase	Congo	European	Iron	Iron		Copper	Lithics		Notes
			decorated	undecorated	1	2	Historic	trade	slag	object	tuyere		chert	quartzite	
49,50e,40s		10–20													
49,50e,40s		20–30													
49,50e,40s		30–40													
49,50e,40s		40–50													
49,50e,40s		50–60	1	2											
49,50e,9s		0–10													
49,50e,9s		10–20													
49,50e,9s		20–30													
49,50e,9s		30–40													
49,50e,9s		40–50		7											
49,50e,9s		50–60		1											1 frag. Sandstone
49,50e,9s		60–70		10						1					1 frag. granite
59–60e,0		0–10					1								
59–60e,0		10–20		1											
59–60e,0		20–30													
59–60e,0		30–40													
59–60e,0		40–50	2	6		2								2	
59–60e,0		50–60	2	15	2									5	
59–60,0		60–70													
5,6w,51s		0–10													
5,6w,51s		10–20													
5,6w,51s		20–30	4	32	4										
5,6w,50s		0–10													
5,6w,50s		10–20													
5,6w,50s		20–30	11	58	11									1	ceramics corroded
5,6w,50s		30–40	2	35	3										1 lower grindstone
9–10w,0		0–10		1											
9–10w,0		10–20													
9–10w,0		20–30													
9–10w,0		30–40		1											large chunk molded clay-unfired
9–10w,0		40–50	1		1										

Provenience							1 sherd with mica temper
9–10w,0 50–60							
9–10w,0 60–70							
18–19w,0 40–50		3					
18–19w,0 50–60	12	141	12				
18–19w,0 60–70							
18–19w,0 70–80							
19–20 w,0 0–10							
19–20w,0 10–20							
19–20w,0 20–30							
19–20w,0 30–40							
19–20w,0 40–50	10	115	10	1		1	
19–20w,0 50–60	8	73	8				
19–20w,0 60–70							
20w,5n 0–40							
20w,5n 40–50		4					
20w,5n 50–60		14					
20w,10n 0–30							
20w,10n 30–40		7					
20w,10n 40–50.	6	96	6				
20w,10n 50–60		3					
20w,10n 60–70							1
20w,19n 0–30					2		
20w,19n 30–40		6			6		
20w,19n 40–50	8	80	8				
20w,20n 0–10							
20w,20n 10–20							
20w,20n 20–30							
20w,20n 30–40		2					
20w,20n 40–50	25	192	25		8	1	1
21w,20n 0–30							
21w,20n 30–40					2		
21w,20n 40–50	8	56	8		1		
59.60w,0 0–10							
59.60w,0 10–20		3					
59.60w,0 20–30							
59.60w,0 30–40							
59.60w,0 40–50							
59.60w,0 50–60							

(continued)

Table A.3. *(continued)*

Unit	Feature	Depth	Ceramics decorated	Ceramics undecorated	Phase 1	Phase 2	Congo Historic	European trade	Iron slag	Iron object	tuyere	Copper	Lithics chert	Lithics quartzite	Notes
50.51e,20n		0–10													
50.51e,20n		10–20													
50.51e,20n		20–30													
50.51e,20n		30–40													
50.51e,20n		40–50	8	20	1	7									Phase 2 bowl
50.51e,20s		0–10													
50.51e,20s		10–20	2				2								lozenge decoration
50.51e,20s		20–30													
50.51e,20s		30–40													
50.51e,20s		40–50	1	3		1									
50.51e,20s		50–60	1	4		1									
50.51e,21n		0–10													
50.51e,21n		10–20		2											
50.51e,21n		20–30		12											
50.51e,21n		30–40	1	30											
50.51e,21n		40–50	5	27		4									2 bowls
50.51e,21n		50–60	4	11	2	1									
50.51e,21n		60–70	1	4	1										1 bowl
50.51e,30n		0–10													
50.51e,30n		10–20													
50.51e,30n		20–30													
50.51e,30n		30–40													
50.51e,30n		40–50		1											
50.51e,30n		50–60	5	50	2	1									
50.51e,30n		60–70		3											
50.51e,30s		0–10													
50.51e,30s		10–20													
50.51e,30s		20–30													
50.51e,30s		30–40													
50.51e,30s		40–50	1	9		1									
50.51e,30s		50–60	2	11											
50.51e,31n		0–10													
50.51e,31n		10–20													

									blue and white annular glass bead
50.51e,31n	20–30								
50.51e,31n	30–40								
50.51e,31n	40–50								
50.51e,31n	50–60	1						6	1
50.51e,40n	0–10								
50.51e,40n	10–20								
50.51e,40n	20–30								
50.51e,40n	30–40								
50.51e,40n	40–50			1					1
50.51e,40n	50–60							3	1
50.51e,40n	60–70							2	1
50.51e,40n	70–80								
50.51e,40n	80–90								1
59.60e,1s	0–10								
59.60e,1s	10–20								
59.60e,1s	20–30								
59.60e,1s	30–40								
59.60e,1s	40–50	2						17	
6.7w,50s	0–10								
6.7w,50s	10–20								
6.7w,50s	20–30								
6.7w,50s	30–40							4	1
64.65e.1s	0–10								
64.65e.1s	10–20								
64.65e.1s	20–30								
64.65e.1s	30–40						1	29	1
64.65e.1s	40–50						1	6	1
64.65e.1s	50–60	2			2		2	10	2
76.77e,34s	0–10				2			2	2
76.77e,34s	10–20				2			2	2
76.78e,33s	0–10	2	2	1	2		2	3	3
77.78e,33s	10–20								
77.78e,33s	20–30								
77.78e,33s	30–40					4		8	4
77.78e,33s	40–50					14		21	14
77.78e,33s	50–60								
77.78e,33s	60–70								
77.78e,33s	70–80							5	2

(continued)

Table A.3. *(continued)*

Unit	Feature	Depth	Ceramics		Phase	Phase	Congo	European	Iron	Iron		Copper	Lithics		Notes
			decorated	undecorated	1	2	Historic	trade	slag	object	tuyere		chert	quartzite	
77-78e,13s		0–10		3				1							blue sponge ware
77-78e,13s		10–20													
77-78e,13s		20–30													
77-78e,13s		30–40													
77-78e,13s		40–50	17	30	1	17									
77-78e,13s		50–60	2	15	2										
77-78e,13s		60–70	8	21	9										
77-78e,13s	Pit 1	70–145	15	42					3					5	
77-78e,14s		0–10	1				1	1							blue and white annular glass trade bead
77-78e,14s		10–20					1								
77-78e,14s		20–30													
77-78e,14s		30–40													
77-78e,14s		40–50	15	9	1	13									
77-78e,14s		50–60	20	5	3	16									
77-78e,14s		60–70	5	14	2	3								2	
77-78e,14s		70–80	5	5	4	1								7	
77-78e,14s		80–90		4											
77-78e,14s		90–100													
77-78e,14s		100–110		11										2	
77-78e,14s	Pit 1	70–80	1	9	1				1						in squares 77,78e,13–14s and 78,79e,13–14s
77-78e,15s		0–10	1	1	1										
77-78e,15s		10–20													
77-78e,15s		20–30	1	2	1		2								ceramics very eroded
77-78e,15s		30–40													
77-78e,15s		40–50													
77-78e,15s		50–60		12		12									ceramics tempered with talc and mica
77-78e,15s		60–70													
77-78e,15s		70–80	11	11	1	10								2	

Context	Depth	1	2	3	4	
77.78e,15s	80–90	12	2	1	1	
78–79e,0	0–20				1	micaceous sherds with talc temper
78–79e,0	20–30					
78–79e,0	30–40	1				
78–79e,0	40–50	23	55			
78–79e,0	50–60	6	6			
78–79e,0	60–70					
78–79e,2s	0–20					
78–79e,2s	20–30				2	
78–79e,2s	30–40		3			
78–79e,2s	40–50	20	37	20		
78–79e,2s	50–60	1	3	1		
78–79e,2s	60–70		2			
78–79e,2s	70–80					
78–79e,3s	0–20					
78–79e,3s	20–30					
78–79e,3s	30–40					
78–79e,3s	40–50	6	9	6	4	
78–79e,3s	50–60	8	14	8	1	
78–79e,3s	60–70	1	8	1	1	
78–79e,3s	70–80					
78–79e,4s	0–20					NIL:
78–79e,4s	20–30					
78–79e,4s	30–40		11	1	1	large decorated lug
78–79e,4s	40–50	1	10	1		
78–79e,4s	50–60	1		3	2	
78–79e,4s	60–70	3	12		1	
78–79e,4s	70–80		1			
78–79e,4s	80–90		2			
78–79e,4s	90–100	1		1		
78–79e,4s	100–110		1			
79–80e,0	0–20					
79–80e,0	20–30	2	1	2		
79–80e,0	30–40		1			mica and talc temper
79–80e,0	40–50	4	14		1	
79–80e,0	50–60	1	14			

(continued)

Table A.3. (continued)

Unit	Feature	Depth	Ceramics		Phase		Congo Historic	European trade	Iron slag	Iron object	tuyere	Copper	Lithics chert	Lithics quartzite	Notes
			decorated	undecorated	1	2									
79–80e,2s		0–20													
79–80e,2s		20–30													
79–80e,2s		30–40	1	4		1									
79–80e,2s		40–50	11	53		11								2	1 large dec rim
79–80e,2s		50–60	8	15	8									7	
79–80e,2s		60–70	2	33	2								3	11	
79–80e,3s		0–20													
79–80e,3s		20–30													
79–80e,3s		30–40				1								3	
79–80e,3s		40–50	12	19	0	12									
79–80e,3s		50–60	4	6	4									2	
79–80e,3s		60–80		8									1	20	
79–80e,4s		0–20.													
79–80e,4s		20–30													
79–80e,4s		30–40													
79–80e,4s		40–50	11	16		11								1	
79–80e,4s		50–60		4											
79–80e,4s		60–70		2						5				15	
79–80e,4s		70–80		1										6	
79–80e,4s		80–90											8	197	
79–80e,4s		90–100											15	210	
79–80e,4s		100–110												8	
80–81e,4s		0–20													
80–81e,4s		20–30													
80–81e,4s		30–40	1			1									
80–81e,4s		40–50	28	62	28										
80–81e,4s		50–60	3	25	3										
78.79e,13s		0–10	1				1								
78.79e,13s		10–20													
78.79e,13s		20–30		18											
78.79e,13s		30–40	6	33	5	6									
78.79e,13s		40–50	7			2			1		1			2	tuyere mouth
78.79e,13s		50–60													
78.79e,13s		60–70		18						1				1	
78.79e,14s		0–10													
78.79e,14s		10–20													

78.79e,14s	20–30											
78.79e,14s	30–40											
78.79e,14s	40–50	2	3		2							
78.79e,14s	50–60		4					1				
78.79e,14s	60–70	4	37	4				5	1	3		carbonized cucurbit seed;tuyere mouth
78.79e,14s	70–80	7	18		7						1	
78.79e,14s	80–90											
78.79e,14s	90–100											
78.79e,14s	100–110		3									
78.79e,15s	0–10											
78.79e,15s	10–20											
78.79e,15s	20–30											
78.79e,15s	30–40											
78.79e,15s	40–50											
78.79e,15s	50–60											
78.79e,15s	60–70	4	10							2	4	corroded ceramics
78.79e,15s	70–80	2	18		1			1			1	corroded ceramics
78.79e,15s	80–90	3	13	1						1	1	sandstone
78.79e,15s	90–100	1	2	1								decorated on interior of lip
78.79e,15s	100–110	1	2									
78.79e,33s	0–10	1	1			1	1					green sponge ware
78.79e,33s	10–20		1			1						
78.79e,33s	20–30											
79.80e,10n	0–10											
79.80e,10n	10–20											
79.80e,10n	20–30											
79.80e,10n	30–40	7	8		7							mica temper
79.80e,10n	40–50	2	8		2							
79.80e,10n	50–60		11		1						1	mica temper
79.80e,10n	60–70		10		1							mica temper
79.80e,10n	70–80		7									
79.80e,10n	80–90		7									ceramics corroded
79.80e,10n	90–100	1	12									pot with a flat base
79.80e,10n	100–110	3	23					1			1	

(continued)

Table A.3. *(continued)*

Unit	Feature	Depth	Ceramics decorated	Ceramics undecorated	Phase 1	Phase 2	Congo Historic	European trade	Iron slag	Iron object	tuyere	Copper	Lithics chert	Lithics quartzite	Notes
79.80e,15s		0–10	1					1							
79.80e,15s		10–20													
79.80e,15s		20–30													
79.80e,15s		30–40		1											
79.80e,15s		40–50	9	3											
79.80e,15s		50–60	8	20											
79.80e,15s		60–70	1	17											
79.80e,15s		70–80	4	6											
79.80e,15s		80–90		2											
79.80e,15s		90–100													
79.80e,15s		100–110		1										1	
79.80e,20n		0–10													
79.80e,20n		10–20													
79.80e,20n		20–30													
79.80e,20n		30–40													
79.80e,20n		40–50		5											
79.80e,20n		50–60		5						1					
79.80e,20n		60–70		2											
79.80e,20n		70–80		4											
79.80e,20n		80–90													
79.80e,20n		90–100													
79.80e,20n		100–110		1											
79.80e,20n		110–120													
79.80e,25s		0–10													
79.80e,25s		10–20									13					13 fragments from "ivory" handled pocket knife
79.80e,25s		20–30													
79.80e,25s		30–40													
79.80e,25s		40–50		1											
79.80e,25s		50–60		8											
79.80e,25s		60–70	1	7											

														Notes
79.80e,35s	0–10	3	10				3							2 glass frags; 1red and green sponge ware
79.80e,35s	10–20	1	4				1							red and green sponge ware
79.80e,35s	20–30													
79.80e,35s	30–40	1			1									micaceous sherd
79.80e,35s	40–50		1											
79.80e,35s	50–60	1	127		2									2 micaceous sherds
79.80e,35s	60–70							3						
79.80e,55s	0–10		4				1							red and brown spongeware
79.80e,55s	10–20		4											
79.80e,55s	20–30		1				2							red and green spongeware
79.80e,55s	30–40													
79.80e,55s	40–50													
79.80e,55s	50–60													
79.80e,55s	60–70													
79.80e,55s	70–80													
79.80e,5s	0–10													
79.80e,5s	10–20													
79.80e,5s	20–30													
79.80e,5s	30–4–													
79.80e,5s	40–50	2	2											hard surface
79.80e,5s	50–60		4											
79.80e,5s	60–70		1											
79.80e,5s	70–80		1											
80.81e,10n	0–10													
80.81e,10n	10–20													
80.81e,10n	20–30													
80.81e,10n	30–40	6	10		5									
89.90e,20n	0–10													
89.90e,20n	10–20													
89.90e,20n	20–30													
89.90e,20n	30–40	1												
89.90e,20n	40–50	1	7										1	bowl
Total		749	3840	370	304	21	13	26	47	7	2	31	569	

Appendix

Table A.4. Provenience of materials recovered from the Lac Ndembo excavations

	Unit	Depth	Diagnostic sherds	Quartzite flakes & fragments	Quartzite cobble	Burned limestone	Rounded pebble	Iron slag	Iron artifact
Area A	16N, 19E	20–30	5						
	16N, 19E	30–40	2						
	16N, 19E	40–50				2			
	16N, 20E	30–40	1						
	17N, 18E	40–50	7						
	17N, 19E	30–40	2						
	17N, 19E	40–50	2			1	2		
	17N, 20E	30–40	2	1		2			
	17N, 20E	40–50				2			
	17N, 21E	40–50	2						
	18N, 18E	40–50	1						
	18N, 19E	40–50	1						
	18N, 20E	30–40	2						
	18N, 20E	40–50	6						
	18N, 21E	30–40	4						
	18N, 21E	40–50			1		2	1	
	18N, 19E	30–40					1		
	18N, 19E	40–50				2			
	19N, 18E	40–50	1						
	19N, 19E	40–50	2				2		
	19N, 20E	20–30	1						
	19N, 20E	40–50	2						
	19N, 21E	30–40	2						
	19N, 21E	40–50	2						
	20N, 16E	30–40	3	1					
	20N, 17E	30–40	1						
	20N, 17E	40–50	1						
	20N, 18E	30–40	2						
	20N, 19E	30–40	1						
	20N, 19E	40–50	2						
	20N, 20E	40–50	5			3			
	20N, 21E	40–50	2						
	20N, 40E	10–20						1	
	21N, 17E	30–40	1						
	21N, 18E	40–50	1		1				
	21N, 19E	40–50	1						
	21N, 20E	40–50	1						
	21N, 21E	30–40			1				
Area B	19N, 40W	30–40	2						1 ring
	20N, 39W	30–40	1						
	20N, 40W	30–40	4						1
	20N, 41W	30–40	1						
	20N, 60W	30–40			1	1			
Total			76	2	4	13	7	2	2

Notes

1. Behind the Scenes of Research

1. There is some uncertainty about the origin of the name Pointe Indienne, which forms the southern end of Loango Bay. According to E. Ravenstein (1901: 651, 629), after leaving Mayumba Bay in southern Gabon, Diogo Cão passed the "Paps of Bamba" (*os duos montes*) at the mouth of the Kouilou River and entered Loango Bay, which he named "Praia Formosa de S. Domingos." Ravenstein (1901: 629) suggests this may mean he landed there on that saint's day, August 4, 1483. Concerning the name of the point and the bay he later adds that, "Castillo, guided by Pimental, identifies [Jew's Bay] with Kilongo bay … and this I accept, although the G. do Judeu of Behaim's [who accompanied Cao] globe seems to represent Loango bay, whilst his Golfo de S. Nicolao … occupies the place of Kilongo. The Jew, later on, was converted into an Indian, and hence already on Reinel's chart (ca. 1520), the bay between the Cabo Segundo and the Duas moutas at the Kuilu, was called Golfo do Indio. The Repertorio dos Tempos (1521), however, has an Angra da Judia two degrees to the north of the Congo, and Reinel's position only suits Kilongo bay. Later authorities distinguish between a Golfo do Judeu and a G. do Indio, identifying the latter with Loango Bay. This I believe to be a duplication due to corrupt spelling."

2. In March 2012 another large munitions store exploded on the outskirts of Brazzaville, killing more than 200 people. In this instance the suburbs of Brazzaville had over the years been allowed to grow and surround the storage facilities, which dated to the colonial era. Similar concerns about political unrest caused unease among the population.

3. In the spelling system created by Dennett, he used the letter *X* to stand for what is today *Tch* so, for example, Xissanga is his term for present-day Tchissanga, the location of one of the archaeological sites excavated. His spelling will henceforth be used in the quotations from Dennett, but the modern spellings will be used elsewhere.

4. "Congo-Brazzaville Rail Wreck: Toll Rises," *iol news* (June 23 2010), http://www.iol.co.za/index. php?from=rss_Africa&set_id=1&click_id=68&art_id=nw20100623093049604C736702 (accessed April 6, 2013).

5. Use of the term *Neolithic* is fraught with problems in Central Africa. Although the term was originally coined to refer to populations with a Stone Age tool technology, but practicing some form of food production, in Central Africa direct evidence for food production in the form of carbonized seeds, pollen, or phytoliths from domesticated plants is often missing. Nonetheless, the term is commonly used, particularly in the French literature (cf. Clist 2005), to refer to early sites containing stone tools along with pottery and deep pits filled with organic refuse that suggest a less mobile hunting-and-gathering lifestyle. In southern Africa (Lombard et al. 2012) and parts of West Africa (Stahl 1994), sites with similar materials would generally be referred to as "Ceramic Later Stone Age," or CLSA. In less-widespread use is the term "Stone to Metal Age" (SMA), referring to sites with similar constellations of ceramics, deep pits containing evidence for intensive use of oil palms, and sometimes occasional

traces of iron working (Lavachery et al. 2010). Because of its applicability to the wider variety of cases in Central and southern Africa discussed in this book, the term *Ceramic Later Stone Age* is used.

2. Pride and Prejudice: Big Oil, Eucalyptus, and the People without History

1. A description of this episode can be found at "Nigeria Waste Imports from Italy (NIGERIA)," n.d., http://www1.american.edu/TED/nigeria.htm (accessed on April 6, 2013).

2. There is debate about the safety of Roundup in the environment (Williams, Kroes, and Munro 2000; Goldstein et al. 2002; Benachour and Séralini 2009).

3. This is my own slightly loose translation of President Sarkozy's words. Here is the French text of that portion of his speech. "Le drame de l'Afrique, c'est que l'homme africain n'est pas assez entré dans l'histoire. Le paysan africain, qui depuis des millénaires, vit avec les saisons, dont l'idéal de vie est d'être en harmonie avec la nature, ne connaît que l'éternel recommencement du temps rythmé par la répétition sans fin des mêmes gestes et des mêmes paroles. Dans cet imaginaire où tout recommence toujours, il n'y a de place ni pour l'aventure humaine, ni pour l'idée de progrès. Dans cet univers où la nature commande tout, l'homme échappe à l'angoisse de l'histoire qui tenaille l'homme moderne mais l'homme reste immobile au milieu d'un ordre immuable où tout semble être écrit d'avance.... Le problème de l'Afrique, ce n'est pas de s'inventer un passé plus ou moins mythique pour s'aider à supporter le présent mais de s'inventer un avenir avec des moyens qui lui soient propres. ... Le défi de l'Afrique, c'est d'entrer davantage dans l'histoire ... c'est de cesser de toujours répéter, de toujours ressasser, de se libérer du mythe de l'éternel retour, c'est de prendre conscience que l'âge d'or qu'elle ne cesse de regretter, ne reviendra pas pour la raison qu'il n'a jamais existé. ... Le problème de l'Afrique, c'est de rester fidèle à elle-même sans rester immobile."

4. "Glyphosate," *Extension Toxicology Network*, May 1994, http://pmep.cce.cornell.edu/profiles/extoxnet/dienochlor-glyphosate/glyphosate-ext.html (accessed on April 6, 2013).

3. Natural and Cultural Environment

1. The ratio of the two stable isotopes of carbon, ^{13}C to ^{12}C, known as $\delta^{13}C$, in a soil sample can be used to differentiate between carbon from plants such as tropical grasses that use C4 carbon fixation in photosynthesis and carbon from trees or shrubs that use C3 fixation. $\delta^{13}C$ can, therefore, be used to measure vegetation shifts from open savannah grasslands to closed forest or mixed forest and shrub habitats over time.

2. For a debate on the evidence for early banana cultivation in Cameroon, see Vansina (2003), Mbida et al. (2003, 2004), and Neumann et al. (2012: 56).

3. The use of *Mundele, mundare* and related variants to refer to both Europeans and maize is found in Western Bantu languages in zones B, C, H, K, L, and R (Bastin et al. 2003), as well as in some Khwe languages such as Kwadi in southern Angola (Bostoen 2007b: 21). Related terms linking Europeans with maize are also found in Ghana where in the Dangme languages of the coast *befo* stands for corn/maize and *Befono* for "corn owner," the term for a white man or westerner. In the Akan language, the word for maize/corn is *bro*, and westerners are known as *Obroni* or "corn people" (William Gblerkpor, personal communication, September 2012).

4. Proyart mistakes this for the pistachio (Proyart 1814: 551). These terms also appear to be the root forms for "Goober" and "Pindar" used in the American South. Van den Broecke describes, "large peas known ... as *ingobos*" in Loango. This is doubtless the origin of the term *goober* in the U.S. South (La Fleur 2000: 101, 101n2). Burton (1876) also attributes the word *pindar* used for peanuts in the southern United States to the Loango term.

4. Preservation: Heritage and Reconnaissance

1. According to Jan Vansina (personal communication, June 2012) the *Loa* in Loango and Loandjili may be a connective referring to an unstated noun beginning with the prefix *lu*, perhaps *luvila* meaning "clan."

5. Ceramic Later Stone Age Excavations

1. Important exceptions to this generalization are dates for banana phytoliths in Cameroon as early as 500 BC (De Langhe, Swennen, and Vuylsteke 1994–1995; Mbida et al. 2001, 2004). Even earlier dates come from Uganda on the eastern side of the tropical forest, where they are dated to approximately 3000 BC (Lejju, Robertshaw, and Taylor 2006; Neumann and Hildebrand 2009). Bananas were first domesticated in Indonesia, so these early dates for their transfer to Africa imply much greater antiquity for Indian Ocean trade than was once thought.

2. For a general discussion see Alpern 2005. More recently, Augustin Holl and E. Zangato (2010) have argued that iron working was independently invented in sub-Saharan Africa in the second millennium BC. The entire 2010 issue of *Journal of African Archaeology*, vol. 8, no. 1, is devoted to a discussion of this from both positive and negative standpoints. Clist (2012b) updates this debate and argues that the "more robust evidence" would place the inception of iron smelting in West, Central, and East Africa after 800 cal BC. In an interesting speculation, Clist (2012b: 79–80) also suggests the possibility that iron smelting technology could have been introduced independently to East Africa via sources from south Asia traveling across the Indian Ocean. One scenario suggests such Asiatic trade networks could even be related to early contacts that brought bananas to East Africa in the last two millennia BC (De Langhe et al. 1994/1995; Mbida et al. 2004; Lejju et al. 2006) and, moving in the opposite direction, millet (*P. glaucum*) to India by the middle of the second millennium BC (Weber 1998).

6. The Early Iron Age

1. UTM (Universal Transverse Mercator) GPS coordinates for BP 113 and Lac Ndembo were kindly provided by Dr. Ibrahima Thiaw, Nexus Heritage/IFAN, BP206, Dakar-Fann, Senegal.

2. The mango tree is said to have arrived in East Africa as early as the tenth century AD from Asia. Ibn Battuta, a Muslim geographer with a fondness for describing local cuisine during his travels, mentions it in his visit to Mogadishu in the fourteenth century (Watson 1983: 72–73). I am unsure of the date of its arrival on the Atlantic coast of Central Africa. Although the trees can live to an age of more than 300 years, during the archaeological reconnaissance they appeared to be consistently associated only with younger sites dating to the nineteenth and twentieth centuries. They were never found growing wild on the savanna, only in former habitation areas. During the reconnaissance, old mango trees acted as convenient markers for the locations of nineteenth century settlements.

3. Aromatic copal was exported from East Africa to India and America in the nineteenth century to be used for incense and varnish (Sunseri 2009). It was also burned as ceremonial incense by pre-Columbian Mayan societies in Mesoamerica (Stross 1997).

7. Later Iron Age Sites and the Historic Period

1. The original reads "ils vont quérir en des mines fort éloignées, comme à Sondi qui est sur le chemin de Pombo au devant du pays des Abyssins. Au mois de septembre une troupe de forgerons part pour Sondi, et étant arrivés vers les montagnes où sont les mines de cuivre, y font travailler leurs esclaves.

Ils fondent et purifient ce cuivre sur les lieux […] Ces forgerons s'en retournent au mois de mai apportant outre le cuivre quelques dents d'éléphants" (Dapper 1686).

8. Opening Pandora's Box: From Loango to the Okavango

1. Seed samples identified by J.M.J. de Wet, University of Illinois, in a 1985 personal communication to Denbow.
2. Seed samples identified by J.M.J. de Wet in a 1985 personal communication to Denbow.

Bibliography

Alpern, S. 2005 Did they or didn't they invent it? Iron in sub-Saharan Africa. *History in Africa* **32**:41–94.

Alves, I., Coelho, M., Gignoux, C., Damasceno, A., Prista, A., and Rocha, J. 2011 Genetic homogeneity across Bantu-speaking groups from Mozambique and Angola challenges Early Split scenarios between East and West Bantu populations. *Human Biology* **83**(1):13–38.

Anciaux de Faveaux, E., and de Maret, P. 1984 Premières datations pour la fonte du cuivre au Shaba (Zaïre). *Bulletin Société Royale Belge d'Anthropologie et de Préhistoire* **95**:5–20.

Andriamirado, S. 1984 *Le Défi du Congo-Océan: ou l'épopée d'un chemin de fer.* Turin: G. Canale.

Arazi, N. 2009 Cultural research management in Africa: challenges, dangers and opportunities. *Azania: Archaeological Research in Africa* **44**(1): 95–106.

Badenhorst, S. 2002 The ethnography, archaeology, rock art, and history of goats (*Capra hircus*) in Southern Africa: an overview. *Anthropology of Southern Africa* **25**(3–4):96–103.

Bahuchet, S. 1992 *Histoire d'une Civilisation Forestière I: dans la forêt d'Afrique Centrale, les pygmées Aka et Baka.* Louvain: Peeters.

Bahuchet, S. 1993a *Histoire d'une Civilisation Forestière II: La rencontre des agriculteurs. Les pygmées parmi les peuples d'Afrique Centrale.* Louvain: Peeters.

Bahuchet, S. 1993b History of the inhabitants of the Central African rain forest: perspectives from comparative linguistics. In *Tropical Forests, People and Food. Biocultural Interactions and Applications to Development.* C. Hladik, A. Hladik, O. Linares, H. Pagezy, A. Semple, and M. Hadley, eds. Pp. 37–54. Man and the biosphere series. Paris: UNESCO.

Barbour, J. and Wandiba, S. 1989 *Kenyan Pots and Potters.* Nairobi: Oxford University Press.

Bassani, E. and Monzino, C. 1987 *Un Cappuccino Nell'Africa nera del Seicento: I disegni dei manoscritti araldi del Padre Giovanni Antonio Cavazzi da Montecuccolo.* Milan: Associazione degli Amici dell'Arte Extraeuropea.

Bastin, Y., Coupez, A., and Mann, M. 1999 *Continuity and Divergence in the Bantu Languages: Perspectives from a Lexicostatistic Study.* Annales 162. Tervuren: Royal Museum for Central Africa.

Bastin, Y., Coupez, A., Mumba, E., and Schadeberg, T. 2003 Reconstructions lexicales Bantoues 3. Online database: http://linguistics.africamuseum.be/BLR3.html.

Benachour, N., and Séralini, G. 2009 Glyphosate formulations induce apoptosis and necrosis in human umbilical, embryonic, and placental cells. *Chemical Research in Toxicology* **22**(1):97–105.

Bisson, M. 2000 Precolonial copper metallurgy: sociopolitical context. In *Ancient African Metallurgy: The Socio-Cultural Context.* J.C. Vogel, ed. Walnut Creek, CA: AltaMira Press.

Blench, R. 1999 Are the Pygmies an ethnographic fiction? In *Central African Hunter-Gatherers in a Multidisciplinary Perspective: Challenging Elusiveness.* K. Biesbrouck, S. Elders, and R. Gerda, eds. Pp. 41–60. Leiden: University of Leiden.

Blench, R. 2006 *Archaeology, Language and the African Past.* Lanham, MD: Altamira Press.

Bordes, F. 1979 *Typologie du Paléolithique.* Paris: Éditions du Centre National de la Recherche Scientifique.

Bostoen, K. 2005 Linguistic evidence for early plant food-processing: observations from Bantu pottery and oil palm vocabulary. *Proceedings of the 12th Panafrican Archaeologial Association for Prehistory and Related Studies.* Gaborone, Botswana, July 2005.

Bostoen, K. 2006/2007 Pearl millet in early Bantu speech communities in Central Africa: a reconsideration of the lexical evidence. *Afrika und Übersee* **89**:183–213.

Bibliography

Bostoen, K. 2007a Pots, words and the Bantu problem: on lexical reconstruction and early African history. *Journal of African History* **28**(2):173–199.

Bostoen, K. 2007b Bantu plant names as indicators of linguistic stratigraphy in the Western Province of Zambia. In *37th Annual Conference on African Linguistics, University of Oregon.* D. Payne and J. Peña, eds. Pp. 16–29. Somerville, MA: Cascadilla Proceedings Project.

Bostoen, K. and Sands, B. 2012 Clicks in South-western Bantu languages: contact-induced vs. language-internal lexical change. In *Proceedings of the 6th World Congress of African Linguistics.* M. Brenzinger and A. Fehn, eds. vol. 5. Pp. 129–140. Cologne: Köppe Verlag.

Bousman, C. 1998 The chronological evidence for the introduction of domestic stock into Southern Africa. *African Archaeological Review* **15**(2):133–150.

Brncic, T., Willis, K., Harris, D., and Washington, R. 2007 Culture or climate? The relative influences of past processes on the composition of the lowland Congo rainforest. *Philosophical Transactions of the Royal Society B: Biological Sciences* **362**(1478):229–242.

Browne, W. 1898 *A Treatise on the Law of Trade-marks and Analogous Subjects: Firm-Names, Business-Signs, Good-Will, Labels, &c.* Boston: Little, Brown, and Co.

Burton, R. F. 1876 *Two Trips to Gorilla Land and the Cataracts of the Congo.* Vol 2. London: Sampson, Low, Marston, Low and Searle.

Campbell, A., Robbins, L., and Taylor, M., eds. 2010 *Tsodilo Hills: Copper Bracelet of the Kalahari.* East Lansing: Michigan State University Press.

Campbell, J. 1835 *Journal of Travels in South Africa.* London: Religious Tract Society.

Childe, V. G. 1925 *The Dawn of European Civilization.* London, New York: K. Paul, Trench A. A. Knopf.

Clark, J. D. 1966 *The Distribution of Prehistoric Culture in Angola.* Subsídios para a história, arqueologia e etnografia dos povos da Lunda. 79. Dundo, Angola: Publicações Culturais da companhia de diamantes de Angola.

Clark, J. D. 1968 *Further Paleo-anthropological Studies in Northern Lunda.* Lisbon: Companhia de Diamantes de Angola (Diamang) Servi.

Clark, J. D. 1970 *The Prehistory of Africa.* London: Thames & Hudson.

Clist, B. 1986 Le Néolithique en Afrique Centrale: état de la question et perspective d'avenir. *L'Anthropologie* **90**(2):217–232.

Clist, B. 1987 La fin de l'Age de la Pierre et les débuts de la métallurgie du fer au Gabon: résultats prélimi-naires 1986–1987. *Nsi: Bulletin de Liaison des CICIBA* **2**:24–28.

Clist, B. 1989 Archaeology in Gabon, 1886–1988. *African Archaeological Review* **7**(1):59–95.

Clist, B. 1995 Archaeological work in Gabon during 1993 and 1994. *Nyame Akuma* **43**: 18–21.

Clist, B. 2005 Des premiers villages aux premiers Européens autour de l'estuaire du Gabon: quatre millé-naires d'interactions entre l'homme et son milieu. PhD dissertation, Faculté de Philosophie et Lettres, Université Libre de Bruxelles.

Clist, B. 2012a Pour une archéologie du royaume Kongo: la tradition de Mbafu. *Azania: Archaeological Research in Africa* **47**(2):175–209.

Clist, B. 2012b Vers une réduction des préjugés et la fonte des antagonismes: un bilan de l'expansion de la métallurgie du fer en Afrique sud-Saharienne. *Journal of African Archaeology* **10**(1):71–84.

Clist, B., and Lanfranchi, R. 1992 Contribution a l'étude de la sédentarisation en République Populaire d'Angola. *Leba* **7**:245–268.

Coelho, M., Sequeira, F., Luiselli, D., Beleza, S., and Rocha, J. 2009 On the edge of Bantu expansions: mtDNA, Y chromosome and lactase persistence genetic variation in Southwestern Angola. *BMC Evolutionary Biology* **9**, 80 (DOI: 10.1186/1471–2148–9–80).

Comaroff, J. and Comaroff, J. L. 1997 *Of Revelation and Revolution: The Dialectics of Modernity on a South African Frontier.* Vol. 2. Chicago: University of Chicago Press.

Connor, R. 1994 African animal trypanosomiases. In *Infectious Diseases of Livestock with Special Reference to Southern Africa,* J. Coetzer, G. Thomson, and C. Tustin, eds. Pp. 167–205. Cape Town: Oxford University Press.

Cruz de Carvalho, E., Vieira da Silva, J., and Morais, J. 1973 *The Agricultural Regions of Angola.* Vol. 10. Los Angeles: University of California Press.

Daines, S. 1991 Geomorphology of the Kouilou basin in Congo. In *Flore et Faune du Bassin du Kouilou (Congo).* R. Dowsett and F. Dowsett-Lemaire, eds. Pp. 13–16. Jupille-Liège, Belgium: Tauraco Press.

Dapper, O. 1686 *Description de l'Afrique.* Amsterdam: Wolfgang, Waesberge, Boom et Van Someren.

de Filippo, C., Bostoen, K., Stoneking, M., and Pakendorf, B. 2012 Bringing together linguistic and genetic evidence to test the Bantu expansion. *Proceedings of the Royal Society B* (23 May) (DOI: 10.1098/rspb.2012.0318).

de Langhe, E., Swennen, R., and Vuylsteke, D. 1994/1995 Plantain in the early Bantu world. *Azania* **29–30**:147–160.

de Luna, K. 2012 Surveying the boundaries of historical linguistics and archaeology: early settlement in South Central Africa. *African Archaeological Review* **29**:209–251.

de Maret, P. 1982a New survey of archaeological research and dates for West-Central and North-Central Africa. *Journal of African History* **23**(1):1–15.

de Maret, P. 1982b The Iron Age in the West and South. In *The Archaeology of Central Africa*. F. van Noten, D. Cahen, P. de Maret, E. Mieyersons, and E. Roche eds. Pp. 77–96. Graz, Austria: Akademishe Druk.

de Maret, P. 1986 The Ngovo group: an industry with polished stone tools and pottery in lower Zaire. *African Archaeological Review* **4**:103–133.

de Maret, P. 1994/1995 Pits, pots and the far-west streams. *Azania* **29–30**:318–323.

Degrandpré, L. 1801 *Voyage a la Cote Occidentale d'Afrique, faites dans les Années 1786 et 1787*. Paris: Dentu.

Delègue, M., Fuhr, M., Schwartz, D, Mariotti, A., and Nasi, R. 2001 Recent origin of a large part of the forest cover in the Gabon coastal area based on stable isotope data. *Oecologia* **129**(1): 106–113.

Denbow, J. 1983 Iron Age Economics: herding, wealth and politics along the fringes of the Kalahari Desert during the Early Iron Age. PhD dissertation, Anthropology Department, Indiana University.

Denbow, J. 1986 After the flood: a preliminary account of recent geological, archaeological and linguistic investigations in the Okavango region of northern Botswana. In *Contemporary Studies on Khoisan*. R. Vossen and K. Keuthmann, eds. Pp. 181–214. Hamburg: H. Buske.

Denbow, J. 1990 Congo to Kalahari: data and hypotheses about the political economy of the Western Stream of the Early Iron Age. *African Archaeological Review* **8**:139–176.

Denbow, J. 1999 Heart and soul: glimpses of ideology and cosmology in the iconography of tombstones from the Loango Coast of Central Africa. *Journal of American Folklore* **112**:404–423.

Denbow, J. 2008 Kalahari Margins. In *Encyclopedia of Archaeology*. D. Pearsall, ed. Pp. 74–83. vol. 1. New York: Academic Press.

Denbow, J. 2011 Excavation at Divuyu, Tsodilo Hills. *Botswana Notes and Records* **43**:76–94.

Denbow, J. 2012 Pride, prejudice, plunder and preservation: archaeology and the re-envisioning of ethnogenesis on the Loango Coast of the Republic of Congo. *Antiquity* **86** (332):383–408.

Denbow, J., and Campbell, A. 1986 The early stages of food production in Southern Africa and some potential linguistic correlations. *Sprache und Geschichte in Afrika* **7**(1):83–103.

Denbow, J., and Miller, D. 2007 Metal working at Bosutswe, Botswana. *Journal of African Archaeology* **5**(2):3–46.

Denbow, J., and Thebe, P. C. 2006 *Culture and Customs of Botswana*. Westport, CT: Greenwood Press.

Denbow, J., and Wilmsen, E. 1986 The advent and course of pastoralism in the Kalahari. *Science* **234**:1509–1515.

Denbow, J., Manima-Moubouha, A., and Sanviti, N. 1988 Archaeological excavations along the Loango Coast. *NSI: Bulletin de Liaison des CICIBA* **3**:37–42.

Denbow, J., Mosothwane, M. N., and Ndobochani, N. 2008a Finding Bosutswe: archaeological encounters with the past. *History in Africa* **35**:145–190.

Denbow, J., Smith J., Atwood, K., Mathibidi, N. and Miller, D. 2008b Excavations at Bosutswe, Botswana: cultural chronology, paleo-ecology and economy. *Journal of Archaeological Science* **35**(2):459–480.

Dennet, R. E. 1968 (1906) *At the Back of the Black Man's Mind: Or Notes on the Kingly Office in West Africa*. London: Frank Cass and Co.

Dennett, R. E. 1887 *Seven Years among the Fjort; Being an English Trader's Experiences in the Congo District*. London: S. Low, Marston, Searle, & Rivington.

Dennett, R. E. 1898 *Notes on the Folklore of the Fjort (French Congo)*. London: Published for the Folklore Society by David Nutt.

Dick, C., Bermingham, E., Lemes, M., and Gribel, R. 2007 Extreme long-distance dispersal of the lowland tropical rainforest tree *Ceiba pentandra L. (Malvaceae)* in Africa and the Neotropics. *Molecular Ecology* **16**:3039–3049.

Digombe, L., Schmidt, P., Boukosso, V., and Locko, M. 1988 The development of an Early Iron Age prehistory in Gabon. *Current Anthropology* **29**(1):179–184.

dos Santos Jr., J., and Ervedosa, C. 1970 A estação arqueológica de Benfica, Luanda, Angola. *Ciências Biológicas* **1**(1):31–51.

Bibliography

Dowsett-Lemaire, F., and Dowsett, R. 1991 Observations complémentaires sur quelques grands mammifères dan le bassin du Kouilou au Congo. In *Flore et Faune du Bassin du Kouilou (Congo) et leur Exploitation*. R. Dowsett and F. Dowsett-Lemaire, eds. Pp. 291–296. Jupille-Liège, Belgium: Tauraco Press.

Droux, G., and Kelley, H. 1939 Recherches Préhistoriques dan la Région de Boko-Songho et a Pointe-Noire. *Journal de la Société des Africanistes* **9**:71–84.

Dupré, M., and Pinçon, B. 1997 *Métallurgie et Politique en Afrique Centrale : deux mille ans de vestiges sur les plateaux Batéké (Gabon, Congo, Zaïre)*. Paris: Karthala.

Eggert, M. 1984 Imbonga und Lingonda: Zur frühesten Besiedelung des äquatorialen Regenwaldes. *Beitrage zur Allgemeinen und Vergleichenden Archäologie* **6**:247–288.

Eggert, M. 1987 Imbonga and Batalimo: ceramic evidence for early settlement of the equatorial rain forest, *The African Archaeological Review* **5**:129–145.

Eggert, M. 1992 The Central African rain forest: Historical speculation and archaeological facts. *World Archaeology* **24**:1–24.

Eggert, M. 1994/1995 Pots, farming and analogy: early ceramics in the Equatorial Forest. *Azania* **29**–30:332–338.

Eggert, M. 1995 Central Africa and the archaeology of the equatorial rainforest: reflections on some major topics. In *The Archaeology of Africa: Food, Metals and Towns*. T. Shaw, P. Sinclair, B. Andah, and A. Okpoko, eds. Pp. 289–329. New York: Routledge.

Eggert, M., Hohn, A., Kahlheber, S., Meister, C., Neumann, K., Scweizer, A. 2006 Pits, graves and grains: archaeological and archaeobotanical research in southern Cameroon. *Journal of African Archaeology* **4**:273–298.

Ehret, C. 1974 Agricultural history in Central and Southern Africa, ca. 1000 BC to ca. AD 500. *Transafrican Journal of History* **4**(1/2): 1–25.

Ehret, C. 1998 *An African Classical Age: Eastern and Southern Africa in World History, 1000 B.C. to A.D. 400*. Charlottesville: University of Virginia Press.

Ehret, C. 2002 *The Civilizations of Africa: A History to 1800*. Charlottesville: University of Virginia Press.

Ehret, C. 2008 The early livestock-raisers of Southern Africa. *Southern African Humanities* **20**:7–35.

Ekholm, K. 1972 *Power and Prestige: the rise and fall of the Kongo Kingdom*. Uppsala: Skriv Service.

Ekoya, A., Ongoka, P., Toua, B., Ouabonzi, A., Ouamba, J.-M., Diatewa, M., and Abena, A. 2006 Isolement de trois triterpenes de *Melletia versicolor baker*. *Journal de la Société Ouest-Africaine de Chimie* **21**:73–76.

Ervedosa, C. 1980 *Arqueologia Angolana*. Lisbon: Edicoes 70.

Fennell, C. 2007 BaKongo identity and symbolic expression in the Americas. In *Archaeology of Atlantic Africa and the African Diaspora*. A. Ogundiran and T. Falola, eds. Pp. 199–232. Bloomington: Indiana University Press.

Fu-Kiau, A. 1969 *Le Mukongo et le Monde qui l'Entourait: cosmogonie-Kongo*. Kinshasa: Office National de la Recherche et de Développement.

Geertz, C. 1973 *The Interpretation of Cultures: selected essays*. New York: Basic.

Gibson, G. D., Larson, T. J., and C. McGurk 1981 *The Kavango Peoples*. Wiesbaden: Steiner.

Gifford-Gonzalez, D. 2000 Animal disease challenges to the emergence of pastoralism in sub-Saharan Africa. *African Archaeological Review* **17**:95–139.

Gilbert, G., and Sénéchal, J. 1989 L'économie forestière. In *Revue des Connaissances sur le Mayombe*. J. Sénéchal, M. Kabala, and F. Fournier, eds. Pp. 249–294. Paris: UNESCO.

Goldstein, D., Acquavella, J. Mannion, R., and Farmer, D. 2002 An analysis of glyphosate data from the California Environmental Protection Agency Pesticide Illness Surveillance Program. *Journal of Toxicology – Clinical Toxicology* **40**(7):885–92.

Gosselain, O. P. 1988 *Sakusi: fouille d'un premier village du néolithique et de l'âge des métaux au Zaïre*, Mémoire de Licence, Université Libre de Bruxelles.

Gosselain, O. P. 2002 *Poteries du Cameroun Méridional: styles techniques et rapports à l'identité*. CRA Monographies, 26. Paris: CNRS Editions.

Gradstein, F., Ogg, J., and Smith, A. eds. 2004 *A Geologic Time Scale*. Cambridge: Cambridge University Press.

Güldemann, T. 2008 A linguist's view: Khoe-Kwadi speakers as the earliest food- producers of Southern Africa. *Southern African Humanities* **20**:93–132.

Güldemann, T., and E. Elderkin 2010 On external genealogical relationships of the Khoe family. In *Khoisan Languages and Linguistics: Proceedings of the 1st International Symposium January 4–8, 2003*. M. Brenzinger and C. König, eds. Pp. 15–52. Cologne: Rüdiger Köppe.

Güldemann, T. forthcoming Changing profile when encroaching on hunter-gatherer territory: towards a history of the Khoe-Kwadi family in southern Africa. In *Hunter-gatherers and Linguistic History: A Global Perspective*. T. Güldemann, P. McConvell, and R. Rhodes, eds. Cambridge: Cambridge University Press.

Guthrie, M. 1967/71 *Comparative Bantu: An Introduction to the Comparative Linguistics and Prehistory of the Bantu Languages*. 4 vols. Letchworth UK & Brookfield VT: Gregg International.

Hagenbucher-Sacripanti, F. 1973 *Les Fondements Spirituels du Pouvoir au Royaume de Loango, République Populaire du Congo*. Paris: O.R.S.T.O.M. [Office de la recherche scientifique et technique outre-mer].

Hargus, R. 1997 Ceramic evidence of the 4th Century BC to the 6th Century AD Bantu expansion in the People's Republic of Congo. MA thesis, Anthropology Department, University of Texas at Austin.

Heine, B., Hoff, H. and Vossen, R. 1977 Neuere Ergebnisse zur Territorialgeschichte der Bantu. In *Zur Sprachgeschichte und Ethnohistorie in Afrika*. W. Möhlig, R. Rottland, and B. Heine, eds. Pp. 57–72. Berlin: Dietrich Reimer.

Henn, B. M., Gignoux, C., Lin, A. A., Oefner, P. J., Shen, P., Scozzari, R., Cruciani, F., Tishkoff, S. A., Mountain, J. L., and Underhill, P. A. 2008 Y-chromosomal evidence of a pastoralist migration through Tanzania to Southern Africa. *Proceedings of the National Academy of Sciences* **105**(31): 10693–10698.

Herbert, E. 1984 *Red Gold of Africa: Copper in Precolonial History and Culture*. Madison: University of Wisconsin Press.

Herbert, E. 1993 *Iron, Gender, and Power: Rituals of Transformation in African Societies*. Bloomington: Indiana University Press.

Holl, A. and Zangato, E. 2010 On the iron front: new evidence from North-Central Africa. *Journal of African Archaeology* **8**(1): 7–23.

Huffman, T. N. 1986 Archaeological evidence and conventional explanations of southern Bantu settlement patterns. *Africa: Journal of the International African Institute* **56**(3): 280–298.

Huffman, T. N. 1989 *Iron Age Migrations. The Ceramic Sequence in Southern Zambia: Excavations at Gundu and Ndonde*. Johannesburg: Witwatersrand University Press.

Huffman, T. N. 1993 Broederstrom and the Central Cattle Pattern. *South African Journal of Science* **89**:220–226.

Huffman, T. N. 1994 Toteng pottery and the origins of Bambata. *Southern African Field Archaeology* **3**:3–9.

Huffman, T. N. 2005 The stylistic origin of Bambata and the spread of mixed farming in Southern Africa. *Southern African Humanities* **17**: 57–79.

Huffman, T. N. 2007 *Handbook to the Iron Age: The Archaeology of Pre-Colonial Farming Societies in Southern Africa*. Scottsville, South Africa: University of KwaZulu-Natal Press.

Huffman, T. N. 2008 Climate change during the Iron Age in the Shashe-Limpopo Basin, Southern Africa. *Journal of Archaeological Science* **35**:2032–2047.

Hume, I. 1970 *A Guide to Artifacts of Colonial America*. New York: Knopf.

Huysecom, E., and Agustoni, B. dirs. 1998 *Inagina: The Last House of Iron*. Film.

Jacobson-Widding, A. 1979 *Red – White – Black as a Mode of Thought: A Study of Triadic Classification by Colours in the Ritual Symbolism and Cognitive Thought of the Peoples of the Lower Congo*. Stockholm: Almquist and Wiksell International.

Jarvis, J., Scheinfeldt, L., Soi, S., Lambert, C., Omberg, L., Ferwerda, B., Froment, A., Bodo, J., Beggs, W., Hoffman, G., Mezey, J., and Tishkoff, S. 2012 Patterns of ancestry, signatures of natural selection, and genetic association with stature in Western African Pygmies. *PLOS Genetics* **8**(4): e1002641. DOI:10.1371/journal.pgen.1002641.

Kahlheber, S., Bostoen, K., and Neumann, K. 2009 Early plant cultivation in the Central African rain forest: first millennium BC pearl millet from South Cameroon. *Journal of African Archaeology* **7**(2): 253–272.

Khama, S. 1970 Graduation address to the University of Botswana, Lesotho and Swaziland. *Botswana Daily News*, May 19, 1970.

Kimfoko-Maddungou, J. N.d. *Guide au Musée Ma-Loango*. Mimeographed, Musée Régional Ma-Loango, Direction Régionale des Affaires Culturelles.

Klieman, K. A. 2003 *"The Pygmies Were Our Compass": Bantu and Batwa in the History of West Central Africa, Early Times to c. 1900 C.E.* Portsmouth, NH: Heinemann.

Kose, E. 2009 New light on ironworking groups along the middle Kavango in Northern Namibia. *South African Archaeological Bulletin* **64**(190): 130–147.

Kose, E., and Richter J. 2007 The prehistory of the Kavango People. *Sprache und Geschichte in Afrika* **18**:103–129.

Bibliography

La Fleur, J., ed. 2000 *Pieter van den Broecke's Journal of Voyages to Cape Verde, Guinea and Angola (1605–1612)*. London: The Hakluyt Society.

Laidler, P. 1929 Hottentot and Bushman pottery of South Africa. *South African Journal of Science* **26**:93–172.

Laidler, P. 1938 South African native ceramics: their characteristics and classification. *Transactions of the Royal Society of South Africa* **26**:99–172.

Laman, K. 1953–68 *The Kongo*. 4 vols. Uppsala: Almquist and Wiksells.

Lamikanra, A., Ogundaini, A., and Ogungbamila, F. 2006 Antibacterial constituents of *Alchomea cordifolia* leaves. *Phytotherapy Research* **4**(5):198–200.

Lanfranchi, R., and Manima-Moubouha, A. 1984 Première datation 14C d'un bas fourneau de fonte de cuivre en R.P. du Congo. *Cahiers Congolais d'Anthropologie et d'Histoire* **9**:7–12.

Lanfranchi, R., Clist, B., and de La Croix, Y. 1991 *Aux Origines de l'Afrique Centrale*. Libreville: Centre International des Civilisations Bantu.

Lavachery, P., MacEachern, S., Bouimon, T., and Mindzie, C. 2010 *Komé-Kribi: archéologie préventive le long de l'oléoduc Tchad– Cameroun, 1999–2004*. Journal of African Archaeology Monograph Series 5. Frankfurt: Africa Magna.

Leiju, B., Robertshaw, P. and Taylor, D. 2006 Africa's earliest bananas? *Journal of Archaeological Science* **33**(1): 102–113.

Livingstone, D. 1858 *Missionary Travels and Researches in South Africa*. New York: Harper and Brothers.

Lombard, J. 1931 Matériaux préhistoriques du Congo Français. *Journal de la Société des Africanistes* **1**:49–60.

Lombard, M., Wadley, L., Deacon, J., Wurz, S., Parsons, I., Mohapi, M., Swart, J., and Mitchell, P. 2012 South African and Lesotho Stone Age sequence updated. *South African Archaeological Bulletin* **67** (105): 123–144.

Lopes, D., Pigafetta, F. and Hutchinson, M. 1881 *A Report of the Kingdom of Congo: And of the Surrounding Countries; Drawn out of the Writings and Discourses of the Portuguese, Duarte Lopez*. London: John Murray.

MacEachern, S. 2001 Cultural resource management and Africanist archaeology. *Antiquity* **75**:866–871.

MacGaffey, W. 1977 Economic and social dimensions of Kongo slavery. In *Slavery in Africa: Historical and Anthropological Perspectives*. S. Miers and I. Kopytoff, eds. Pp. 235–257. Madison: University of Wisconsin Press.

MacGaffey, W. 1983 *Modern Kongo Prophets: Religion in a Plural Society*. Bloomington: Indiana University Press.

MacGaffey, W. 1986 *Religion and Society in Central Africa: The Bakongo of Lower Zaïre*. Chicago: University of Chicago Press.

Maley, J. 2004 Les variations de la végétation et des paleoenvironnements du domaine forestier africain au cours du Quaternaire récent. In *Evolution de la Végétation depuis Deux Millions d'Années*. A. M. Sémah and J. L. Renault-Miskovsky, eds. Pp. 143–178. Paris: Editions Artcom.

Maley, J. and Brenac, P. 1998 Vegetation dynamics, paleoenvironments and climatic changes in the forests of West Cameroon during the last 28,000 years BP. *Review of Paleobotany and Palynology* **99**:157–187.

Mankowitz, W. 1957 *The Concise Encyclopedia of English Pottery and Porcelain*. New York: Hawthorn.

Martin, P. 1972 *The External Trade of the Loango Coast, 1576–1870; The Effects of Changing Commercial Relations on the Vili Kingdom of Loango*. Oxford: Clarendon Press.

Martin, P. 1986 Power, cloth and currency on the Loango Coast. *African Economic History* **15**:1–12.

Martins, R. 1976 A estação arqueológica da antiga Banza Quibaxe. *Contribuição para a Estudo da Antropologia Portuguesa* **9**(4):204–306.

Mbida, C., Doutrelepont, L., Vrydaghs, R., Swennen, R., Beeckman, H., de Langhe, E., and de Maret, P. 2001 First archaeological evidence of banana cultivation in Central Africa during the third millennium before present. *Vegetation History and Archaeobotany* **10**:1–6.

Mbida, C., Doutrelepont, L., Vrydaghs, R., Swennen, R., Beeckman, H., de Langhe, E., and de Maret, P. 2003 The initial history of bananas in Africa. A reply to Jan Vansina. *Azania* **40**: 128–135.

Mbida, C., Doutrelepont, L., Vrydaghs, R., Swennen, R., Beeckman, H., de Langhe, E., and de Maret, P. 2004 Yes, there were bananas in Cameroon more than 2000 years ago. *InfoMusa* **13**(40–42).

Meister, C. 2007 Recent archaeological investigations in the tropical rain forest of South–West Cameroon. In *Dynamics of Forest Ecosystems in Central Africa during the Holocene: Past-Present-Future*. J. Runge, ed. Pp. 43–57. London: Taylor and Francis.

Meister, C. and M. Eggert 2008 On the Early Iron Age in southern Cameroon: the sites of Akonétye. *Journal of African Archaeology* **6**(2):183–202.

Mercader, J., Garcia-Heras, M. and Gonzalez-Alvarez, I. 2000 Ceramic tradition in the African forest: characterization analysis of ancient and modern pottery from Ituri, D.R. Congo. *Journal of Archaeological Science* **27**:163–182.

Michczynski, A. 2004 Problems of construction of a radiocarbon chronology for the time period 900–300 cal BC. In *Impact of the Environment on Human Migration in Eurasia*. E. M.Scott, ed. Pp. 117–123. Dordrect/Boston/London: Kluwer.

Miers, S., and Kopytoff, I. 1979 *Slavery in Africa: Historical and Anthropological Perspectives*. Madison: University of Wisconsin Press.

Miller, D. 1996 *The Tsodilo Jewelry: Metal Work from Northern Botswana*. Rondebosch, South Africa: University of Cape Town Press.

Miller, J. 1988 *Way of Death: Merchant Capitalism and the Angolan Slave Trade 1730–1830*. Madison: University of Wisconsin Press.

Mitchell, P. 2010 Genetics and Southern African prehistory: an archaeological view. *Journal of Anthropological Sciences* **88**:73–93.

Mitchell, P. 2011 Reply to Rocha: a note on erroneous ethnolinguistic affiliations in genetic studies of southern Africa. *Journal of Anthropological Sciences* **89**:1–2.

Mortelmans, G. 1959 Préhistoire et protohistoire du Bas-Congo Belge: une esquisse.Volume de homenagem ao Prof. Doutor Mendes Correa. *Trabalhos de Antropologia e Etnologia* **17**:329–344.

Mortelmans, G. 1962 Archéologie des grottes Dimba et Ngovo (Région de Thysville, Bas-Congo). In *Actes du 4ème Congrès Panafricain de Préhistoire et de l'étude du Quaternaire*, III. Pp. 407–425. Tervuren: Musée Royal de l'Afrique Centrale.

Mosothwane, M. N. 2011 Dietary stable Carbon isotope signatures of the Early Iron Age inhabitants of Ngamiland. *Botswana Notes and Records* **43**:115–129.

Neumann K., Bostoen K., Höhn A., Kahlheber S., Ngomanda A., and Tchiengué, B. 2012 First farmers in the Central African rainforest: a view from Southern Cameroon. *Quaternary International* **249**: 53–62.

Neumann, K. 2006. Ölpalme, Perlhirse und Banane: Wie kam die Landwirtschaft in den Regenwald Zentralafrikas. *Forschung Frankfurt* **2**–3:38–41.

Neumann, K., and Hildebrand, E. 2009 Early bananas in Africa: the state of the art. *Ethnobotany Research and Applications* **7**:3 53–362.

Ngomanda, A., Neumann, K., Schweizer, A., Maley, J. 2009 Seasonality change and the third millennium BP rainforest crisis in Southern Cameroon (Central Africa). *Quaternary Research* **71**:307–318.

Nsondé, Jean de Dieu 1995 *Langues, Culture et Histoire Kongo aux XVII et XVIII Siècles: à travers les documents linguistiques*. Paris: Volume Editions L'Harmattan.

Oslisly, R., and Peyrot, B. 1988 Synthèse des données archéologiques des sites de la moyenne vallée de l'Ogooué (provinces du Moyen-Ogooué et de l'Ogooué-Ivindo), Gabon. *Nsi* **3**:63–98.

Pechuël-Loesche, E. 1907 *Volkskunde von Loango*. Stuttgart: Strecker and Schröder.

Phillipson, D. 1977 *The Later Prehistory of Eastern and Southern Africa*. London: Heinemann.

Phillipson, D. 2005 *African Archaeology*. Cambridge: Cambridge University Press.

Phillipson, G., and S. Bahuchet 1994/1995 Cultivated crops and Bantu migrations in Central and Eastern Africa: a linguistic approach. *Azania* **29**/30:103–120.

Piton, B., Pointeau, J. H., and Wauthy, B. 1979 *Donnés Hydro-climatiques à Pointe-Noire (Congo) 1953–1977*. Pointe Noire: OSTROM.

Pleurdeau, D., Imalwa, E. Dé troit, F., Lesur, J., Veldman, A., Bahain, J. and Marais, E. 2012 "Of sheep and men": earliest direct evidence of Caprine domestication in Southern Africa at Leopard Cave (Erongo, Namibia). *PLOS One* **7** (7): e40340 DOI: 10.1371/journal.pone.0040340

Plug, I. 1996 Seven centuries of Iron Age traditions at Bosutswe, Botswana: a faunal perspective. *South African Journal of Science* **92**:91–97.

Proyart, Abbé 1814 History of Loango, Kakongo and other kingdoms in Africa. In *A General Collection of the Best and Most Interesting Voyages and Travels in All Parts of the World, Many of which Are Now First Translated into English*. J. Pinkerton, ed.Vol. 16. Pp. 548–597. London: Longman, Hurst, Rees, Orme, and Brown.

Prévost, A. 1748 *Histoire Générale des Voyages. Description de la Guinée, Royaume de Benin, Royaumes de Loango, de Congo, d'Angola, de Benguela, et des Pays Voisins: Volume 6*. The Hague: de Hondt.

Purchas, Samuel 1617 *Purchas his Pilgrimage, or, Relations of the World and the Religions Observed in All Ages and Places Discovered, from the Creation unto this Present: Part 2*. London: Printed by William Stansby for Henry Fetherstone.

Purdy, J. 1855 *Laurie's Sailing Directory for the Ethiopic or Southern Atlantic Ocean; including the Coasts of Brazil, etc., to the Rio de la Plata, the Coast thence to Cape Horn, and the African Coast to the Cape of Good Hope, etc.; including the Islands between the Two Coasts*. London: Richard Holmes Laurie.

Bibliography

Rat Patron, P. 1993 *L'histoire du Congo lue dans les cartes géographiques*. Pointe Noire: ORSTROM.

Ravenstein, E. 1901 *The Strange Adventures of Andrew Battell of Leigh, in Angola and the Adjoining Regions*. London: The Hakluyt Society.

Rice, P. 1987 *Pottery Analysis: A Sourcebook*. Chicago: University of Chicago Press.

Robbins, L. H., Brook, G. A., Murhpy, M. L., Campbell, A. C., Melear, N., and Downey, W. S. 2000b Late Quaternary archaeological and palaeo-environmental data from sediments at Rhino Cave, Tsodilo Hills, Botswana. *Southern African Field Archaeology* **9**:17–31.

Robbins, L. H., Murphy, M. L., Brook, G. A., Ivester, A. H., Campbell, A. C., Klein, R. G., Milo, R. G., Stewart, K. M., Downey, W. S., and Stevens, N. J. 2000a Archaeology, palaeoenvironment, and chronology of the Tsodilo Hills White Paintings Rock Shelter, Northwest Kalahari Desert, Botswana. *Journal of Archaeological Science* **27**:1085–1113.

Robbins, L., A. Campbell, M., Murphy, G. A., Brook, R., Liang, S., Skaggs, P., Srivastava, A. Mabuse, and Badenhorst, S. 2008 Recent archaeological and paleontological research at Toteng, Botswana: early domesticated livestock in the Kalahari. *Journal of African Archaeology* **6**(1):131–149.

Robbins, L., M. Murphy, and A. Campbell 1998 Intensive mining of specular hematite in the Kalahari ca. AD 800–1000. *Current Anthropology* **39**(1):144–149.

Robbins, L. H., Campbell, A. C., Murphy, M. L., Brook, G. A., Srivastava, P., and Badenhorst, S. 2005 The advent of herding in Southern Africa: early AMS dates on domestic livestock from the Kalahari Desert. *Current Anthropology* **46**(4): 671–677.

Robertshaw, P. 2006 Africa's earliest bananas. *Archaeology* **59**(5): 25–29.

Rouvier, M., and Geisendörfer, J. 1887 *Itinéraire de Loango a Zilengoma d'après les travaux de M. M. Rouvier, Capitaine de Frégate et Pleigneur, Capitaine d'Infanterie de Marine*. Paris: Lemercier et Cie.

Rudner, J. 1976 An archaeological reconnaissance tour of Angola. *South African Archaeological Bulletin* **31**:99–111.

Runge, R., Eisenberg, J., and Sangen, J. 2006 Eiszeit im tropischen Regenwald: Der ewige Wald – eine Legende? *Forschung Frankfurt, Sonderheft Afrika* **2**:34–37.

Sadr, K. 1997 Kalahari archaeology and the Bushman debate. *Current Anthropology* **38**:104–112.

Sadr, K. 2008 Invisible herders? The archaeology of Khoekhoe pastoralists. *Southern African Humanities* **20**:179–203.

Sahlins, M. 1965 *On the Sociology of Primitive Exchange*. Vol. 1. London: Social Anthropologists Monographs.

Scheermeyer, C. 2005 A changing and challenging landscape: heritage resources management in South Africa. *South African Archaeological Bulletin* **60**(182):121–123.

Schlebusch, C. M., Skoglund, P., Sjödin, P. Gattepaille, L., Hernandez, D., Jay, F., Li, S., De Jongh, M., Singleton, A., Blum, M., Soodyall, H., and Jakobsson, M. 2012 Genomic variation in seven Khoe-San groups reveals adaptation and complex African history. *Science* **338**(6105):374–9.

Schmidt, P., and McIntosh, S. 1996 *Plundering Africa's Past*. Bloomington: Indiana University Press.

Schofield, J. 1948 *Primitive Pottery: An Introduction to South African Ceramics, Prehistoric and Protohistoric*. Cape Town: South African Archaeological Society.

Schrag, N. 1990 *Changing Perceptions of Wealth among the BaMboma (Lower Zaïre)*. African Studies Program mimeograph. Phyllis Martin, ed. Bloomington: Indiana University Press.

Schwartz, D. 1992 Assèchement climatique vers 3000 B.P. et expansion Bantu en Afrique Centrale Atlantique: quelques réflexions. *Bulletin de la Societé Géologique de France* **163**(3):353–361.

Schwartz, D., de Foresta, H., Dechamps, R., and Lanfranchi, R. 1990 Découverte d'un premier site de l'Age du Fer Ancien (2110 B.P.) dan le Mayombe Congolaise. Implications paléobotaniques et pédologiques. *Comptes Rendus de l'Académie des Sciences Paris T.* **310** (Série II): 1293–1298.

Schwartz, D., De Foresta, H., Mariotta, A., Balesdent, J., Massimba, J. P., and Girardin, C. 1996 Present dynamics of the savanna-forest boundary in the Congolese Mayombe: a pedological, botanical and isotopic (13C and 14C) study. *Oecologia* **116**:516–524.

Seidel, F., Kose, E., and Möhlig, W 2007 Northern Namibia – overview of its historiography based on linguistic and extralinguistic evidence. In *Atlas of Cultural and Environmental Change in Arid Africa*. O. Bubenzer, A. Bolten, and F. Darius, eds. Pp. 152–155. Koln: Heinrich Barth Institut.

Shillington, K. 1995 *History of Africa*. New York: St. Martin Press.

Simpson, R., and Pitcher, M. 1988 The Congo Archaeological Project, pp. 8, Houston.

Sitou, L., Schwartz, D., Mielton, M., and Tchicaya, J. 1996 Histoire et dynamique actuelle des cirques d'érosion du littoral d'Afrique Centrale. Une étude de cas: les cirques du littoral Ponténégrin (Congo). *Dynamique à Long Terme des Écosystèmes Forestiers Intertropicaux*. Bondy: CNRS-ORSTOM.

Smith, A. 2005 The concepts of "Neolithic" and "Neolithisation" for Africa. *Before Farming* **1**(2): 1–6.

Smith, A. 2006 *Excavations at Kasteelberg, and the Origins of the Khoekhoen in the Western Cape, South Africa.* BAR International Series 1537. Oxford: British Archaeological Reports.

Smith, A. 2008 Pastoral origins at the Cape, South Africa: influences and arguments. *Southern African Humanities* **20**:49–60.

Smith, J. 2005 Climate change and agro-pastoral sustainability in the Shashe/Limpopo River basin from AD 900. PhD dissertation, Department of Archaeology, University of the Witwatersrand, Johannesburg.

Soper, R. 1985 Roulette decoration on African pottery: technical considerations, dating and distributions. *The African Archaeological Review* **3**:29–51.

Soret, M. 1978 *Histoire du Congo.* Paris: Berger-Levrault.

Sowunmi, M.A. 1999 The significance of the oil palm (*Elaeis guineensis Jacq.*) in the late Holocene environments of West and West Central Africa: a further consideration. *Vegetation History and Archaeobotany* **8**:199–210.

Stahl, A. 1993 Intensification in the West African Late Stone Age. In *The Archaeology of Africa: Food, Metals, and Towns.* T. Shaw, P. Sinclair, B. Andah, and A. Okpoko, eds. Pp. 261–273. London: Routledge.

Stahl, A. 1994 Innovation, diffusion, and culture contact: the Holocene archaeology of Ghana. *Journal of World Prehistory* **8**:51–112.

Stross, B. 1997 Mesoamerican copal resins. In *U-Mut Maya and Reports and Readings Inspired by the Advanced Seminars led by Linda Schele and the University of Texas at Austin, 1994–1996* C. Jones and T. Jones, eds. Pp. 177–186. Austin: University of Texas.

Stuiver, M. and P. Reimer, P. 1993 Extended ^{14}C data base and revised CALIB 3.0 ^{14}C age calibration program. *Radiocarbon* **35**: 215–230.

Sunseri, T. 2009 *Wielding the Ax: State Forestry and Social Conflict in Tanzania, 1820–2000.* Athens: Ohio University Press.

Swartz, B.K. 1996 The McKern "Taxonomic" system and archaeological culture classification in the Midwestern United States: a history and evaluation. *History of Archaeology* **6**(1): 3–9.

Teugels, G.G., Snoeks, J, De Vos, L. and Diakanou-Matongo, J.C. 1991 Les Poissons du bassin inférieur de Kouilou (Congo). In *Flore et Faune du Bassin du Kouilou (Congo) et leur Exploitation.* R. Dowsett and F. Dowsett-Lemaire, eds. Pp. 109–139. Jupille-Liège, Belgium: Tauraco Press.

Thomas, S., and Shaw, P. 1991 *The Kalahari Environment.* New York: Cambridge University Press.

Thompson, R., and Cornet, J. 1981 *The Four Moments of the Sun: Kongo Art in Two Worlds.* Washington: National Gallery of Art.

Tlou, T. 1985 *A History of Ngamiland, 1750 to 1906: The Formation of an African State.* Gaborone, Botswana: Macmillan Botswana.

Turner, G. 1987a Early Iron Age herders in Northwestern Botswana: the faunal evidence. *Botswana Notes and Records* **19**:7–23.

Turner, G. 1987b Hunters and herders of the Okavango Delta, Northern Botswana. *Botswana Notes and Records* **19**:25–40.

Valdeyron, N., and Da Silva Domingos, S. 2009 Nouvelles données sur la Préhistoire récent angolaise: le gisement de Cabolombo à Benfica revisité. In *De Méditerranée et d'ailleurs … Mélanges offert à Jean Guilaine.* Centre de Recherches sur la Pré- et Protohistoire de la Méditerranée, eds. Pp. 737–749. Toulouse: Archives d'Écologie Préhistorique.

Van Noten, F., Cahen, D., de Maret, P., Moeyersons, E., and Roche, E. 1982 *The Archaeology of Central Africa.* Graz, Austria: Akademische Druck.

Van Waarden, C. 1996 The pre-development archaeology programme of Botswana. In *Aspects of African Archaeology: Papers from the 10th Congress of the PanAfrican Association for Prehistory and Related Studies.* G. Pwiti and R. Soper, eds. Pp. 829–836. Harare: University of Zimbabwe Press.

van Zyl, W., Badenhorst, S., Denbow, J., and Wilmsen, E. 2013 The archaeofauna from Xaro on the Okavango Delta in Northern Botswana. *Annals of the Ditsong National Museum of Natural History* **3**:49–58.

Vansina, J. 1966 *Kingdoms of the Savanna.* Madison: University of Wisconsin Press.

Vansina, J. 1984 Western Bantu expansion. *Journal of African History* **25** (2):129–45.

Vansina, J. 1990 *Paths in the Rainforests: Toward a History of Political Tradition in Equatorial Africa.* Madison: University of Wisconsin Press.

Vansina, J. 1995 New linguistic evidence and "the Bantu expansion." *Journal of African History* **36**:173–195.

Vansina, J. 1997 Histoire du manioc en Afrique Centrale avant 1850. *Paideuma* **43**:255–279.

Bibliography

Vansina, J. 1998 Raffia cloth in West Central Africa, 1500–1800. In *Textiles: Production, Trade and Demand: The European Impact on World History, 1450–1800.* M. F. Mazzaoui, ed. Pp. 263–81. Aldershot: Variorum.

Vansina, J. 2003 Bananas in Cameroun c. 500 BCE? Not proven. *Azania* **38**:174–176.

Vansina, J. 2004 *How Societies Are Born: Governance in West Central Africa before 1600.* Charlottesville: University of Virginia Press.

Vansina, J. 2010. *Being Colonized: The Kuba Experience in Rural Congo, 1880–1960.* Madison: University of Wisconsin Press.

Vincens, A., Schwartz, D., Bertaux, J., Elenga, H., and de Namur, C. 1998 Holocene climatic changes in Western Equatorial Africa inferred from pollen from Lake Sinda, Southern Congo. *Quaternary Research* **50**:34–45.

Vogel, J. O. 1971a *Kamangoza: an Introduction to the Iron Age Cultures of the Victoria Falls Region.* Zambia Museum Papers (no. 2). Lusaka, Zambia: Oxford University Press.

Vogel, J. O. 1971b *Kumadzulo, an Early Iron Age Village Site in Southern Zambia.* Zambia Museum Papers, (no. 3). Lusaka, Zambia: Oxford University Press.

Vogel, J. O. 1973 The Early Iron Age Site at Sioma Mission, Western Zambia. *Zambia Museums Journal* **4**:153–169.

Vogel, J. O. 1975 *Simbusenga: The Archaeology of the Intermediate Period of the Southern Zambian Iron Age.* Lusaka: Zambia Museum Papers.

Volavka, Z., and Thomas, W. 1998 *Crown and Ritual: the Royal Insignia of Ngoyo.* Toronto: University of Toronto Press.

Von Oppen, A. 1991 "The lazy man's food"? Indigenous agricultural innovation and dietary change in Northwestern Zambia, ca. 1650–1970. *Food and Foodways* **5**(1):15–38.

Vossen, R. 1997 What click sounds got to do in Bantu: reconstructing the history of language contacts in southern Africa. In *Human Contact through Language and Linguistics.* B. Smieja and M. Tasch, eds. Pp. 353–366. Frankfurt am Main: Peter Lang.

Vossen, R., Keuthmann, K., and Köhler, O. 1986 *Contemporary Studies on Khoisan: In Honour of Oswin Köhler on the Occasion of his 75th Birthday.* Quellen zur Khoisan-Forschung, Bd. 5, 1–2. 2 vols. Hamburg: H. Buske.

Walker, N. 1983 The significance of an early date for pottery and sheep in Zimbabwe. *South African Archaeological Bulletin* **38**:88–92.

Watson, A. 1983 *Agricultural Innovation in the Early Islamic World: The Diffusion of Crops and Farming Techniques, 700–1100.* Cambridge: Cambridge University Press.

Weber, S. 1998 Out of Africa: the initial impact of millets in South Asia. *Current Anthropology* **39**(2): 267–274.

White, C. M. N. 1962 *Tradition and Change in Luvale Marriage.* Lusaka, Zambia: Rhodes Livingstone Institute.

Williams, G., Kroes, R., and Munro, I. 2000 Safety evaluation and risk assessment of the herbicide Roundup and its active ingredient, glyphosate, for humans. *Regulatory Toxicology and Pharmacology* **31**(2): 117–165.

Willoughby, W. C. 1928 *The Soul of the Bantu; a Sympathetic Study of the Magico-Religious Practices and Beliefs of the Bantu Tribes of Africa.* Garden City, NY: Doubleday, Doran & Company.

Wilmsen, E. 2011 Nqoma: an abridged review. *Botswana Notes and Records* **43**:95–114.

Wilmsen, E. and Denbow, J. 2010 Early Villages at Tsodilo: the introduction of livestock, crops, and metalworking. In *Tsodilo Hills: Copper Bracelet of the Kalahari.* L. Robbins, A. Campbell, and M. Taylor, eds. Pp. 72–81. East Lansing: Michigan State University Press.

Wilmsen, E., Killick, D., Rosenstein, D., Thebe, P. and Denbow, J. 2009 The social geography of pottery in Botswana as reconstructed by optical petrography. *Journal of African Archaeology* **7**: 3–39.

Wilson, V.J., and Wilson, B.L.P. 1991 La chasse traditionelle et commerciale dans le Sud-ouest du Congo. In *Flore et Faune du Bassin du Kouilou (Congo) et leur Exploitation.* R. Dowsett and F. Dowsett-Lemaire, eds. Pp. 279–289. Jupille-Liège, Belgium: Tauraco Press.

Wolf, E. 1982 *Europe and the People Without History.* Berkeley, London: University of California Press.

Wotzka, H.P. 1995 *Studien zur Archäologie des zentralafrikanischen Regenwalds: Die Keramik des inneren Zaïre-Beckens und ihre Stellung im Kontext der Bantu-Expansion.* Cologne: Heinrich-Barth Institut.

Index

Index

Index

Index